A-LEVEL
PSYCHOLOGY

colourful and concise revision
guide for **AQA psychology**
(7182) years 1 and 2

CHRISTIAN B. FEEST

Copyright © 2023 by Christian B. Feest

All rights reserved. No part of this book may be reproduced or used in any manner without written permission of the copyright owner except for the brief use of quotations.

First paperback edition April 2023

ISBN: 9798387512025

CONTENTS

Paper 1	Social Influence		4
	Memory		10
	Attachment		17
	Psychopathology		24
Paper 2	Approaches in Psychology		32
	Biopsychology		44
	Research Methods		52
Paper 3	Issues and Debates		71
	Pick 1 of 3	Relationships	77
		Gender	85
		Cognition and Development	94
	Pick 1 of 3	Schizophrenia	102
		Eating Behaviour	110
		Stress	118
	Pick 1 of 3	Aggression	127
		Forensic Psychology	135
		Addiction	144
Extra Bits	Exam Format and Assessment Objectives		153
	Practice Questions		160
	Bibliography and References		172
	Glossary		182

SOCIAL INFLUENCE - CONFORMITY

Conformity: A form of social influence where a person changes their beliefs and behaviour to fit – or *conform* – to those of a group (also called *majority influence*).

Kelman (1958) identified **3 *types* of conformity**	
Compliance:	**Compliance** is the *weakest* type of conformity. It's where a person *publicly changes their behaviour and beliefs* to fit the group and avoid disapproval. But privately, the person doesn't accept them – they just comply with the beliefs. *Example:* Pretending to like a film you actually dislike in order to fit in.
Identification	**Identification** is a stronger type of conformity than compliance because it involves the person *both publicly and privately* changing their behaviour and beliefs to fit that of a group they want to be part of. But the person only identifies with these beliefs as long as they're associated with the group – after leaving the group, the original behaviours and beliefs return. *Example:* Adopting the same music and fashion as your friendship group. But when you move away, you revert back to your old clothes and music.
Internalisation	**Internalisation** is the *strongest* type of conformity. It is where a person both publicly and privately changes their behaviour and beliefs to those of a group – but *permanently*. So, individuals who internalise beliefs and behaviours maintain those beliefs and behaviours even after leaving the group. *Example:* A genuine religious conversion. This person will still pray and believe in God even if they move away from the social group of the church.

Deutsch and Gerard (1955) give **2 *explanations* of conformity**	
Informational Social Influence (ISI)	People like to feel that their opinions and beliefs are **correct** – this is **informational social influence**. This desire to be correct motivates individuals to copy and conform to the group. *Example:* Conforming to others' behaviour at a formal restaurant. You don't know which cutlery is the correct set to use, so you just copy someone else who seems to know what they're doing.
Normative social influence (NSI)	People want to be **accepted** by others and not be rejected – this is **normative social influence**. This desire to fit in motivates individuals to conform to the beliefs and opinions of a group so as not to stand out. *Example:* Agreeing with the group's opinions on politics so they like you.

SOCIAL INFLUENCE - CONFORMITY

	Key study: **Asch (1955)** Conformity Experiments
Aim	To investigate the extent to which people conform to an incorrect majority consensus.
Method	**123 male participants** were told they were taking part in a study of visual perception. Participants were put in groups with between 7 and 9 confederates (i.e. fake subjects pretending to be part of the experiment too). Each participant completed 18 trials where they would be shown sets of lines like the ones opposite (A, B, or C) and then asked which one was closest to the original line. In the 12 critical trials, **the confederates would all give the same *wrong* answer** – the participant was always asked to give their answer last (or second to last) so as to hear the group's answers first. The **control group** for this experiment consisted of 36 participants. In the control trials, participants were asked the same questions as above – but this time **alone**. Is A, B, or C closest in length to the other line? Participants would often give the wrong answer in order to fit in.
Results	Across all critical trials, **participants conformed to the incorrect group consensus 32% of the time.** 75% of participants conformed to *at least one* wrong answer, and 5% of participants conformed to *every* wrong answer in the 12 critical trials. This is compared to an error rate of just 0.04% in the control trials.
AO3	• **Questions of ecological validity:** Guessing the length of lines is a specific task so the findings might not be valid when applied to conformity in the real world. • **Gender bias (beta bias):** All the participants in Asch's study were *male*. As such, they may not be valid when applied to *female* conformity. • **Ethical concerns:** Asch lied to participants and said it was a study of *visual perception* (not conformity). This means they didn't give informed consent.

Asch did other variations to determine **variables affecting conformity:**

- **Unanimity:** Conformity declined from 32% to 5.5% when one 'partner' confederate was instructed to give the correct answer and break the unanimous consensus of the majority.
- **Group size:** Increasing the size of the group tended to increase conformity – up to a point. In trials with 2 confederates, conformity was 12.8% but this went up to 32% for trials with 3 confederates. Beyond this extra confederates (4, 8, or 16) did not increase conformity.
- **Difficulty:** Asch adjusted the lengths of the lines in the study above to make it either more easy or more difficult to see which line was closest in length to the original line. Increasing the difficulty of the task was also found to increase conformity.

SOCIAL INFLUENCE – CONFORMITY TO SOCIAL ROLES

Different social situations have different expectations for behaviour – different **social norms**. These norms create **social roles** we conform to.

Example: The social role of employee requires you to be on time and do the work.

	Key study: **Zimbardo (1973)** Stanford Prison Experiment
Aim	To investigate whether people will conform to the social roles of prisoner and guard in a prison situation. To compare **dispositional** vs. **situational** explanations of conformity.
Method	The study was a **controlled observation** scheduled to last for 2 weeks. Zimbardo and his team converted the basement of the psychology department at Stanford University into a prison. 21 male participants (selected from 75 for mental stability) were randomly divided into two groups: **10 'guards'** and **11 'prisoners'**. **Prisoners** were arrested by real police and then subjected to fingerprinting and mug shots. They were put in cells in groups of 3 and confined throughout the experiment. The prisoners wore jackets with their number on, and a chain around one ankle. **Guards** worked 8-hour shifts and referred to prisoners by assigned numbers rather than names. A prison routine was established with meal times, etc. Guards wore khaki uniforms, mirrored sunglasses to prevent eye contact, and had handcuffs and batons.
Results	The guards became increasingly sadistic e.g. forcing prisoners to continually repeat their assigned numbers and making them go to the toilet in buckets in their cells. As punishments, guards refused to allow prisoners to empty these buckets, took away their mattresses and made them sleep on the floor, and took away their clothes. The prisoners became increasingly submissive. Many stopped questioning the guards behaviour and sided with the guards against rebellious prisoners. After 35 hours, one prisoner had a breakdown and was released. 3 other prisoners were released for similar reasons throughout the experiment. It got so bad that **Zimbardo stopped the observation after 6 days** instead of the planned 2 weeks. **Conclusion:** *People conform to social roles to a significant extent. This supports a **situational** explanation of conformity rather than a **dispositional** one.*
AO3	• **Practical applications:** Zimbardo's research prompted reform in the way juvenile prisoners were treated (at least initially). • **Individual differences:** Only some guards were 'brutal' – most weren't. This suggests both situational *and* dispositional factors are needed to explain conformity. • **Demand characteristics:** Subjects knew they were taking part in a study – some said they were just acting. As such, this study may not have *ecological validity*. • **Ethical concerns:** The study caused participants high levels of stress.

Social Influence

SOCIAL INFLUENCE - OBEDIENCE

Obedience: When someone complies with *(obeys)* an order of an authority figure.

	Key study: **Milgram (1963)** Obedience Experiments
Aim	To investigate the extent to which people obey the orders of an authority figure.
Method	40 American male participants aged 20-50 were told they were taking part in a study of the effects of punishment on memory and learning.
	The '**experimenter**' (the authority figure) told the participant he'd been randomly assigned the role of '**teacher**' and that another participant (a confederate) had been assigned the role of '**learner**'. The participant had to give increasingly powerful **electric shocks** to the learner from a machine in the room next door. Each time the learner got a word wrong, the participant had to increase the shock – starting at 15 volts and increasing by 15 volts each time all the way up to **450 volts** (labelled 'XXX').
	The learner started shouting at 150 volts and the protests increased in intensity with the increasing voltage (it was actually just a pre-recorded tape). After 330 volts, the learner went silent. If the participant asked to stop, the experimenter would give verbal prods such as "please continue", and "the experiment requires that you continue" and, finally, "you have no other choice, you must go on.".
Results	**26 out of 40 participants (65%) administered shocks all the way up to the maximum of 450 volts** and 40 out of 40 participants (100%) administered shocks up to 300 volts.
	Conclusion: *People will obey the demands of an authority even if it means going against their own moral code and even if it means killing someone.*
AO3	• **Reliable:** Milgram's results have been replicated several times over the decades (e.g. Burger (2009)), which suggests the results are *reliable*. • **Practical applications:** For example, there are several examples of (typically junior) doctors and nurses knowingly following orders that have injured or killed patients. Training junior doctors and nurses of the dangers of obedience (as demonstrated by Milgram's experiments) could avoid this. • **Ethical concerns:** Milgram was criticised by the American Psychological Association for the extreme stress placed upon the participants (3 suffered seizures). However, participants were debriefed after so it can be argued that the valuable findings of the experiments outweigh the harm caused.

SOCIAL INFLUENCE – OBEDIENCE

Milgram did different versions to determine **variables affecting obedience**

- **Proximity:** Obedience declined when the participant was physically closer to the learner. For example, when the participant and the learner were in the *same room*, obedience fell to 40% from 65%. The proximity of the authority figure also affects obedience – when the authority figure gave instructions *via phone*, obedience fell to just 21% from 65%.
- **Location:** Obedience increases in official-seeming environments. For example, Milgram's original experiment was done at Yale University. But when Milgram (1974) replicated the experiment in an office in a bad part of town obedience dropped to 47.5% from 65%.
- **Uniforms:** In Milgram's original version, the experimenter wore a lab coat. But in another variation, the experimenter was replaced by someone wearing ordinary clothes. In this version, obedience was only 20% rather than 65%. The influence of uniform is also supported by Bickman (1974), who found 38% of participants obeyed orders given by someone wearing a security guard's uniform but only 14% obeyed when the same person wore a milkman uniform.

There are various *explanations* of obedience

Agentic state: The person sees themselves as a tool of the authority figure.	Ordinarily, we are in an **autonomous state:** Freely in control of our actions and taking responsibility for them. But according to Milgram (1974), people in an **agentic state** become de-individuated and consider themselves an agent (tool) of an authority figure and mentally *hand over responsibility* for their actions to the authority figure. This means they will obey instructions that go against their moral compass because they don't take responsibility.
Legitimacy of authority: The authority figure has a right to give orders.	We're taught that obedience to **legitimate authority figures** (e.g. parents, teachers, police) is necessary for an orderly society. Some variables in Milgram's experiments clearly added to the perceived legitimacy of the experimenter's authority (e.g. wearing a lab coat). If a person accepts an authority figure as legitimate, the person will feel they have to obey them.
The authoritarian personality: An inherent *disposition* towards obedience.	This is an **internal explanation** of obedience because it explains obedience as part of someone's *personality* rather than an external one that explains obedience as a result of situational factors in the *environment* they are in. Erich Fromm proposed the **authoritarian personality**: people whose *disposition* makes them submissive to authority and dominating of lower-status people. Adorno *et al* (1950) created the F-scale personality test to measure the authoritarian personality. Elms and Milgram (1966) found people who were obedient in the Milgram experiments scored higher on the F-scale.

AO3: All explanations here have *some* research support, but no single factor explains obedience. A combination of **situational** *and* **dispositional** (i.e. internal) factors is needed.

Social Influence

RESISTANCE TO SOCIAL INFLUENCE AND SOCIAL CHANGE

	There are various **explanations of *resistance* to social influence**
Social support: Having someone on your side.	**Conformity:** Conformity in Asch's experiments (page 5) fell from 32% to 5.5% when one of the confederates *went against* the group and said the correct answer. This confederate provided **social support** for the participant. **Obedience:** In a variation of Milgram's experiments, participants did the experiment **with two other (confederate) teachers**. When the other teachers refused and left, participant obedience dropped from 65% to 10%.
Internal **locus of control:** Rotter's (1966) scale measures if a person believes their own choices shape their life.	**Conformity:** A meta-analysis by Avtgis (1998) found that people with an *internal* **locus of control** (i.e. people who felt their own choices shaped their life) were less likely to conform than people with an *external* locus of control. **Obedience:** Research linking obedience and locus of control is mixed but generally suggests that having an internal locus of control reduces obedience. For example, Blass (1991) analysed data from participants who took part in Milgram's experiments. Using statistical analysis, he found that participants with an internal locus of control were less likely to deliver lethal shocks.

Social change: Establishment of new social norms.

Example: The suffragette movement and womens' voting rights. Social change is often a **snowball effect** as more people become converted to a minority viewpoint and convert others. Eventually, people *internalise* (page 4) the new norms and forget old norms (***social cryptoamnesia***).

	Key study: **Moscovici et al (1969)** Minority Influence
Method	Participants were divided into 3 groups of 6 (4 real participants and 2 confederates) and told they were taking part in a study of visual perception. The participants were shown 36 shades of **blue** and asked to say out loud what the colour was. In one group (*inconsistent* minority), the confederates said **24/36** colours were green. In another group (*consistent* minority) confederates said **36/36** colours were green.
Results	In the control group (no confederates), participants said green **0.25%** of the time. In the inconsistent minority group, participants said green **1.25%** of the time. In the consistent minority group, participants said the colours were green **8.4%** of the time. **Conclusion:** *Consistent* and ***committed*** minority influence is more effective.
As well as consistency and commitment, **flexibility** also improves minority influence. Nemeth (1986) divided participants into groups of 4 (with 1 confederate) to negotiate how much money to pay someone. She found confederates who were *flexible* were **more effective** at persuading the majority to accept a low amount than confederates who inflexibly stuck to a low amount.	

MEMORY – THE MULTI-STORE MODEL

Atkinson and Shiffrin (1968) devised the **Multi-Store Model of memory**.

The **Multi-store Model (MSM)** is a *cognitive* model that explains memory as information passing through **3 storage systems:** Sensory register, short-term memory, and long-term memory.

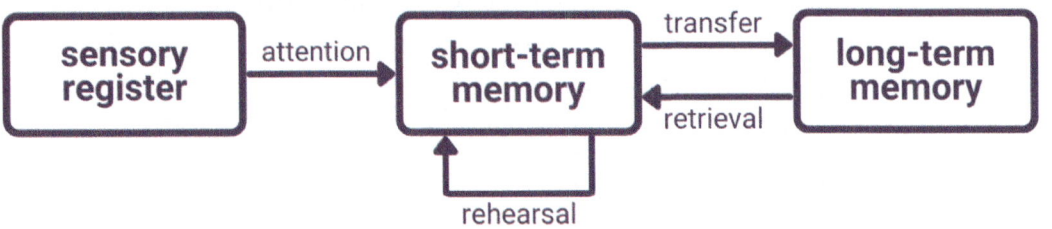

The **sensory register** processes *raw data* coming in from the senses

Information enters the sensory register **coded** in a raw and unfiltered format via sense organs such as the eyes and ears. This information is processed by dedicated stores. For example, visual information goes to the iconic store and auditory information (sound) goes to the echoic store. There is a lot of constantly changing information that passes through these stores, and so the sensory register has a very large **capacity**.

But most information that comes in to the sensory register is quickly forgotten, so its **duration** is very short. However, if a person *pays attention* to information coming in via the sensory register, it gets passed on to the next storage system of the MSM – short-term memory.

Short-term memory contains the information a person is *currently thinking of*

Information from the sensory register is passed on to short-term memory (STM) where it is **coded** into a format that is more easily digestible. For example, the words 'ice cream' could be coded visually (e.g. a picture of ice cream) or acoustically (e.g. repeating the words 'ice cream').

Jacobs (1887) suggests short-term memory has a **capacity** for between 5 and 9 (7 ± 2) items. However, this can be extended by '**chunking**': Grouping items into *semantically similar* groups. For example, '1066007420' = 3 items: Battle of Hastings (1066), James Bond (007), weed (420).

The **duration** of short-term memory is about 30 seconds. This can be extended, though, via rehearsal (i.e. repetition). E.g. repeating a phone number to yourself so you don't forget it.

The duration of **long-term memory** can *last a lifetime...*

...and can be **coded** visually, acoustically, olfactorily (smell), semantically – in many ways.

The **capacity** of long-term memory is very large – possibly infinite. Studies haven't determined the limit of how many long-term memories can be stored (although we do forget – see page 15).

Long-term memories can be *retrieved* and transferred to STM (e.g. thinking of a happy memory).

MEMORY – MODELS OF MEMORY

AO3: **Strengths** of the Multi-Store Model

- **Supporting evidence:** Several case studies and experiments support separate stores for sensory register, short-term, and long-term memory. For example, with amnesia, people are either unable to store *short-term* memories (anterograde amnesia) or *long-term* memories (retrograde amnesia), but not both. This suggests they are separate stores.
- **Influential:** As the first cognitive explanation of memory, the MSM has been influential. Later research has refined the MSM to better explain and understand memory.

AO3: **Weaknesses** of the Multi-Store Model

- **Overly simplistic:** Both short-term and long-term memory are more complex than the Multi-Store Model suggests. For example, the Working Memory Model (see below) shows how short-term memory consists of many different components rather than just a single store. Similarly, there are many different types of long-term memory (e.g. semantic and procedural) that are stored and processed in completely different ways.

Baddeley and Hitch (1974) proposed the **Working Memory Model**.

The **working memory model (WMM)** adds more detail to the **short-term memory** component of the Multi-Store Model, breaking it down into 4 separate components: The central executive, the phonological loop, the episodic buffer, and the visuo-spatial sketchpad.

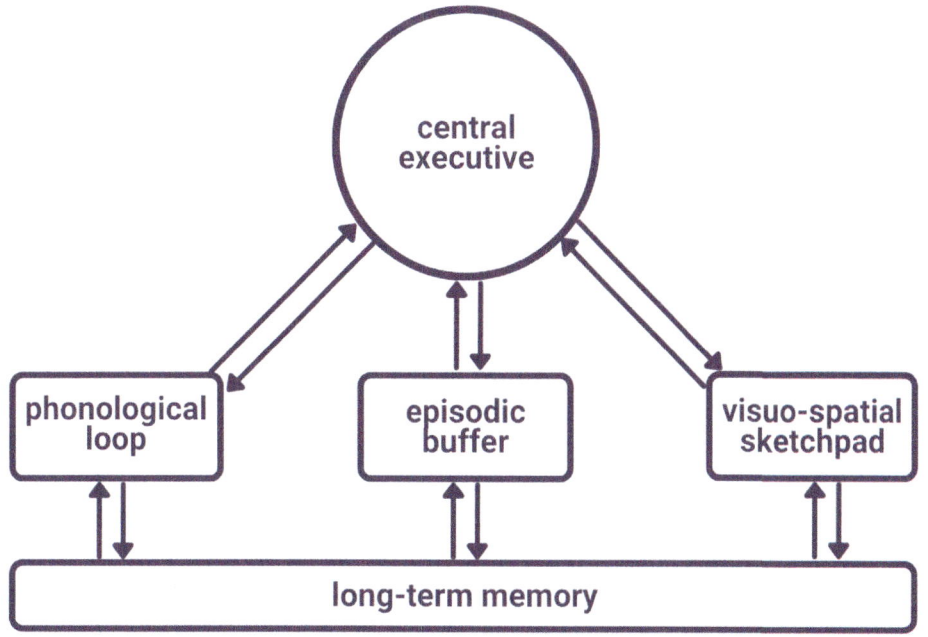

Memory

MEMORY – THE WORKING MEMORY MODEL

The **central executive** co-ordinates the other components of working memory

Working memory is just another word for *short-term* memory. The central executive co-ordinates the various components of working memory and processes information **coded** in all forms (auditory, visual, etc.) and directs this information to **3 slave systems** (see below).

The central executive has a limited **capacity**. Baddeley (1996) found people couldn't perform two tasks (e.g. generating lists of random numbers and switching between pressing letters and numbers on a keyboard) *simultaneously*, because the tasks used up central executive resources.

So, the central executive directs information to other systems for processing. For example, the central executive may direct information required for *driving* to the *visuo-spatial sketchpad*, and direct information required for *talking* would be directed to the *phonological loop*. This enables a person to drive and talk simultaneously.

The **phonological loop** deals with *sound* – particularly words

The phonological loop is divided into **2 sub-systems:**
- **Phonological store:** A short-term store that briefly retains words and the order they appeared in (sometimes called the *inner ear*)
- **Articulatory loop:** Repeats (rehearses) words to keep them within the phonological loop (sometimes called the *inner voice*)

Research suggests the **capacity** of the phonological loop is limited to *how long* words are rather than *how many* words there are. For example, one long word (e.g. floccinaucinihilipification) is harder to store in the phonological loop than three short words (e.g. cat, boat, and happy).

The **visuo-spatial sketchpad** is the mind's inner *eye*

Visual and spatial information is **coded** by the visuo-spatial sketchpad as mental pictures.

Logie (1995) suggests it can be further divided into *visual cache* (for visual information, e.g. *colour*) and *inner scribe* (for spatial information, e.g. location of *objects* relative to each other).

The **episodic buffer** is a temporary store for information coded in all forms

The original WMM didn't include the episodic buffer. But because the central executive has no storage capacity, and the phonological loop and visuo-spatial sketchpad are only able to store and process *specific types* of information, Baddeley (2000) added it to explain how people can **combine and store** information from the various components of short- and long-term memory.

For example, the working memory of a story will likely contain visual, semantic, *and* chronological information (i.e. the order of events). These different types of information would be combined in the episodic buffer to form a coherent story in short-term memory.

Memory

MEMORY – MODELS OF MEMORY

AO3: **Strengths** of the Working Memory Model

- **Supporting evidence:** Penney (1975) observed that short-term recall of words is far better when learned verbally (i.e. using the phonological loop) vs. visually (i.e. using the visuo-spatial sketchpad), suggesting they are separate stores. Further, brain scans conducted by Smith and Jonides (1997) show increased activity in the left hemisphere when doing verbal tasks whereas spatial tasks resulted in increased activity in the right hemisphere.
- **More accurate and detailed:** Whereas the Multi-Store Model explains short-term memory as a single unit, the working memory model accounts for the many different types of short-term memory (e.g. words vs visual information) and the different ways they are processed.

AO3: **Weaknesses** of the Working Memory Model

- **Overly simplistic:** For example, Miyake et al (2000) found that some executive tasks are impaired by brain damage but not others, suggesting separate parts. This suggests the central executive consists of multiple parts - not just the one proposed by the WMM.

There are also different types of **long-term memory (LTM)**

For example, *explicit* LTM is conscious and easy to put into words – such as remembering your first day at school (**episodic**), or a fact such as "Paris is the capital of France" (**semantic**). *Implicit* LTM is subconscious and includes abilities such as knowing how to ride a bike (**procedural**).

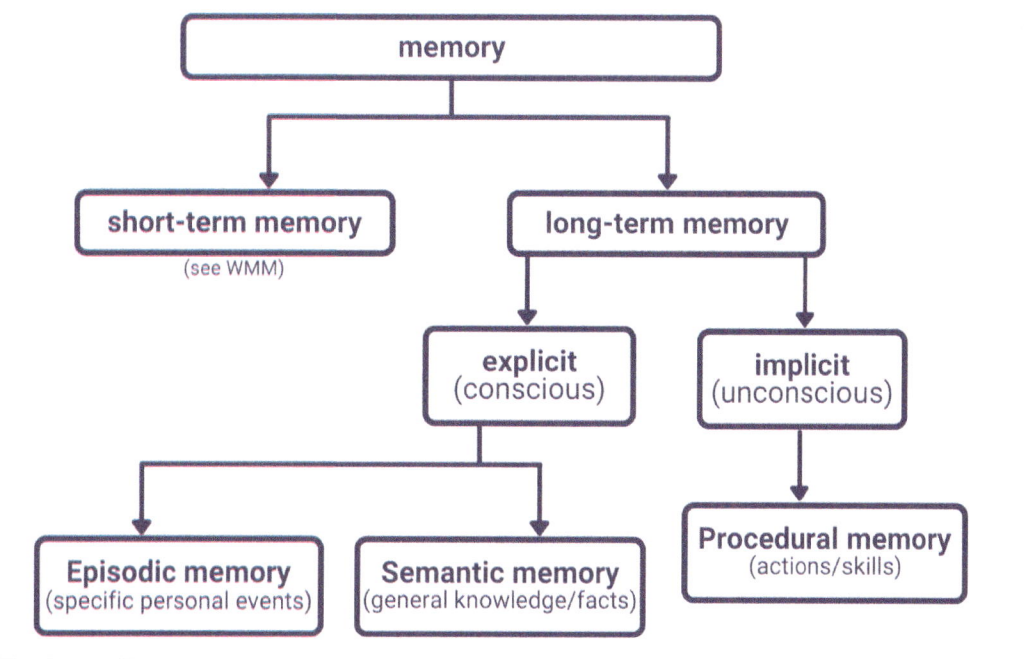

Memory

MEMORY – LONG TERM MEMORY

Episodic LTM covers the story of our lives - i.e. events or *episodes*

For example, remembering your first day at school, or a holiday you went on a few years back, or some embarrassing memory of falling over are all examples of **episodic** long-term memory. It includes context (e.g. time and place), details of what happened, and the emotions felt.

Strong emotions (positive or negative) cause episodic memories to be **coded** more strongly. And if episodic memories are highly **processed** (e.g. by rehearsal) they'll be coded more strongly too.

Semantic LTM is memory of *facts* and *meaning*

Semantic long-term memory covers meaning, understanding, and general knowledge. Examples of semantic memory would be facts like "the Battle of Hastings was in 1066" and general understanding of concepts like dogs as 4-legged mammals that run around and bark.

Procedural LTM is memory of *skills* and *abilities*

Procedural long-term memory covers how to do things – actions, skills, abilities, etc. For example, remembering how to juggle, ride a bicycle, or drive a car. We star forming procedural memory early on – things like knowing how to walk and talk are stored as procedural memory.

Although procedural memories are easy to act out, they are difficult/impossible to *consciously explain in words*. So, unlike semantic and episodic LTM, procedural memory is **implicit**. The fact that procedural memories do not require conscious thought means they can be recalled while simultaneously performing other cognitive activities – for example, trying to remember what the tallest mountain is (semantic, explicit) while walking along the road (procedural, implicit).

AO3: **Strengths** of this model of different types of long-term memory

- **Supporting evidence:** Multiple studies and examples support the distinction between different types of long-term memory. For example, patients with retrograde amnesia may completely forget episodic details of their lives (e.g. childhood events) while still retaining perfect procedural knowledge (e.g. how to ride a bike).

AO3: **Weaknesses** of this model of different types of long-term memory

- **Redundant distinctions:** While a distinction between implicit (procedural) and explicit memory is clearly established, the difference *within* explicit types of LTM (i.e. between semantic and episodic) is less clear. Semantic memory seems to originate *within* episodic memory, and there is significant overlap between the two categories. For example, if you are remembering a semantic fact for a test (e.g. the capital of France) you might do so by recalling your experience (episodic) of looking at a map the night before.

MEMORY – EXPLANATIONS OF FORGETTING

Forgetting: The inability to recall information from long-term memory.

There are 2 **explanations of forgetting** you need to know (well, 4 actually)		
Interference: When *existing* information stored in memory disrupts recall. This may be newer information disrupting older info *(retroactive)* or vice versa *(proactive)*.	**Proactive interference:** When *older* information interferes with your ability to remember something *newer*. *Example:* You're trying to remember the new login password you set but you keep thinking of your previous one.	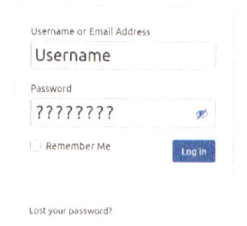
	Retroactive interference: *Newer* information disrupts *older* information. *Example:* You're trying to remember your home address from 10 years ago but you keep thinking of your home address from 2 years ago.	
	AO3: Interference only explains forgetting in cases where two types of information are similar, such as the address and password examples above. But a lot of what we forget (e.g. events that happened in the past) can't be explained by interference. So, other explanations of forgetting are needed.	
Absence of cues: When information can't be accessed because there is nothing to *trigger* the memory. Tulving and Thomson (1973) say forgetting is more likely when the context is different to the context when the memory was created.	**Context-dependent failure:** When the *external* environment does not provide the cues necessary to recall a memory. *Example:* You're able to remember your bank card pin code when you have to type it in an ATM but can't remember when walking along a beach.	
	State-dependent failure: When a person's *internal* mental state during recall is different to the internal state when they coded the memory. *Example:* Darley et al (1973) observed that participants who forgot where they hid money while high on cannabis were more likely to remember where they hid that money once they got high again compared to when they were sober.	
	AO3: There is more research supporting cue-dependent forgetting than interference and some psychologists see it as the main reason for forgetting. However, psychological research on forgetting due to absence of cues is often based on experiments in artificial (laboratory) settings and so the findings might not transfer to ordinary examples of forgetting.	

Memory

MEMORY – EYEWITNESS TESTIMONY

Misleading information can reduce the accuracy of eyewitness testimony (EWT)

Key study: **Loftus and Palmer (1974)** Leading Questions and EWT

Method	45 participants were divided into 5 groups and shown the same video clips of car crashes. After each clip, they were asked questions about the car crash. Each group was asked the same question – *"How fast were the cars going when they **X** each other"* – but with a different verb: **"Contacted"**, **"hit"**, **"bumped"** **"collided"**, or **"smashed"**.
Results	Asking the question using a more intense verb (e.g. "smashed") rather than a less intense verb (e.g. "contacted"), **influenced** the participant to estimate a higher speed. **Conclusion:** *This suggests that asking leading questions reduces the accuracy of EWT.*

Anxiety can affect the accuracy of eyewitness testimony in different ways

Deffenbacher (1983) conducted a meta-analysis that supports an **"inverted-U" hypothesis** where a *medium* amount of anxiety produces the most accurate and detailed EWT. However, too much anxiety (too scared) or too little anxiety (too calm) *reduces* the accuracy of EWT.

AO3: Research on the inverted-U hypothesis is conflicting. For example, in interviews with bank robbery witnesses, Christianson and Hubinette (1993) found no relationship between anxiety and accuracy of testimony, weakening support for the inverted-U hypothesis.

The cognitive interview is supposed to increase the accuracy of EWT

Context reinstatement	Remembering the *external* environment (e.g. the building & weather) and the individual's *internal* state (e.g. the emotions felt). These contextual details may provide **cues** that help trigger more memories.
Recall from a different perspective	For example, what another witness was seeing, or what the culprit saw. This reduces potential bias from the witness' **schema**.
Recall in a different chronological order	For example, starting from the end and working backwards. This also helps reduce potential bias from the witness' **schema** (see page 36).
Report everything…	…even unimportant details. Memories have different retrieval paths so recalling these details may provide **cues** to trigger more memories.

AO3: Evidence generally supports the cognitive interview. Geiselman et al (1985) found the cognitive interview increased the accuracy and detail of recollection compared to standard police interviews. A meta-analysis by Kohnken et al (1999) also found this, but found the cognitive interview also increased the number of *inaccurate* details too. Milne and Bull (2002) found some features of the cognitive interview are more important than others: Context reinstatement and reporting everything appear to be the most important factors for an accurate and detailed EWT.

ATTACHMENT – CAREGIVER AND INFANT INTERACTIONS

Attachment: An emotional connection between people (e.g. baby to its mother).

Caregiver-infant interactions have typical **features** that build attachment

Reciprocity: Both sides are involved and engaged.	Interactions between caregivers and infants not one-way, they are **reciprocal**. For example, when the baby smiles, it will often make the mother smile back and vice versa. These kinds of reciprocal interactions strengthen the emotional connection between infant and caregiver.
Interactional synchrony: Interactions between infant and caregiver are somewhat *synchronised* – a bit like a conversation.	For example, the mother might pull a funny face, the baby laughs, and then the mother laughs back. These kinds of interactions are rhythmic and co-ordinated, with both infant and caregiver '**taking turns**' in a similar way to how adults take turns to speak in conversations.
	AO3: Condon and Sander (1974) analysed videos of infants and caregivers. They saw that infants moved and reacted to caregivers in rhythm, supporting the idea of interactional synchrony. Isabella et al (1989) found interactional synchrony is correlated with *secure* attachment styles (see page 21).
Other features	Mimicking, physical contact, and **motherese** (slow, high-pitched, 'baby talk').

Schaffer and Emerson (1964) identified 4 **stages of attachment**

Pre-attachment	Birth – 3 months	From very early on, babies enjoy the company of other people and prefer humans over objects and other non-human things. But the baby can't yet tell different human faces apart.
Indiscriminate attachment	3 months – 8 months	The baby starts to prefer familiar people. However, the baby will allow a stranger to handle them without getting upset.
Specific attachment	8 months onwards	The baby's attachment to its primary caregiver (e.g. its mother) is very strong. The baby has separation anxiety (distress from being away from its primary caregiver) and a fear of strangers.
Multiple attachments	10 months onwards	The baby begins forming attachments to other familiar faces, such as grandparents and other children. However, the strongest emotional attachment is with the primary caregiver.

33% of the time, a baby's primary attachment figure will be its **father**...

… according to Schaffer and Emerson (1964). Geiger (1996) argues that mothers typically occupy the **caregiving** and **nurturing** role to infants, whereas fathers are typically a **playmate** who provides physical and exciting play. However, societal changes (such as more mothers going to work) may affect this and it is increasingly common for a man to be an infant's primary caregiver.

BEHAVIOURISM AND SOCIAL LEARNING THEORY

AO3: **Strengths** of behaviourism

- **Scientific:** Behaviourism focuses on what is observable, measurable, and repeatable, which lends credibility to the study of psychology as a science.
- **Practical applications:** Behaviourism has several useful psychological applications. For example, the behaviourist treatment of phobias (see page 27) is highly effective.

AO3: **Weaknesses** of behaviourism

- **Ignores internal factors:** By focusing only on environmental *inputs* (stimulus) and behavioural *outputs* (responses), behaviourism neglects the mental events in the middle such as thoughts, reflections, and emotions. This makes it difficult for behaviourism to explain behaviours such as memory, which happen internally and so cannot be observed.
- **Animal studies:** Humans are very different – both physically and cognitively – to animals such as dogs and rats. As such, the conclusions drawn from studies on animals (e.g. Pavlov and Skinner) may not be valid when applied to human psychology.

The **basic assumptions** of the **social learning theory (SLT)** are...

...similar to behaviourism (page 33) in that SLT says behaviours are *learned* from experience. However, SLT adds a *social* dimension: We learn not only from consequences of our own behaviour, but by **observing** and **imitating other peoples' behaviour**.

Key study: **Bandura et al (1961)** Bobo the Doll

Aim	To investigate whether children will imitate the behaviours of a **role model**.
Method	**Laboratory experiment** with **independent groups** design. 36 boys and 36 girls aged between 3 and 6 years old were individually put in a room with an **inflatable doll** (Bobo) and **observed** an adult role model interact with the doll for 10 minutes. The subjects had been separated into **3 groups** with different **independent variables**: 1. **Aggressive:** Role model hits the doll with a hammer and shouts abuse at it 2. **Non-aggressive:** Role model does not hit the doll or shout at it 3. **Control:** No role model After observing the role model for 10 minutes, the participants were taken to a room with toys (including a Bobo doll) and left to play with them for 20 minutes.
Results	Children who had **observed an aggressive** role model **acted more aggressively** (e.g. hitting the Bobo doll) than children who had observed a non-aggressive role model.
AO3	• **Controlled:** As a lab experiment, Bandura was able to control extraneous variables. • **Low ecological validity:** But a lab scenario is *artificial*, so the results may not be *valid* in real life. For example, perhaps the children wouldn't be aggressive in *school*.

Approaches in Psychology

ATTACHMENT – ANIMAL STUDIES

A lot of early research into attachment was conducted on **animals**. Whenever you're discussing animal studies, there are a few trusty *evaluation* (**AO3**) points you can always make:

- A **strength** of animal studies is they are generally more ethical than human studies.
- But a **weakness** is animals are not humans so the findings may not be *valid* in humans.

Key study: **Lorenz (1935)** Imprinting

Method	Lorenz split a clutch of goose eggs into two groups: One hatched naturally by the mother, and the other hatched in an incubator and **Lorenz himself was the first moving object the newborn goslings saw**. After hatching, the goslings from both groups were placed under a box. When the box was lifted up, their behaviour was recorded.
Results	The naturally hatched goslings followed their mother immediately after birth, but the incubator goslings followed Lorenz. In the box test, the naturally hatched goslings went straight to their mother, whereas the incubator goslings went straight to Lorenz. **Conclusion:** *This demonstrates **imprinting** - the goslings attached to the first moving object they encountered regardless of whether it was their biological mother.*
AO3	**Relation to other theories:** Imprinting always occurred within 4-25 hours after birth. This could provide support for Bowlby's concept of a *critical period* (see page 20).

Key study: **Harlow (1959)** Food vs. Comfort

Aim	To test whether attachment is based solely on food (as learning theory might suggest).
Method	**Laboratory experiments** where baby rhesus monkeys were separated from their natural mothers and raised in cages with **surrogate mothers** made from either **metal wire** or a **soft towel**. In some variations, the *wire* mother produced milk to feed the baby monkeys and in other variations the *towel* mother produced milk. Harlow recorded how much time the monkeys spent with each mother. He would sometimes expose them to loud noises to see which mother they went to under stress.
Results	Monkeys who had access to *both* mothers always spent more time with the soft towel mother and went to it when stressed – **regardless of whether it produced food**. Monkeys with only a wire mother showed physical symptoms of stress (e.g. diarrhoea). **Conclusion: *Comfort** is more important for attachment (in monkeys) than **food**.*
AO3	**Relation to other theories:** *Learning theory* (see page 19) argues that attachment is a conditioned response to feeding, but Harlow's study is evidence against this theory.

Attachment

LEARNING THEORY EXPLANATION OF ATTACHMENT

Learning theory explains attachment as a *conditioned* (learned) response

Before learning

The **unconditioned stimulus** (food) causes an **unconditioned response** (pleasure)

During learning

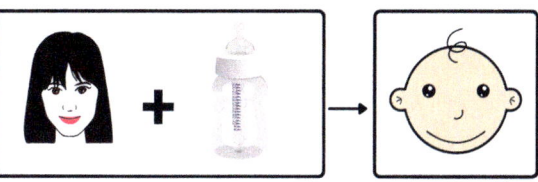

Baby *learns* to associate the pleasurable stimulus (food) with the **neutral stimulus** (caregiver) during feeding because they occur **at the same time**

After learning

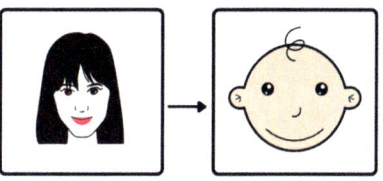

The formerly neutral stimulus (caregiver) in now a **conditioned stimulus** that creates a **conditioned response**: *Pleasure*. **Learning theory says this is how attachment forms.**

The explanation above is an example of **classical conditioning,** but there may also be *operant* **conditioning** (page 33) involved too. For example, *reducing unpleasant feelings* (i.e. hunger) may also *negatively reinforce* attachment to the caregiver.

AO3: **Strengths** of the learning theory explanation of attachment

- **Theoretical support:** The principles of classical conditioning have theoretical support. For example, Pavlov's experiments on dogs (see page 33), may apply to human behaviour.

AO3: **Weaknesses** the learning theory explanation of attachment

- **Conflicting evidence:** Schaffer and Emerson (1964) found 39% of infants developed a primary attachment to someone other than the mother (the person who fed them). Further, Fox (1977) studied attachments in Israeli kibbutzim, where babies were fed by caregivers called metapelets. Despite being *fed* by the metapelets, most babies were more attached to their mothers.
- **Reductionist:** Learning theory ignores all other factors that might influence attachment, such as cognitive processes and emotions. So it may be an overly reductive explanation.

BOWLBY'S MONOTROPIC EXPLANATION OF ATTACHMENT

Bowlby's (1951) **monotropic theory of attachment** is evolutionary

It says humans **evolved** an innate capacity to form an attachment to **one** (hence **mono**tropic) persom from birth – i.e. the mother. The reason for this is that in a dangerous environment, infants would die if left to fend for themselves. And so, nature **selects** for babies who behave in ways that form bonds with caregivers who'll protect them. These behaviours aren't *learned*, as learning theory (page 19) says, but are pre-programmed from birth (**innate**).

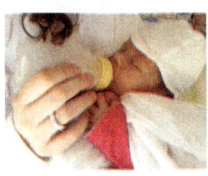

There is a **critical period** within which babies must develop attachments

After this period, the infant will have difficulty forming attachments at all. For most infants, this critical period is **12 months after birth**. Although some infants may develop attachments after this time, Bowlby believed all infants must develop attachments within 3 years for healthy psychological development. Bowlby's maternal deprivation hypothesis (page 22) describes what happens if an infant fails to develop attachments in the critical period.

Early monotropic attachments form an **internal working model**...

...for all *future* attachments. In other words, an infant's monotropic (primary) attachment forms a **template** for all relationships that follow. This includes *friendships* and *romantic* relationships.

The internal working model is a cognitive framework through which the individual understands themself and their expectations for relationships to other people. It also creates consistency between emotional experiences in early life and in later relationships (see page 23 for more).

AO3: **Strengths** of Bowlby's monotropic theory of attachment

- **Supporting evidence:** Several studies discussed so far support Bowlby's montropic theory. Fox (1977) (page 19) demonstrates how babies formed monotropic attachments to their biological mothers despite being fed by metapelets. And the imprinting seen in Lorenz (1935) (page 18) was also monotropic: The goslings became attached to a single person.

AO3: **Weaknesses** Bowlby's monotropic theory of attachment

- **Conflicting evidence:** Schaffer's stages of attachment (page 17) show that most babies develop *multiple* attachments after 10 months, rather than just one monotropic one as proposed by Bowlby. Further, Rutter's Romanian orphan studies (page 22) suggest that infants can form attachments *after* the critical period and be psychologically healthy.
- **Stereotypical:** Bowlby's monotropic theory assumes the *mother* is the primary attachment figure. However, it's common for fathers to be an infant's primary attachment (see page 17).

Attachment

ATTACHMENT - TYPES OF ATTACHMENT

Key study: **Ainsworth et al (1978)** The Strange Situation		
Method	\multicolumn{2}{l	}{**Controlled observation:** An infant is exposed to 8 'episodes' (~3 mins each) during which different people enter and leave a room. The infant's behaviour is observed.}
	M & I & O	**Observer** takes **mother** and **infant** into the room and leaves.
	M & I	**Mother** allows the **infant** to explore the room with her present.
	M & S & I	A **stranger** enters the room. The stranger is silent at first then talks to the **mother**. Then the stranger approaches the **infant** and mum leaves.
	S & I	The **stranger** interacts with the **infant** (this is the 1st *separation* episode).
	M & I	The stranger leaves, the **mother** returns and plays with the **infant** for a while (this is the 1st *reunion* episode) and then leaves again.
	I	The **infant** is left alone in the room (this is the 2nd *separation* episode).
	S & I	The **stranger** returns to the room and interacts with the **infant.**
	M & I	**Mother** returns and comforts **infant** (2nd *reunion* episode), stranger leaves.

Ainsworth et al (1978) identified **3 types of attachment** in the strange situation

Secure	High *stranger* anxiety, high *separation* anxiety. **Happy** when reunited.
Insecure-avoidant	Low *stranger* anxiety, low *separation* anxiety. **Indifferent** when reunited.
Insecure-resistant	High *stranger* & *separation* anxiety. Reunion: Seeks but **pushes mum away**.
\multicolumn{2}{l	}{*70% of infants had secure attachments, 15% insecure-avoidant, and 15% insecure-resistant.*}

Van Ijzendoorn and Kroonenberg (1988): **Cultural variations** in attachment

Ainsworth's strange situation has been replicated many times and in many **different countries**. Van Ijzendoorn and Kroonenberg (1988) conducted a meta-analysis of 32 studies (1990 mother-child pairs total) across several countries. Below is a *partial* table of some of the results:

Country	# Studies	Secure	I-Avoidant	I-Resistant	
USA	18	65%	21%	14%	**AO3:** These results suggest culture *does* play a part in attachment styles. Western cultures (USA, Germany) may have higher insecure-avoidant attachments than e.g. Japan.
Germany	3	57%	35%	8%	
Japan	2	68%	5%	27%	

However, in many cases, *intra*-cultural differences were bigger than *inter*-cultural differences. For example, one USA study had 94% insecure-avoidant, whereas another USA study had just 47%.

DISRUPTION OF EARLY ATTACHMENT

Bowlby's **maternal deprivation hypothesis** (MDH)...

... says if attachments between infants and their mothers are broken for a long time during the *critical period* (see page 20) it causes **psychological damage** (e.g. aggression and depression).

The MDH is supported by Bowlby's (1944) **44 thieves** study where he interviewed 44 children who had been referred to him for stealing and compared them to a control group of 44 'emotionally disturbed' children who did not steal. Of the 44 *thieves*, **17 (39%) had been separated from their mothers before age 2** whereas just 2 children in the control group **(4.6%)** had been separated from their mothers before age 2. Further, Bowlby diagnosed 14 of the thieves as '*affectionless psychopaths*' – and 12 of these 14 **(86%)** had experienced maternal deprivation before age 2.

Strengths:	• **Supporting evidence:** Goldfarb (1943) found children raised in orphanages for the first 3 years of life suffered intellectually and socially in later life.
Weaknesses:	• **Reversible:** The MDH says psychological damage is permanent but Rutter's orphan studies (below) suggest these effects are largely reversible. • **Correlation does not prove causation:** Bowlby (1944) and Goldfarb (1943) could be explained by poor conditions in orphanages (e.g. poverty, crowding, etc.) rather than maternal deprivation specifically.

Institutionalisation is the psychological effects of being raised in an institution

Effects of institutionalisation may include delayed language development, low IQ, disinhibited attachment, reduced physical growth, and difficulties forming relationships in adulthood.

Key study: **Rutter et al (1998)** Romanian Orphan Studies

Aim	To observe the effects of early deprivation and see whether they can be reversed.
Method	A **longitudinal study** and **natural experiment** that followed 111 children who'd been placed in Romanian orphanages (an environment of **extreme deprivation**) before 2 weeks of age. These children were adopted into British families at different ages. The control group consisted of 52 *British* orphans adopted into British families.
Results	By age 4, the Romanian orphans adopted *before* 6 months old had caught up (physically and cognitively) with the British orphan control group. The Romanian orphans adopted *after* 6 months old had made significant progress but had not fully caught up with the control group – many demonstrated disinhibited attachments (e.g. treating strangers the same way they would their primary caregiver). **Conclusion:** *Institutionalisation can be mostly reversed. But the longer an infant goes without an attachment, the more likely psychological effects will be permanent.*
AO3	**High ecological validity:** Natural experiments are likely to reflect real-world effects.

THE INFLUENCE OF EARLY ATTACHMENT

Bowlby's **continuity hypothesis** is based on the internal working model...

...that is *learned* in childhood (see page 20 for more). And there is a lot of psychological research to support a **consistency** between early infant attachments and attachments later on.

Early attachment experiences may influence **friendships** in childhood

For example, Youngblade and Belsky (1992) conducted a longitudinal study of 73 children. They found that children who had demonstrated **secure attachment styles** (see page 21) at 1 year old were **more likely to have close friendships** and get along well with other children by ages 3-5.

And there is also continuity between early attachments and **adult relationships**

	Key study: **Hazan and Shaver (1987)** Love Quiz
Method	The researchers had a 'love quiz' printed in a newspaper. **620 participants** answered questions that would determine which of Ainsworth's **attachment styles** they had as infants, as well as their experiences and views of **romantic relationships** as adults.
Results	The researchers found **correlations** between infant attachment styles and romantic relationships in adulthood. For example, participants who were identified as **securely attached** infants from the childhood questions tended to have **longer lasting relationships and lower divorce rates** as adults. Those with either of the insecure attachment styles in infancy were more likely to be lonely as adults. **Conclusion:** *The authors took these findings to support Bowlby's continuity hypothesis.*
AO3	**Biased sample:** Certain kinds of people are unlikely to respond to a 'love quiz' in a newspaper, so this volunteer sampling method could have created a biased sample.

*Bonus: Bailey et al (2007) found continuity in infant attachments and **parenting style** as adults.*

AO3: **Strengths** of the continuity hypothesis

- **Supporting evidence:** The studies above all support the continuity hypothesis.

AO3: **Weaknesses** of the continuity hypothesis

- **Alternative explanations:** Correlations between infant attachment and adult relationships could be explained *biologically* rather than via a learned internal working model. For example, Kagan and Snidman (2004) argue for a *temperament hypothesis:* That humans have innate and biologically determined personality traits. These innate character traits would be consistent into adulthood, influencing both infant and adult relationship styles.

PSYCHOPATHOLOGY – DEFINITIONS OF ABNORMALITY

Psychopathology: The study of mental disorders and conditions that are considered psychologically *abnormal*. **(But *abnormal* is not easy to define!)**

The **deviation from social norms** definition of abnormality

Examples of **social norms** would be wearing clothes in public and respecting people's personal space. We can define *abnormality* as behaviour that **deviates** from these social norms. For example, going up and touching random strangers or walking around naked is **abnormal**.

Strengths:	• **Practically useful:** The social dimension of this definition can help both the abnormal individual and wider society. For example, intervening when someone breaks social norms may protect people from the potentially dangerous behaviours of abnormal individuals.
Weaknesses:	• **Subjective:** Social norms are not objective facts of which behaviours are most healthy, they are subjective (and sometimes arbitrary) rules created by people. • **Changing:** Social norms change and so what is considered a mental disorder today might not be in the future. For example, homosexuality was diagnosed as a mental disorder by the American Psychiatric Association until 1973. • **Deviation =/= mental illness :** Deviating from social norms might just be eccentric rather than *abnormal*. For example, it's against social norms to dress in 18th century clothes today, but it's not exactly a mental disorder.

Failure to function adequately means a person struggles in everyday life

Rosenhan and Seligman (1989) give various **features of dysfunction,** including: Personal distress (e.g. anxiety, depression, excessive fear), maladaptive behaviour (i.e. behaviour that prevents the person achieving goals), irrationality, unpredictability, and discomfort to others. A person who demonstrates any of these features is failing to function adequately and thus **abnormal**.

Strengths:	• **Objective and quantifiable:** The Global Assessment of Functioning (GAF) scale provides a way to quantify (from 0 to 100) the extent to which a mental disorder affects an individual's ability to function adequately. • **Anecdotal support:** Most people who seek help for psychological disorders do so *because* they're failing to function adequately. So, this definition is supported by the individuals themselves who suffer from mental disorders.
Weaknesses:	• **Successful functioning does not mean psychologically healthy:** There are many people who *are* psychologically abnormal but who function well in society. For example, there have been many instances of serial killers who managed to maintain a normal – or even highly successful – life despite being psychopaths. 

Psychopathology – Chapter 4

PSYCHOPATHOLOGY – DEFINITIONS OF ABNORMALITY

The **statistical infrequency** definition of abnormality...

...is a **mathematical** one. It defines abnormality as statistically rare characteristics and behaviours. The further from the mathematical average, the more **abnormal** it is.

Strengths:	• **Objective:** Statistical infrequency provides a clear and objective way of determining whether something is abnormal or not. It is not just the subjective opinion of one person, but something that can be measured and quantified. • **Useful:** Statistical infrequency is a good measure for many psychological disorders. For example, intellectual disability has historically been defined as having an IQ lower than 70 (2 standard deviations below the mean).
Weaknesses:	• **Infrequency =/= psychological disorder:** For example, having an IQ above 140 is *statistically infrequent*, but it's not a mental disorder and is actually quite desirable. And **vice versa:** Many abnormal mental disorders (such as depression and anxiety) are *statistically* quite common. • **Not all psychological disorders can be quantified:** Some psychological disorders are difficult to measure objectively and so hard to quantify as statistically infrequent. For example, how do you *quantify* how depressed or anxious someone is to determine whether they're statistically infrequent?

The **deviation from ideal mental health** definition of abnormality

Jahoda (1958) identified **6 features of ideal mental health:** A positive attitude towards oneself, self-actualisation (see page 42), autonomy (i.e. being independent), ability to resist stress, an accurate perception of reality, and mastery of environment (e.g. successful work, social life, etc.). If a person does not meet these 6 criteria, they are said to be **abnormal** by this definition.

Strengths:	• **Holistic:** This definition focuses on the *entire person* rather than *atomised elements*. This may provide a more effective and long-lasting means of treating mental disorders. For example, a person with depression might have low self-esteem and not be achieving self-actualisation. Addressing these issues might be more effective than e.g. prescribing drugs just so they function adequately.
Weaknesses:	• **Subjective:** Jahoda's criteria are somewhat subjective and hard to measure. For example, it is hard to quantify how much a person is self-actualising, or the extent to which they are able to master their environment. There are methods for measuring such characteristics (e.g. patient self-reports) but these may be unreliable, as each individual is likely to have different standards. • **Too demanding:** Very few people meet *all* 6 of Jahoda's features above. For example, Maslow believed only around *1%* of people achieve self-actualisation, which would mean that 99% of people would be classified as abnormal!

PSYCHOPATHOLOGY – BEHAVIOURIST APPROACH TO PHOBIAS

Phobia: An anxiety disorder characterised by extreme and irrational fear towards a stimuli. For example, *arachno*phobia = extreme fear of *spiders*.

Characteristics of phobias	
Emotional	Extreme, uncontrollable **fear** and **anxiety** when confronted with their phobia.
Behavioural	**Screaming, crying, freezing,** or **running away** from the feared stimuli. Attempts to avoid the feared stimuli – e.g. someone with *aero*phobia will avoid airports.
Cognitive	Most people with phobias **recognise** that their fear is disproportionate and irrational but this does little to reduce the fear the phobic person feels.

The syllabus focuses on a *behaviourist* explanation of phobias…	
…which is called the **two-process model** because there are 2 parts: *Classical* and *operant*.	
1. Phobias are *acquired* through **classical conditioning** (see page 33 for more on this)	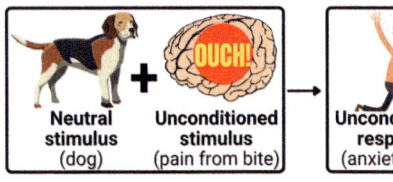   Humans naturally fear pain. But when this natural (unconditioned) response is *associated* with a neutral stimulus (e.g. a dog) through experience (e.g. a dog biting them)… …then a person can become **conditioned** to associate the response (fear) with the stimulus (dogs).
2. *Maintained* through **operant conditioning**	See operant conditioning on page 33 for the different types of reinforcement. *Example:* A person with a phobia of dogs will feel anxiety (an unpleasant feeling) in the presence of dogs. And so, avoiding dogs (e.g. by avoiding parks) will lessen this anxiety, which **negatively reinforces** these dog-avoiding behaviours.
Strengths:	• **Supporting evidence:** Watson and Rayner (1920) were able to induce a phobia of rats in a baby – Little Albert – by making a loud noise when the rat was near.
Weaknesses:	• **Alternative explanations:** The cognitive approach explains phobias in terms of thought processes. For example, there is evidence that phobic people may have an attentional bias (i.e. disproportionate focus of thought) towards the scariest features of the stimuli (e.g. a dog's teeth or a spider's venom). • **Exceptions:** Not everyone who has an unpleasant experience at the same time as a neutral stimulus goes on to develop a phobia. For example, a person who gets bitten by a dog will not always develop a phobia of dogs.

PSYCHOPATHOLOGY – BEHAVIOURIST TREATMENT OF PHOBIAS

Systematic desensitisation *gradually* exposes people to their phobias

One behaviourist treatment for phobias is **systematic desensitisation**. This involves **gradually** increasing exposure to the feared stimuli until it no longer induces anxiety.

Example: Someone with arachnophobia may initially be asked to *imagine* spiders while being guided through relaxation strategies to stay calm. Then, the process is repeated with *pictures* of spiders, then *real-life* spiders in cages, until the subject actually *hold* the spider.

Systematic desensitisation is another example of **classical conditioning:** the subject is conditioned to *associate* the object with relaxation instead of anxiety.

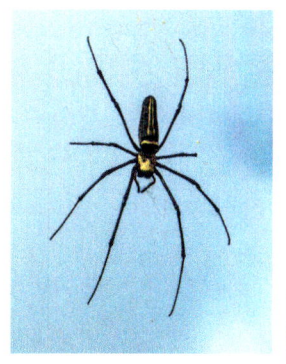

Whereas **flooding** chucks the phobic person in at the deep end

Another behavioural approach to treating phobias is **flooding**. Whereas systematic desensitisation increases exposure step-by-step, flooding involves exposing the subject to the **most extreme scenarios** straight away.

Example: Locking someone with a phobia of dogs in a room with one until their anxiety subsides.

The idea behind flooding is that **extreme anxiety cannot be maintained** indefinitely. Eventually, through flooding, the fear subsides and (in theory) so does the phobia.

AO3: **Strengths** of behaviourist treatment of phobias

- **Evidence supporting systematic desensitisation:** In Jones (1924), a 2 year old boy – Peter – had a phobia of white rats and similar stimuli. Jones was able to remove Peter's phobia over several sessions with him by progressively increasing his exposure to a white rabbit.
- **Evidence supporting flooding:** Wolpe (1969) cured a girl's phobia of cars by driving her around in a car for four hours until she calmed down and her phobia disappeared.

AO3: **Weaknesses** of behaviourist treatment of phobias

- **Ethical concerns:** Treating phobias with flooding may raise ethical concerns. For example, forcing a girl with a phobia of cars into one for hours (as Wolpe (1969) did) may be seen as cruel. Systematic desensitisation is perhaps the more ethical of the two treatments.
- **Doesn't work for all phobias:** Although behaviourist treatments are highly effective for treating *simple* phobias (such as spiders or dogs), they are much less effective for phobias such as agoraphobia (fear of open spaces or fear of leaving one's house) and social phobias (such as fear of public speaking).

PSYCHOPATHOLOGY – COGNITIVE APPROACH TO DEPRESSION

(Unipolar) **Depression:** A mood disorder characterised by feelings of low mood, loss of motivation, and inability to feel pleasure.

Characteristics of depression	
Emotional	Persistent feelings of **sadness** and hopelessness. Feelings of worthlessness and a **lack of enthusiasm**. Low mood may come and go in cycles lasting months/years.
Behavioural	Low energy, **reduced activity**, and reduced social interaction. Depressed people may also have **irregular sleep patterns** (either sleeping too much or too little (insomnia)) and **gain or lose weight** from over- or under-eating.
Cognitive	Exaggerated or **delusional negative thoughts** about self and world. **Difficulty concentrating** and remembering. Sometimes thoughts of death or suicide.

The syllabus focuses on *cognitive* explanations of depression…	
…so these say depression is caused by irrational **thoughts** and **beliefs** (i.e. irrational *cognitions*).	
Beck's (1979) negative triad	Beck argues that depression is caused by a **negative triad** of beliefs about: The **self** (e.g. *"I'm useless"*) the **world** (e.g. *"everyone hates me because I'm useless"*) and the **future** (e.g. *"things won't improve, I'll always be useless"*).
	He argues that this negative triad results from and is maintained by two cognitive processes: **Negative schema** (see page 36) and **cognitive biases**. E.g. an attentional bias towards negative experiences while ignoring positive ones.
Ellis' (1962) ABC model	Ellis explains depression as **activating event** (A), **belief** (B), and **consequence** (C). Compare the *beliefs* in the examples below – left is *rational*, right *depressed*:

A: Losing a game of chance	**A:** Losing a game of chance
B: *"It's not my fault, it's just chance"*	**B:** *"I always lose, I'm such a failure"*
C: Healthy emotional response	**C:** Negative emotional response

Strengths:	• **Supporting evidence:** Boury et al (2001) observed that depressed participants consistently *misinterpreted* facts and experiences in a negative way, supporting the idea that depression is caused by biased and irrational thought processes. • **Practical applications:** The fact that CBT (see page 29) is an effective treatment for depression provides support for the underlying cognitive *explanation*.
Weaknesses:	• **Alternative explanations:** Wender et al (1986) found that adopted children with depression were 8 times more likely to have biological parents who also had depression. This suggests there is a strong genetic/biological component to depression (rather than simply a cognitive explanation).

Psychopathology

PSYCHOPATHOLOGY – COGNITIVE TREATMENT OF DEPRESSION

The cognitive treatment for depression is **cognitive behavioural therapy (CBT)**

The cognitive approach sees depression as caused by negative, irrational, and maladaptive thought patterns (see page 28). So **CBT treats depression by changing these thoughts**.

CBT therapists help patients to **identify** depressed thought patterns. The therapist then encourages the patient to **recognise** these depressed thought patterns as irrational, false, and unhelpful. The patient is then encouraged to **replace** these irrational thoughts with more accurate and helpful ones. Changing their **thoughts** changes their **behaviour** and **emotions**. The *behavioural* component of CBT may involve exercises (e.g. scheduled activities, journal writing).

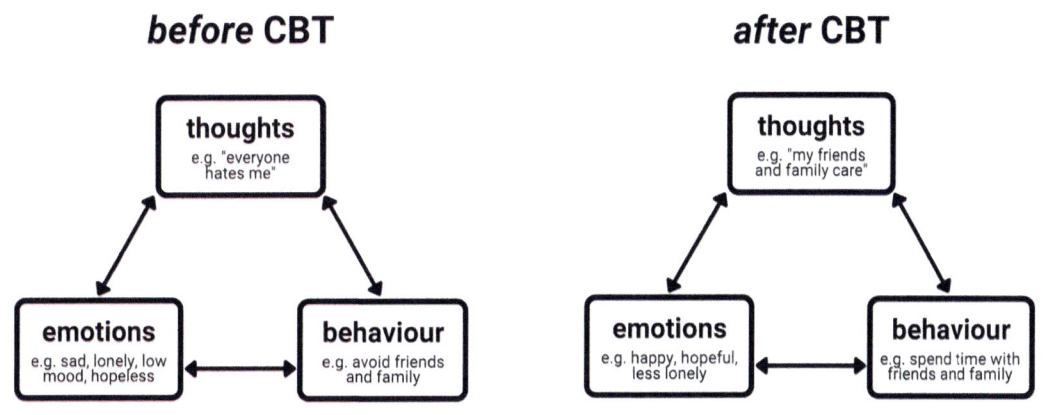

AO3: **Strengths** of cognitive behavioural therapy for depression

- **Supporting evidence:** Many clinical studies have shown that CBT is highly effective for treating depression. For example, a meta-analysis by Beltman et al (2010) found that CBT significantly reduces depressive symptoms.
- **No side effects:** *Biological* treatments for depression (e.g. SSRI drugs) may cause negative side effects. In contrast, CBT does not cause side effects.

AO3: **Weaknesses** of cognitive behavioural therapy for depression

- **Other treatments:** There is evidence that biological treatments (e.g. drug therapy such as SSRIs) are equally or potentially more effective for treating depression. However, this isn't necessarily a weakness as the two treatment approaches can be combined together.
- **Variations between patients:** Embling (2002) found that CBT is an effective treatment for depression, but that it is more effective for some personality types than others. For example, people who are high in sociotrophy (i.e. who strongly desire social acceptance) and with an external locus of control (see page 9) benefit less from CBT. Embling's study also found that CBT + antidepressant drugs is more effective than antidepressants alone.

PSYCHOPATHOLOGY – BIOLOGICAL APPROACH TO OCD

Obsessive-Compulsive Disorder (OCD): An anxiety disorder characterised by continuous and repeated undesirable thoughts (obsessions) and uncontrollable behaviours and rituals in response to these thoughts (compulsions).

Example: Obsessive thoughts about germs may lead to compulsive hand-washing behaviour and rituals as the individual tries to alleviate these obsessive worries.

	Characteristics of OCD
Emotional	High levels of **anxiety** and **stress** in response to obsessive thoughts.
Behavioural	Continuous **repetition of behaviours** and **rituals** in response to obsessive thoughts. Both the obsessive thoughts and the compulsive behaviours get in the way of everyday tasks, disrupting normal activities such as work and social life.
Cognitive	**Repetitive** and **persistent** thoughts to do with the obsession. Cognitive **biases** that focus attention on the obsession. OCD sufferers are often aware their obsessive thoughts are exaggerated but are still unable to control them.

Genetics are one biological explanation of OCD

Twin studies (see page 38) support a genetic explanation of OCD. A meta-analysis by Grootheest et al (2005) looked at studies comparing **concordance rates** for OCD among *monozygotic* (identical) twins with concordance rates among *dizygotic* (non-identical twins). Based on this, they estimate that genetics are 45%-65% responsible for OCD in children and 27%-47% in adults.

Other studies have used **gene mapping** to identify **correlations** between genes and OCD. For example, Davis et al (2013) compared the genetic profiles of 1500 OCD sufferers with 5500 non-OCD controls and found OCD sufferers often shared similar genetic patterns that were not present in the non-OCD controls.

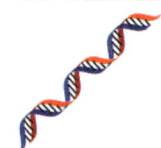

And neural factors are another biological explanation of OCD

Brain structures	Brain scans - e.g. Saxena and Rauch (2000) – suggest OCD sufferers have increased activity in the **orbital frontal cortex,** which is sometimes called the *worry circuit*. This area translates impulses into actions, but overactivity in this area may mean impulses to perform behaviours continue even after performing them, which leads to obsessions and compulsions.
Neuro-chemistry	Several studies – e.g. Hu et al (2006) – suggest OCD sufferers have **lower levels of serotonin** (a *neurotransmitter* – see page 45) compared to controls. Some brain scans also suggest OCD sufferers have **higher dopamine levels** than controls.

PSYCHOPATHOLOGY – BIOLOGICAL APPROACH TO OCD

AO3: **Strengths** of biological explanations of OCD

- **Supporting evidence:** The studies above support biological explanations of OCD.

AO3: **Weaknesses** of biological explanations of OCD

- **Conflicting evidence:** If OCD was entirely determined by genetics, the concordance rate would be 100% among identical twins because they have 100% identical genetics. However, concordance rates for OCD among identical twins are much less than 100%, which weakens the genetic explanation.
- **Other factors:** A holistic explanation of OCD would need to include cognitive factors (e.g. persistent irrational thoughts about germs) and behavioural factors (e.g. alleviation of anxiety through cleaning behaviours negatively reinforces those behaviours).

The main **biological treatment for OCD** is drug therapy

The most common drugs prescribed for OCD are **selective serotonin reuptake inhibitors** (SSRIs) such as fluoxetine (Prozac) and sertraline (Zoloft).

SSRIs are also known as antidepressants and work by **increasing serotonin levels**, which often reduces obsessive thoughts and compulsive behaviours to a level that allows the patient to live a more normal life. The effectiveness of SSRIs fits with the neural explanation of OCD (page 30) that OCD is caused by low serotonin.

If OCD symptoms do not improve with SSRIs, a doctor may also prescribe antipsychotic drugs such as risperidone. One mechanism of risperidone is to **reduce dopamine activity**, which supports the neural explanation that high dopamine contributes to OCD.

AO3: **Strengths** of drug therapy for OCD

- **Supporting evidence:** Multiple studies such as Pigott and Seay (1999) and Soomro et al (2008) have found SSRIs to reduce OCD symptoms, which suggests that biological treatment approaches to OCD are effective.

AO3: **Weaknesses** of drug therapy for OCD

- **Side effects:** SSRIs may cause side effects e.g. nausea, headaches, sleep disruption, and loss of libido. These risks must be weighed against the benefits of reduced OCD symptoms.
- **Other treatments:** A meta-analysis by Jonsson and Hougaard (2009) found CBT to be more effective at reducing OCD symptoms than drug therapy (in some studies). But this isn't necessarily a weakness as drug therapy can be *combined* with CBT. Many studies (e.g. O'Connor et al (1999), O'Kearney et al (2006)) suggest *both* both CBT and drug therapy are effective at reducing OCD symptoms – but *CBT + drug therapy* is most effective.

APPROACHES IN PSYCHOLOGY – THE ORIGINS OF PSYCHOLOGY

Wilhelm Wundt is known as the *'father of experimental psychology'*...

...because he was a pioneer of studying the mind in a **scientific** way. He founded the first psychology laboratory – *the Institute of Experimental Psychology* – in **1879**.

Wundt's **experiments** used **introspection**. Introspection means looking 'inward' and examining one's thoughts, emotions, and sensations. For example, an experiment might involve showing subjects a picture, and they would report back their inner experiences. For Wundt, this was not about reporting whatever random thing the subject felt. It was intended as a highly systematic process – *a science*. Wundt **controlled the environments** and researchers were trained to adopt the right mental state before reporting the specific data Wundt wanted. Despite this, the reports were highly **subjective** and varied from person to person, which meant they were **unreliable**.

Strengths:	• **Scientific:** Wundt tried to apply the scientific method to his studies. For example, controlling the environment where he conducted his introspection experiments would prevent this extraneous variable from skewing the results. • **Influential:** Introspection and Wundt's focus on inner mental processes can be said to have influenced the cognitive approach (see page 36).
Weaknesses:	• **Unscientific:** Despite Wundt's attempts to be scientific, his research can be considered unscientific in many ways. Science is about what is objective, measurable, and repeatable (see page 52) but the private thoughts examined during introspection are subjective and couldn't be measured or replicated.

The emergence of **psychology** *as a science*

1879 vvvvv	*Since Wundt,* a variety of approaches to psychology have emerged – some more **scientific** than others. Ordinarily, science is about what is **objective** and **measurable**, but the subjective dimension of the human mind means people aren't as predictable as things like gravity. This **subjective dimension** led to various different **approaches** to psychology:
1912 vv	**Behaviourism** emerged in the early 20th century and remained the dominant approach to psychology until the 1950s. It rejected Wundt's introspective approach as too subjective, instead focusing only on **externally observable** and **measurable data** – *behaviour*.
1950 vv	The *'cognitive revolution'* of the 1960s saw renewed interest in **inner mental processes**. Although thoughts and feelings are private and unobservable, the **cognitive approach** sought to make *inferences* about these inner mental processes from experiments.
1990 vvvvvvv	Advances in technology (particularly in the early 21st century) have progressively increased the power of a **biological approach** to psychology. For example, the invention of **fMRI brain scanning** in 1990 enabled psychologists to measure brain activity and correlate it with mental processes. Elsewhere, advances in **genome sequencing** since the early 2000s have enabled psychologists to identify a genetic basis for some psychological disorders.

Approaches in Psychology – Chapter 5

LEARNING APPROACHES (BEHAVIOURISM)

The **basic assumptions** of the **behaviourist approach** are...

- The mind is a blank slate at birth and **all behaviour is learned** from experience.
- The study of the mind should focus on **external behaviour**, not internal thought processes, as behaviour is the only thing that can be objectively measured and observed.
- The same processes governing human behaviour also govern animal behaviour (e.g. rats and dogs) so **animal experiments** can yield valid conclusions about human behaviour.

Pavlov's (1927) dogs provide a *classic* example of **classical conditioning**

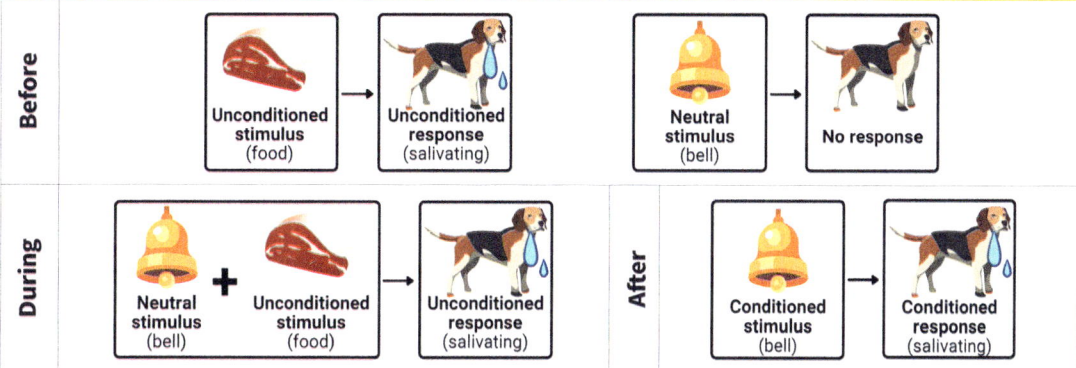

Behaviours are *learned* via **subconscious association**. This key principle of behaviourism may be *valid* in humans, too. E.g. reaching into your pocket when *someone else's* phone goes off.

Skinner's (1938, 1948, 1953) experiments demonstrate **operant conditioning**

Skinner put rats individually in cages, now referred to as **'Skinner boxes'**. In one variation, the rats could press a response lever that caused **food** to come out of a food dispenser. In another variation, the floor was an **electrified grid** and pressing the response lever turned it off.

Positive reinforcement	Doing something that gets a positive consequence. This **increases** the likelihood the behaviour will be repeated.	Food coming from the food dispenser *positively reinforced* pressing the response lever.
Negative reinforcement	Doing something that *avoids* a *negative* consequence. This also **increases** the likelihood the behaviour will be repeated.	Stopping the electric shocks *negatively reinforced* pressing the response lever.
and also, **Punishment**	Negative consequences for behaviour. This **decreases** the likelihood that the behaviour will be repeated.	If pressing the lever turned the electrified floor on instead of off, that would *punish* this behaviour.

Operant conditioning occurs in response to **conscious choices**. Rewards and punishments **reinforce** these choices of behaviour, making them either more or less likely to be **repeated**.

Approaches in Psychology

LEARNING APPROACHES (SOCIAL LEARNING THEORY)

The Bobo studies illustrate the **key concepts of social learning theory**

According to SLT, people **imitate** (copy) behaviours of **role models** they *identify* with (i.e. people they are like or want to be like). This was demonstrated in the study above by the fact that the children were more likely to imitate the behaviour of the role model if the role model was the same gender as them – they were more likely to *identify* with a role model of their own gender.

Bandura and Walters (1963) illustrates another key concept of SLT: **Vicarious reinforcement**, where behaviours are **reinforced by observing others**. In this variation of the Bobo experiment, the role model was either *praised* or *punished* for acting aggressively towards the doll. Children who observed the model **praised** for their aggression toward the doll were *more* **likely to imitate** this aggressive behaviour but *less likely* **to imitate** it if the role model was **punished.**

Mediating processes are *in-between* observing a behaviour and imitating it

So **social learning theory isn't 100% behaviourist** because it invokes inner, private, and *unobservable* cognitive processes. Bandura (1977) describes these **4 mediating processes:**

Attention	The behaviour has to be important/significant so as to grab our **attention**.
Retention	The observed behaviour has to be remembered/**retained**. If you don't remember a behaviour then you can't imitate it.
Reproduction	Our abilities may influence our decision to **physically reproduce** the behaviour. E.g. an elderly lady might desire to reproduce breakdancing behaviour, but won't attempt it because of a lack of physical ability.
Motivation	If we think a potential behaviour will be positively rewarded (e.g. because we've observed vicarious reinforcement), this **motivates** us to imitate the behaviour.

AO3: **Strengths** of social learning theory

- **More holistic:** Whereas behaviourism is limited to stimulus and response only, SLT allows for cognitive processes in explaining behaviour such as thoughts, beliefs, and abilities. This can explain why two people might act differently in response to the same stimulus.
- **Explanatory power:** SLT can explain why, for example, someone might take up smoking: They observe their friends (*role models* they *identify* with) smoking and *imitate* them.

AO3: **Weaknesses** of social learning theory

- **Reductionist:** Although more holistic than behaviourism, SLT still explains all behaviour as *learned* from experience while ignoring other factors. However, even Bandura's own studies suggest other factors: Boys showed more aggression towards the dolls than girls independently of other conditions. This suggests that *biological* factors (e.g. testosterone levels) also play a role in explaining behaviour and that SLT is not, by itself, complete.

Approaches in Psychology

APPROACHES – THE COGNITIVE APPROACH

The **basic assumptions** of the **cognitive approach** are...

- **Inner mental processes** *can* and *should* be studied in a scientific way.
- It's not enough to understand the mind solely in terms of stimulus and response (as behaviourism – page 33 – does). Although a person's inner mental processes can't be *observed*, they can be **inferred** from their external behaviour.
- Mental processes can be modelled like a **computer program**: inputs (e.g. sense data) get processed in the mind (like a computer program) to produce outputs (i.e. behaviour).

Schema are *cognitive frameworks* for organising information

They're basically **mental blueprints** that help us make sense of the world. For example:

Self schema	How you understand yourself. This includes physical characteristics (e.g. "I'm tall" or "I'm ugly") and personality traits (e.g. "I'm competitive" or "I'm kind").
Role schema	Understanding of what people do in certain social roles (see page 6). E.g. "Police catch criminals" or "customers join the queue before paying".
General	E.g. "Dogs have 4 legs", "video games are boring", "dark alleys are dangerous".

Schema cover **a lot** of things. They're formed from experience and change over time. For example, a child might form the schema that *"dog = 4 legged furry animal"*. But this schema would include *cats* too and so the child refines its schemas to become more detailed.

However, once a schema is formed, it can be difficult to change: People are **biased** towards information that *fits* their schema, and often *ignore* or *re-interpret* contradictory information in order to fit their existing schema.

Our schemas are the **cognitive lens** through which we view the world. Because everybody has *different* schema, everybody has a *different perception* of reality.

Cognitive neuroscience looks at brain activity underlying cognitive processes

The cognitive approach started gaining traction in the 1950s. But as technology advanced (most notably with brain-scanning tools such as fMRI – see page 50) from the 1970s onwards, scientists became able to identify **correlations** between certain types of **brain activity** and certain types of **mental processes**.

For example, Braver et al (1997) observed that greater **working memory load** (a *cognitive* concept) is correlated with greater **prefrontal cortex activity** (a *biological* concept). This suggests the underlying biological basis for working memory is situated in that area of the brain. As cognitive neuroscience advances, more cognitive processes can be analysed in biological terms.

So, cognitive neuroscience is a mix between the **cognitive** and **biological** approaches (page 38).

Approaches in Psychology

APPROACHES – THE COGNITIVE APPROACH

The cognitive approach says cognitive processes are like **computer processes**

The cognitive approach thinks of mental processes as similar to computer processes. With a *computer*, data goes in, it gets processed, then you get an output. *The mind* can be said to work in a similar way: **Input** from your senses is processed by the mind to produce an **output**.

	Computer	**Human Mind**
Input	Typing an equation into a spreadsheet (e.g. "2 * 7")	Hearing the auditory data of the teacher asking you "what's 2 x 7?"
Data processing	Data is processed by *electronic circuits* on a computer chip	Data is processed by *neurons* in the brain and you work out the answer
Data output	The spreadsheet updates to display the answer ("14")	You speak out loud and say the answer "14"

These processing steps can be broken down into **theoretical models**, which can be tested against observations using experiments to see if these theoretical models are accurate.

Example: The multi-store model of memory (page 10): It explains how information flows through various components for processing. For example, *paying attention* to sensory information causes it to be transferred (processed) to short-term memory.

AO3: **Strengths** of the cognitive approach to psychology

- **Scientific:** Although mental processes cannot be observed *directly*, the cognitive approach uses scientific methods based on observable data to infer details of these processes.
- **Explanatory power:** The cognitive approach addresses a key issue for behaviourism: Why two people can have different behaviours in response to the same stimulus (e.g. why some children imitated the aggressive role model in Bandura's experiments but others didn't).
- **Practical applications:** Therapies based on the cognitive approach (e.g. cognitive behavioural therapy) have been shown to produce positive results. For example, many studies have shown CBT to improve symptoms of depression (see page 29).

AO3: **Weaknesses** of the cognitive approach to psychology

- **Reductive:** The cognitive approach's analogy between the mind and a computer has its limitations. Although there are similarities between the two types of processing, there are important differences. For example, human emotions (which computers lack) have a significant effect on processing, which is not accounted for in a purely information-processing model (e.g. the effect anxiety has on eyewitness testimony – see page 16).
- **Ecological validity:** Theories based on the cognitive approach (e.g. the working memory model – see pages 11 and 12) are often based on lab studies, but these results might not translate to real-life. For example, Baddeley's (1996) test of the capacity of the central executive is an unusual task that one wouldn't normally perform in real-life.

APPROACHES – THE BIOLOGICAL APPROACH

The **basic assumptions** of the **biological approach** are...

- Psychological processes are, at first, **biological** processes.
- These biological processes include **genetics**, **biological structures** (i.e. the brain and nervous system), and **neurochemistry** (e.g. hormones and neurotransmitters).

Genetic effects are divided into **genotype** and **phenotype**

Genotype: Your *actual* genes.	These are decided at conception and consist of around 100,000 genes that **cannot be changed**.	For example, hair colour. You can *dye* your hair, but it still grows back the same colour that is determined by your genotype. Similarly, you might be born with the SLC1A1 gene, which is linked to OCD.
Phenotype: This is how you genes present...	...in response to **environmental factors**. Even though your genotype *itself* can't change, the way it's *expressed* can vary.	For example, height has a strong genetic component, but a person with *tall genes* could end up having *short height* if they grow up in a malnourished environment. Similarly, a person with the SLC1A1 gene could use cognitive behavioural therapy to overcome this gene and not exhibit OCD behaviours.

Twin studies can show if a psychological trait is genetically determined

The **concordance rate** is the rate at which twins *share* the same trait.

If the concordance rate for a psychological disorder (e.g. OCD) is higher among **identical** twins (monozygotic twins) than **non-identical** twins (dizygotic twins), this suggests a **genetic component** to the disorder.

The reason for this is that identical twins have **100% identical genetics** whereas non-identical twins **only share 50% of their genes**. So, if a disorder is *entirely* determined by genetics, then identical twins would both develop the disorder because they share identical genes. However, because non-identical twins only share 50% of their genes, there's a chance only one will inherit the genetics for the disorder but not the other.

Disorder	Identical twins concordance rate	Non-identical concordance rate
Schizophrenia	48%	17%
Bipolar depression	40-70%	5-10%

The higher concordance rates among identical twins than non-identical twins suggests genetic factors play a role in bipolar depression and schizophrenia. But even among identical twins, the concordance rates are less than 100% - so there must be more to these disorders than genetics.

Approaches in Psychology

APPROACHES – THE BIOLOGICAL APPROACH

If psychological traits are *genetically* determined, then **evolution** plays a role

Example: If there was an **intelligence** gene that made a human better at hunting food, then the human with that gene would be less likely to starve to death and so **more likely to survive to pass on that gene** to its offspring. This shows how psychological traits may **evolve** over time.

Another example of evolved psychological traits could be Bowlby's monotropic theory of attachment (page 20). Bowlby argued that babies evolved to develop an attachment to one person – usually its mother. This behaviour makes the baby **more likely to survive** and **pass on its genes** because a baby that does not develop an attachment will be left to fend for itself in a dangerous environment and probably die before it gets the chance to procreate.

Biological structures and neurochemistry...

...are covered in greater detail in the **biopsychology** topic (page 44).

But just as a quick teaser, some key *biological structures* within the biological approach are the **central nervous system** (i.e. the brain and spinal cord), **neurons**, and the **endocrine system**.

And *neurochemical factors* include **hormones** (like testosterone and estrogen) and **neurotransmitters** (such as serotonin, dopamine, GABA, and glutamate).

AO3: **Strengths** of the biological approach to psychology

- **Scientific:** The biological approach focuses on observable and measurable phenomena such as hormone levels, brain structures, and genes. These biological phenomena can be *measured* using technology (e.g. fMRI scanners) and *tested* using rigorous scientific methods (e.g. randomized double-blind placebo-controlled trials of drugs).
- **Practical applications:** Biological approaches have proven highly successful in treating mental disorders. For example, we saw on page 31 how drugs such as SSRIs are highly effective for treating OCD. Similarly, drug therapy has been successfully used to treat depression, anxiety, and other psychological conditions.

AO3: **Weaknesses** of the biological approach to psychology

- **Reductive:** The biological approach can be said to be overly reductive in that it ignores other factors, such as environment. For example, a person with the same genes is likely to behave differently if raised by a different family or in a different culture. This shows that *genetics* can only go so far in explaining human behaviour.
- **Deterministic:** Biological factors, such as genetics and biological structures, are outside of our control. This leaves no room for free will (page 73), which makes it difficult to hold people responsible for their actions as those actions are just a consequence of biology rather than free choices of the individual. This raises both moral and legal issues: How is it fair to send someone to prison, for example, for something they didn't choose to do?

APPROACHES – THE PSYCHODYNAMIC APPROACH

The **basic assumptions** of the **psychodynamic approach** are...

- The mind consists of multiple parts – some of which are conscious, some **unconscious**.
- These different parts of the mind **conflict** with each other and shape behaviour.
- **Early childhood experience** shape us as adults. Failure to resolve psychological conflicts in childhood can lead to psychological problems as an adult.

Freud's **psychoanalytic theory** emphasises **the role of the unconscious**

According to Freud, there are **3 levels of consciousness:**

- **Conscious:** What we are directly aware of.
- **Pre-conscious:** Things we're currently not aware of but can be accessed if needed (e.g. memories and beliefs).
- **Unconscious:** Everything else (and there's a lot!) including biological drives, instincts, desires, repressed memories, and fears. These cannot easily be accessed.

Most psychological activity happens below the level of consciousness. However, unconscious thoughts often bubble to the surface in things like **dreams** and **Freudian slips** of the tongue (e.g. accidentally calling your girlfriend 'Mum'). **Psychoanalysis** helps *identify* these unconscious thoughts, which then can be addressed to treat psychological disorders.

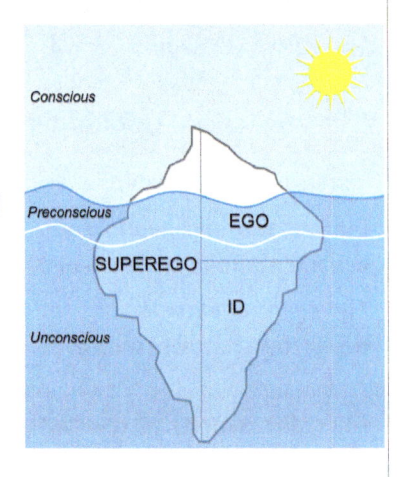

Freud's **tripartite structure of personality** consists of 3 parts

The id	The **primitive**, biological, part of personality. It is present from birth.	Operates on the **pleasure principle**, demanding gratification of its needs.
The ego	The part of personality that **mediates** between the id and the superego. It develops around 1-3 years old.	Operates on the **reality principle** and is able to delay the id's demand for pleasure.
The superego	The **moral** 'higher values' part of personality. It develops at 3-5 years old.	Operates on **the morality principle**, punishing the ego through guilt.

According to Freud's psychoanalytic theory, behaviour is determined by the **interaction** of these three parts – which often have **conflicting demands**. The ego sits in the middle and tries to balance between the id and superego. For example, your *id* might want to kill your annoying neighbour then do a load of drugs and cheat on your wife/husband, but your *superego* tells you that would be morally wrong. So, the ego's job is to keep these competing demands in balance.

Improper balance between the id and superego creates **anxiety** and is the cause of **mental disorders**. One way in which the mind resolves these conflicts is via *defence mechanisms*.

Approaches in Psychology

APPROACHES – THE PSYCHODYNAMIC APPROACH

Defence mechanisms are unconscious strategies to reduce anxiety, including:

- **Repression:** *Hiding* an unpleasant or undesirable thought (e.g. sexual or aggressive urges) or memory (e.g. childhood abuse) from the conscious mind.
- **Denial:** Rejecting and *refusing to accept reality* (e.g. failing to acknowledge that your girlfriend doesn't love you any more after you break up).
- **Displacement:** *Redirecting* emotions from the actual target to a *substitute* (e.g. kicking your cat because you're angry about an episode that happened at work that day).

Normal development involves passing through 5 psychosexual stages

At each stage, a **conflict** must be **resolved** before moving on to the next stage.

Stage	Age	Focus	Description
Oral	0 - 1 years	Mouth	Feeding (mother's breast) is the object of pleasure
Anal	1 - 3 years	Anus	Pleasure from withholding and expelling faeces
Phallic	3 - 5 years	Genitals	Masturbation: Desire focuses on penis or clitoris
Latency	5 - 12 years	Repressed	Sexual desires are repressed
Genital	Puberty	Genitals	Sexual desires are conscious and directed towards sex

These stages are crucial for healthy psychological development. For example, if toilet training is *too harsh* at the anal stage, it manifests as an obsessive and overly tidy personality as an adult. If toilet training is *too relaxed*, it manifests the opposite personality, i.e. messy and disorganised.

AO3: **Strengths** of the psychodynamic approach to psychology

- **Explanatory power and influence:** Freud's theories were among the first to explain how experiences in early childhood influence adult personality. This idea is now common to many other psychological theories, such as Bowlby's continuity hypothesis (see page 23).
- **Practical applications:** There is *some* evidence – often anecdotal – that psychoanalytic therapies (e.g. dream analysis and free association) can help treat some mental disorders.

AO3: **Weaknesses** of the psychodynamic approach to psychology

- **Unscientific:** Science is about what can be measured, observed, and repeated. But unconscious concepts (e.g. the id) are not observable to the individual themself let alone measurable in a lab! Further, Freud's theories were primarily based on his own subjective interpretations of individual case studies rather than measurable and quantified data.
- **Reductive:** The psychodynamic approach explains all mental disorders as the result of conflict between different aspects of the mind. But this ignores other factors (e.g. biological). For example, there are physical differences in both the neurochemistry and biological structures of people with OCD and without. Addressing these physical causes is likely to be more effective than psychoanalysis for many psychological disorders.

Approaches in Psychology

APPROACHES – HUMANISTIC PSYCHOLOGY

The **basic assumptions** of the **humanistic approach** are...

- Human beings have **free will**.
- Each individual is **unique** and so scientific approaches to psychology are flawed.
- Each person should be viewed and treated **holistically**.

The humanistic approach is all about **free will**, **holism**, and the **individual**

Science is typically about identifying *general rules* (e.g. gravity). But because the humanistic approach believes all humans are **unique**, it rejects attempts to identify general rules of human behaviour, making it an **idiographic** approach (see page 76 for more).

Humanistic psychology also **rejects reduction**. The biological approach, for example, would reduce depression to *biological factors* (e.g. neurochemistry) and behaviourism would explain it solely in terms of *experience* (e.g. negative experiences *teach* depression). However, the humanistic approach would acknowledge **all** these factors, which makes it a **holistic** approach.

Free will means humans are able to make choices without being controlled by the influences of biology or environment (see page 73 for more). Humanistic psychology **rejects determinism** and see humans as free to change and make decisions that lead to *self-actualisation*.

Self actualisation means fulfilling your potential...

...but what this looks like will be different for everyone – because each person is *unique*. The humanistic approach believes *all* humans have a **desire** to achieve **self-actualisation**.

Maslow's (1943) view of self-actualisation involves satisfying all **5 levels** in a **hierarchy of needs:**

Pyramid (top to bottom): Self-actualisation | Esteem needs | Social needs | Safety needs | Physiological needs

At the bottom of the hierarchy are the most essential **physiological** needs – without things like food, water, and air to breathe, you die. The next most essential needs are **safety** (e.g. having a home), followed by **social** (e.g. having friends and romantic relationships), and then **esteem** needs (e.g. a job you are good at).

These lower levels of the hierarchy are **deficiency needs**. A person without these basic needs is lacking and must address them before they can reach the top of the pyramid: **self-actualisation.**

Self-actualisation is a *growth* need. It involves fulfilling your full creative, moral, and intellectual potential. A self-actualising person is one who is constantly striving towards and achieving a worthy goal. Maslow gave several examples of self-actualised people, including Albert Einstein, but believed only around **1% of people** truly achieve self-actualisation.

Approaches in Psychology

APPROACHES – HUMANISTIC PSYCHOLOGY

Carl Rogers said self-actualisation requires congruence...

...between a person's **self-image** (i.e. how a person sees themselves now) and **ideal self** (i.e. how they would *like* to be). If these things are too far apart, a person can't achieve self-actualisation.

Rogers also argues that self-actualisation requires **positive self-regard** (i.e. a positive opinion of yourself). If a person's parents imposed **conditions of worth** on them as a child (e.g. only praising and loving them *when they did well in school*), this can cause low self-esteem and poor self-regard. But if their parents treated them with **unconditional positive regard**, they're more likely to have positive self-regard as an adult and will find self-actualisation easier to achieve.

Rogers' counselling psychology is the humanistic approach to treatment

According to Rogers, the 3 core qualities of a good **counselling therapist** are:

- **Genuine:** The therapist doesn't hide behind a professional facade.
- **Unconditional positive regard:** The therapist accepts and values the client for who they are without disapproval or judgement.
- **Empathy:** The therapist tries to understand and appreciate the client's perspective.

The aim of Rogers' counselling psychology (also called *person-centred therapy*) is to **increase congruence** between a client's self-image and ideal self and to **increase feelings of self-worth**.

AO3: Strengths of humanistic psychology

- **Practical applications:** Counselling psychology is commonly used within social work and has helped many people improve their lives. Beyond psychology, Maslow's hierarchy of needs has been influential within the business world to explain improve motivation.
- **Holistic:** Whereas other psychological approaches are *reductive*, the humanistic approach considers all aspects of a person's life. This holistic approach may yield more valid insights and treatment approaches.

AO3: Weaknesses of humanistic psychology

- **Unscientific:** Science is about what can be measured, observed, and repeated. But the *subjective* approach of humanistic psychology means it does not produce this kind of quantifiable or replicable data. As such, it is hard to objectively test the claims of the humanistic approach against reality and say whether they are true or not. Further, science involves developing hypotheses and general theories that explain behaviour, but humanistic psychology is idiographic so rejects such attempts to generalise behaviour.
- **Cultural differences:** Self-actualisation within the humanistic approach focuses entirely on the *individual* achieving their own potential. However, more collectivist cultures emphasise the *common good* and may prefer to focus on achieving community or societal potential rather than individual self-actualisation.

BIOPSYCHOLOGY – THE NERVOUS SYSTEM

The nervous system is divided into 2 parts: central and peripheral

And these 2 parts are divided into further subcategories. The **central nervous system (CNS)** consists of the **brain** and **spinal cord**. The **peripheral nervous system (PNS)** connects the CNS to the rest of the body and the external world and is divided into **autonomic** and **somatic**.

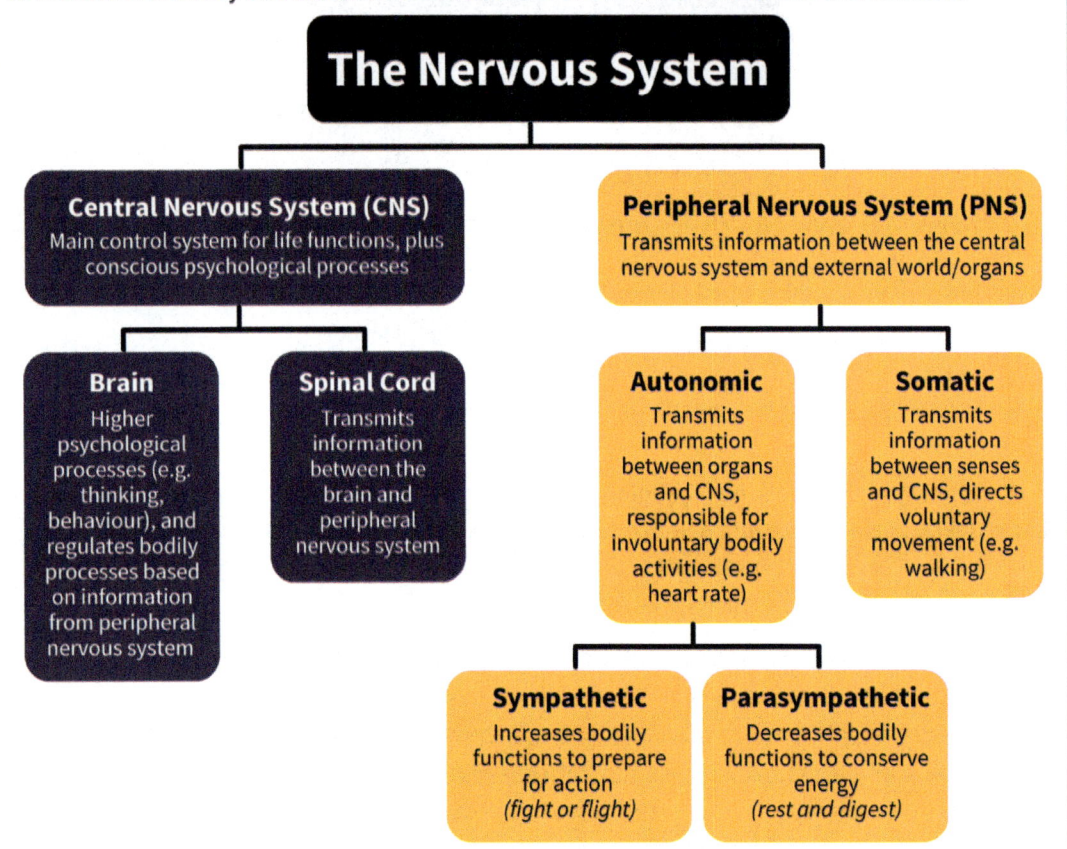

The Nervous System

Central Nervous System (CNS)
Main control system for life functions, plus conscious psychological processes

- **Brain**: Higher psychological processes (e.g. thinking, behaviour), and regulates bodily processes based on information from peripheral nervous system
- **Spinal Cord**: Transmits information between the brain and peripheral nervous system

Peripheral Nervous System (PNS)
Transmits information between the central nervous system and external world/organs

- **Autonomic**: Transmits information between organs and CNS, responsible for involuntary bodily activities (e.g. heart rate)
- **Somatic**: Transmits information between senses and CNS, directs voluntary movement (e.g. walking)

The autonomic system divides into:

- **Sympathetic**: Increases bodily functions to prepare for action (fight or flight)
- **Parasympathetic**: Decreases bodily functions to conserve energy (rest and digest)

The **somatic nervous system** is responsible for **voluntary** movement (e.g. walking) and is under conscious control. The **autonomic nervous system** is **involuntary** and controls various processes in the body – either increasing or decreasing them depending on the situation.

Organ	Sympathetic	Parasympathetic
Heart	Increases heart rate	Decreases heart rate
Digestive system	Decrease digestion	Increase digestion
Eyes	Dilate pupils	Constrict pupils

When a person is under stress, the **sympathetic nervous system** *increases* bodily activities to prepare for action – this is known as the **fight or flight** response (see page 46). Once a threat has passed, the **parasympathetic nervous system** *decreases* bodily activities to conserve energy – this is sometimes called the **rest and digest** response.

Biopsychology – Chapter 6

BIOPSYCHOLOGY – NEURONS AND SYNAPTIC TRANSMISSION

Neurons are how information is transmitted within the nervous system

Within neurons, information is transmitted as **electrical impulses** from one end to the other.

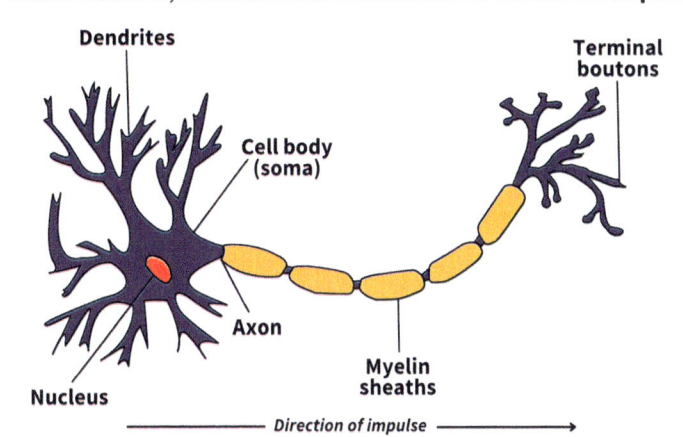

The **dendrites** of the neuron receive a signal and pass it towards the **cell body** (which contains the **nucleus**) and then along an **axon** (which is protected by **myelin sheaths**) to **terminal boutons** at the **axon terminal** (i.e. the end).

Here, **synaptic transmission** passes a signal to the next neuron via **neurotransmitters**.

All neurons have this general structure, but differ slightly depending on their function:

- **Sensory neurons:** Transmit information from the senses (e.g. the eyes) to the CNS.
- **Motor neurons:** Transmit information between the CNS and the organs and muscles (e.g. an instruction to the adrenals to produce adrenaline).
- **Relay neurons:** Connect neurons to other neurons (e.g. motor neurons to sensory neurons) and transmit information within the CNS (also called *interneurons*).

Synaptic transmission is how neurons communicate with each other

Neurons are separated by small gaps called **synapses.** Neurons send **chemical signals** called **neurotransmitters** over these gaps to communicate with each other.

When the electrical signal *within* a neuron reaches the axon terminal of that neuron, **neurotransmitters** are released from **vesicles.** These neurotransmitters cross over the synapse where they are taken up by **receptors** in the dendrites of the other neuron. This then gets converted back to an **electrical signal**.

So, communication *within* neurons is **electric**, but communication *between* neurons is **chemical**.

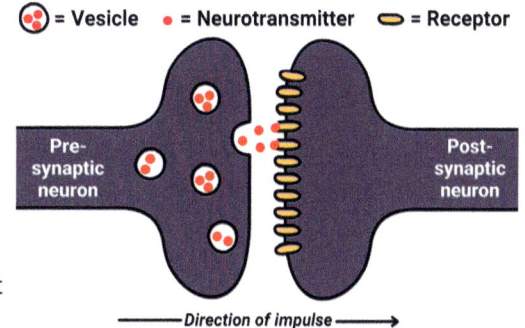

Neurons contain many different types of neurotransmitters such as serotonin, dopamine, GABA, and glutamate. These different neurotransmitters have either **excitatory** or **inhibitory** effects:

- **Excitatory:** *Increase* the likelihood of the neuron firing (e.g. glutamate).
- **Inhibitory:** *Decrease* the likelihood of the neuron firing (e.g. GABA).

BIOPSYCHOLOGY – THE ENDOCRINE SYSTEM

The **endocrine system** is a system of **glands** that release **hormones**

Hormones are **chemicals** that communicate information throughout the body.

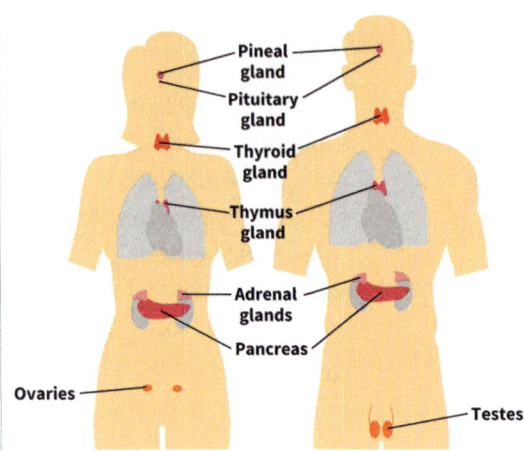

Different hormones are produced and released by different **glands** in the body. The **pituitary gland** (the 'master gland') is linked to the nervous system via the **hypothalamus**, which co-ordinates and regulates the release of hormones from glands.

Hormones affect growth, metabolism, mood, sleep, and just about every other process in the body. They flow through the body and bind to specialised **receptors** in cells. When a hormone binds to a receptor, it can cause an effect in that cell. For example:

Gland	Hormone	Effect(s)
Pituitary	Growth hormone and prolactin	Growth hormone: Growth and cell division Prolactin: Stimulates milk production
Testes	Testosterone	*Male* secondary sex characteristics (e.g. body hair, deeper voice), sperm cell production, increases aggression and muscle size
Ovaries	Estrogen and progesterone	Estrogen: *Female* secondary sex characteristics (e.g. breasts, wider hips), egg maturation Progesterone: Regulates uterus for pregnancy
Thyroid	Thyroxine	Metabolism, growth, and temperature

The endocrine system works *chemically*, so operates **more slowly than the nervous system**.

The **adrenaline** hormone is responsible for the **fight or flight** response...

...which involves activation of the **sympathetic nervous system** (see page 44):
- The brain (specifically the **hypothalamus**) senses a threat.
- The hypothalamus sends a message to the **adrenal glands** (specifically the adrenal medulla) to release **adrenaline**.
- Adrenaline **increases bodily activities** to either fight or flee from the threat
    - E.g. **heart rate increases** to improve blood flow, the bronchioles of **the lungs dilate** to increase oxygen intake, and the **pupils dilate** to increase vision. Other bodily activities that aren't essential for fighting or fleeing are reduced, such as digestion.
- Once the brain senses that the threat has passed, the **parasympathetic nervous system** reduces these activities and returns the body to a resting state (rest and digest).

Biopsychology

BIOPSYCHOLOGY – HEMISPHERIC LATERALISATION OF THE BRAIN

> The brain can be divided **laterally**, i.e. **right** hemisphere and **left** hemisphere...

...which are further divided into **lobes:** frontal, parietal, occipital, and temporal. The two hemispheres do different things. For example, the **left hemisphere** tends to be more involved in **language processing**, whereas the **right hemisphere** tends to be more involved in processing **spatial relationships**.

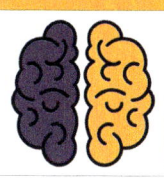

Generally speaking, the hemispheres operate in a **contralateral** fashion: Information from the *left* side of the body is processed by the *right* hemisphere of the brain and vice versa. For example, damage to the motor cortex (see page 48) in the *right* hemisphere will affect the person's ability to move their *left* side, and damage to the auditory cortex (page 48) in the *left* hemisphere will affect a person's hearing in their *right* ear.

The two hemispheres are connected by a bundle of nerve fibers called the **corpus callosum**. In rare cases of extreme epilepsy, a surgeon may *cut* the corpus callosum (**corpus callosotomy**), separating the right and left hemispheres from each other. This contains any epileptic seizures to just one side of the brain, reducing their severity.

Key study: Sperry (1968) Split-brain Patients

Method	**Case studies** and **experiments** on patients who'd undergone corpus callosotomy.
Results	When split-brain patients were shown an image to their *right* visual field, they were able to describe in words what they saw. But when shown the same image to their *left* visual field, they were not able to describe what they saw.
	Despite not being able to describe *in words* the image shown to the left visual field, the split-brain patients could use their *hands* to pick an object associated with that image. E.g. if shown a cigarette, they could use their left hand to pick an ashtray.
	Conclusion: *This suggests different brain hemispheres perform different functions. For example, information presented to the right visual field was processed in the left hemisphere. The fact that the split-brain patients could describe (in words) what they saw suggests language processing happens in the left hemisphere but not the right.*
AO3	• **Small sample size:** Just 11 participants took part in Sperry's experiments and so these findings may not be *valid* when applied to the entire population of humans.
	• **Conflicting evidence:** For example, Gazzaniga (1998) describes the case study of a split-brain patient, J.W., who learned to speak about information presented to his right hemisphere 13 years after undergoing a corpus callosotomy.
	• **Overly simplified:** Sperry's research often leads to the exaggeration and oversimplification of the different functions of the left and right hemispheres. In reality, functions associated with one hemisphere (e.g. the left) can be carried out or shared by the other hemisphere when necessary.

BIOPSYCHOLOGY – LOCALISATION OF BRAIN FUNCTIONS

Different functions are **localised** to specific **areas of the brain**

For example, damage to the auditory cortex in the brain can damage hearing, and damage to the motor cortex may damage movement. This suggests these functions are **localised** in these areas.

- The **motor cortex** is responsible for *voluntary movement*, such as walking. It's located in the **frontal lobes**.
- The **visual cortex** is responsible for *vision*. It's located in the **occipital lobes**.
- The **auditory cortex** is responsible for *hearing*. It's located in the **temporal lobes**.
- There are **two language centres**, both located in the **left hemisphere**.

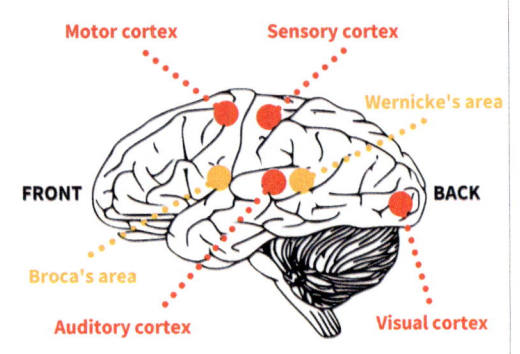

The two language centres are called the Broca's area and the Wernicke's area.

The **Broca's area** is the main area where speech is *produced*. Damage to the Broca's area causes *Broca's aphasia*, a condition characterised by slow speech, lack of fluency, and inability to find the right words. Despite difficulties *producing* speech, people with Broca's aphasia often have normal language comprehension – i.e. they understand what others are saying.

The **Wernicke's area** is primarily responsible for language *comprehension* (both written and spoken). Damage to the Wernicke's area causes *Wernicke's aphasia*. Patients with Wernicke's aphasia typically have no problems producing speech – they speak in a fluent and effortless way – but the content of what they say often lacks meaning and makes little sense.

AO3: **Strengths** of localisation of function

- **Supporting evidence:** Several case studies support localisation of function. For example, Phineas Gage, a 19th century railroad worker, had an iron bar shot straight through his head during an accident while working, which damaged the left frontal lobe of his brain. Before the accident, Gage was calm and polite, but after the accident Gage was violent and rude (however, some accounts claim these characterisations are exaggerated). Gage's doctor believed the damaged area (the left frontal lobe) was responsible for self-control, which was confirmed by later research into localisation of function.

AO3: **Weaknesses** of localisation of function

- **Higher cognitive processes:** Higher cognitive processes such as learning, language, and memory are too complex to be localised within a single area. For example, Lashley (1950) removed different parts of rats brains while they were learning a maze but found no single area was most important. This suggests higher cognitive processes (e.g. learning) are *distributed* in a holistic way within the brain, rather than being *localised* in a single area.
- **Neuroplasticity:** Functional recovery (page 49) suggests functions need not be localised.

Biopsychology

BIOPSYCHOLOGY – NEUROPLASTICITY AND FUNCTIONAL RECOVERY

Neuroplasticity is the ability of the brain to change its physical structure...

...in order to perform different functions. Just like how *plastic* can be moulded and shaped, so too can the brain: **New neuronal connections** can be formed and old ones removed.

In childhood, the brain is highly plastic. This plasticity enables infants and children to quickly learn new skills, adapt to their environment, and recover from brain injury. Neuroplasticity reduces with age, but still remains – unused pathways are removed, commonly used pathways are strengthened, and new pathways can be formed.

Neuroplasticity enables **functional recovery after trauma**

For example, after a serious accident after a stroke, the brain may be damaged, which affects certain functions. To recover these functions, the brain restructures itself in the following ways:

Other areas of the brain adapt to take over damaged areas.	For example, Danelli et al (2013) describes a case study of a boy who had his **entire left hemisphere removed** at age 2 and a half. As language function is primarily localised in this hemisphere, the boy was initially unable to speak. However, his language skills recovered after 2 years, suggesting the right hemisphere adapted to take over this function.
Unused neural pathways are recruited.	Wall (1977) observed that the brain contains many dormant neural connections. When healthy neural connections are damaged, these **previously dormant synapses activate** and form new connections to compensate for the damaged ones.
Axon sprouting.	Damage to the axon of a neuron (see page 45) can break its connections to neighbouring neurons. When this happens, the neighbouring healthy neurons may grow ('sprout') extra nerve endings to **reconnect** with them.

AO3: **Strengths** of neuroplasticity and functional recovery after trauma

- **Supporting evidence:** In addition to the studies above, brain scans by Maguire et al (2000) found London taxi drivers had more grey matter in the posterior hippocampus (an area associated with spatial memory and navigation) compared to controls. This suggests neuroplasticity meant the cab drivers' brains *adapted* to help them with their work.

AO3: **Weaknesses** of neuroplasticity and functional recovery after trauma

- **Variations between people:** Neuroplasticity functional recover differs depending on many factors, such as age. For example, Danelli et al (2013) demonstrates that young people can recover function even after *extensive* damage to the brain, but it's unlikely that an older patient could recover from such extensive damage. However, Bezzola et al (2012) found evidence of neural changes in participants aged 40-60 following 40 hours of golf training, which suggests neuroplasticity still exists to some extent even among older adults.

BIOPSYCHOLOGY – WAYS OF STUDYING THE BRAIN

	There are many different **ways of studying the brain**
fMRI: Brain scans of blood flow.	**Functional magnetic resonance imaging** (fMRI) is a form of brain scanning. When an area of the brain is highly active, that area needs more oxygen and greater blood flow to provide this oxygen. fMRI uses **magnetic fields** to measure these **blood flow and oxygenation** levels in areas of the brain.
Strengths	• **High *spatial* resolution:** fMRI scans are able to identify activity in the brain to within 1mm. This provides a detailed and accurate picture of brain activity.
Weaknesses	• **Expensive:** fMRI scans have high costs (compared to EEG scans). • **Low *temporal* resolution:** It takes several seconds between recording brain activity using fMRI and converting it into an image. This means fMRI generates fewer images per minute and brain activity between each image is not recorded.
EEG and **ERPs:** Brain scans of electrical activity and changes in electrical activity.	An **electroencephalogram** (EEG) is a scan of the brain's **electrical activity**. It's performed by attaching **electrodes** to the scalp or by using a hat with electrodes. The electrodes detect electrical activity in the brain cells directly beneath them. **Event-related potentials** (ERPs) use the same equipment as EEGs but use statistical techniques to measure **changes** in brain activity in response to a stimulus. For example, the EEG could initially provide a baseline picture of brain activity, then researchers could introduce a stimulus (e.g. giving a subject some food) and use ERPs to determine how brain activity changed in response.
Strengths	• **Lower cost:** EEG brain scans are much less expensive than fMRI brain scans. • **Higher *temporal* resolution:** EEG can record several pictures of the brain per second, unlike fMRI.
Weaknesses	• **Lower *spatial* resolution:** EEG only measures *general electrical activity* and so is unable to provide a detailed view of what is happening in the brain. For example, neurons associated with feeling in the hands may be *next to* neurons associated with hearing, but EEG won't be able to differentiate between the two.
Post-mortem: Physical examination of the brain.	A post-mortem is a physical examination of the brain **after a person has died**. By physically analysing a brain (for example, by weighing it, dissecting parts of it, and comparing it to 'normal' brains) and cross-referencing this with the person's behaviour in life (e.g. any psychological disorders the person had) the examiner can learn more about the causes of behaviours and psychological disorders.
Strengths	• **Practical applications:** Post-mortem is how Pierre Paul Broca identified the Broca's area (page 48). By analysing the brains of patients who'd had speaking difficulties, Broca correctly identified the area that controls speech production.
Weaknesses	• **No brain activity:** As the person is dead, a post-mortem does not enable researchers to measure *dynamic* brain activity (unlike fMRI and EEG).

Biopsychology

BIOPSYCHOLOGY – BIOLOGICAL RHYTHMS

Biological rhythms are controlled by **endogenous pacemakers**...

...which are influenced by **exogenous zeitgebers**:
- **Endogenous pacemakers:** Things *within* the body that regulate biological rhythms (your 'body clock'). For example, the suprachiasmatic nucleus of the hypothalamus.
- **Exogenous zeitgebers:** Cues in the *external environment* that inform endogenous pacemakers to regulate biological rhythms. For example, sunlight and darkness influence the sleep/wake cycle.

Circadian rhythms last 24 hours

Example: **The sleep/wake cycle**. You might be awake for 16 hours, then sleep 8 hours at night.

Endogenous pacemakers that control circadian rhythm include systems that release hormones such as melatonin, systems that regulate body temperature, and systems that control digestion and metabolism. The main control system is the **suprachiasmatic nucleus (SCN)**.

These internal processes are influenced by **exogenous zeitgebers** – perhaps the most obvious of which is sunlight. For example, darkness triggers melatonin release, which makes you feel tired.

AO3: Endogenous pacemakers appear to be more important than exogenous zeitgebers for regulating circadian rhythms. For example, Aschoff and Wever (1976) conducted an experiment where participants were kept in a World War 2 bunker without any natural light for four weeks. All participants (except one) maintained a circadian rhythm close to 24 hours.

Infradian rhythms last *more than* than 24 hours

Example: **The human female menstrual cycle**. Women typically ovulate once every 28 days.

As with circadian rhythms, infradian rhythms are controlled by **endogenous pacemakers**. For example, hormones such as estrogen and progesterone are crucial to the menstrual cycle.

Infradian rhythms can also be influenced by **exogenous zeitgebers**. For example, Stern and McClintock (1998) found menstrual cycles change in response to pheromones from other women.

and **Ultradian rhythms** last *less than* 24 hours

Example: **The stages of sleep**. A sleeping person will typically cycle between 5 stages many times:

Stage	Length	Description
1	5 - 15 mins	*Light* sleep. Alpha waves increase and brain activity starts to reduce. Heart rate slows and muscles relax.
2	5 - 15 mins	*Light* sleep. Brain activity reduces with occasional bursts of activity.
3	5 - 15 mins	*Deep* sleep. Delta brain waves increase and brain activity is reduced.
4	~40 mins	*Deep* sleep. Delta waves peak, lowest level of brain activity.
REM	>15 mins	Rapid eye movement (REM). High level of brain activity. Dreams are likely to occur. Body is completely relaxed.

RESEARCH METHODS – FEATURES OF SCIENCE

Science compares **hypotheses** and **theories** against **empirical observations**

For example, Bowlby's maternal deprivation hypothesis (page 22) predicts that children who are separated from their mothers for long periods of time before age 2 will suffer psychological damage. This **hypothesis** can be compared against **empirical observations** in the real world – e.g. by administering psychological tests to adults who suffered maternal deprivation as children and comparing their results against adults who did not suffer maternal deprivation as children.

Good science and **good scientific hypotheses** have the following **features**:
- **Objectivity:** Observations are made from a neutral perspective without bias, rather than the scientist's subjective viewpoint. For example, a tape measure measure provides a more *objective* measurement of distance compared to a researcher's guess.
- **Replicability:** Scientific procedures and experiments can be *repeated* to check the findings are *valid*. For example, Burger (2009) replicated Milgram's experiments (page 7) with similar results.
- **Falsifiability:** Popper (1959) argued that a scientific theory or hypothesis must have *some possible observation* that could prove it false – even if this never actually happens. For example, the hypothesis that "water boils at 100°c" could be falsified by an experiment where you heated water to 999°c and it didn't boil. In contrast, the hypothesis "everything in the universe doubles in size every 10 seconds" could not be falsified by any experiment – because whatever equipment you used to measure everything would also double in size!

There are several different types of scientific **hypothesis**

The **experimental hypothesis** (AKA *alternate hypothesis*) is a prediction of an effect. For example, you might have a hypothesis "that SSRIs will reduce symptoms of depression" or that "subjects will be more likely to comply when orders are issued by someone wearing a uniform".

These examples are both **directional** (sometimes called *one-tailed*) because they predict an effect in a particular direction. But some hypotheses are **non-directional** (*two-tailed*) because they predict an effect in *either* direction. For example, the hypothesis that "caffeine will affect memory" doesn't predict a change either way – caffeine might *increase* memory or *decrease* it.

The **null hypothesis** is a prediction of *no effect*. So, for example, if your experimental hypothesis is that "caffeine will affect memory", the null hypothesis would be that "caffeine won't affect memory". Either the null hypothesis or the experimental hypothesis is proved by the study.

Researchers will often conduct a **pilot study** first

A pilot study is basically a **practice run** of the proposed research project where researchers use a small number of participants and run through the procedure with them. This helps to identify any problems or areas for improvement in the study design *before* conducting the research in full. For example, if it's obvious to participants what the real purpose of an experiment is, then the results may not be *valid*. The pilot study would enable researchers to correct this for the main study.

Research Methods – Chapter 7

RESEARCH METHODS – FEATURES OF SCIENCE

Kuhn (1970) says science progresses through a series of paradigms

Kuhn argues that science is not as unbiased and objective as it seems. Instead, the majority of scientists *just accept* the existing scientific theories (i.e. they accept the existing **paradigm**) as true and then find data that supports these theories while ignoring/rejecting data that refutes them.

Rarely, though, minority voices are able to **successfully challenge** the existing paradigm and replace it with a new one. When this happens it is a **paradigm shift**. An example of a paradigm shift in science is the shift from a geocentric model of the solar system (where the earth is at the centre) to a heliocentric model (where the sun is at the centre).

Within **psychology**, you could perhaps say the shifts from behaviourism to the cognitive approach to the biological approach (see page 32) represent a series of paradigm shifts.

Psychological research has implications for the economy

The following are some examples of how psychological findings may affect the economy:

Attachment	Bowlby's maternal deprivation hypothesis (see page 22) suggests that periods of extended separation between mother and child before age 3 are harmful to the child's psychological development. And if mothers stay at home during this period, they can't go out to work. However, some more recent research challenges Bowlby's conclusions, suggesting that substitutes (e.g. the father, or nursery care) can care for the child, allowing the mother to go back to work sooner and remain economically active.
Psychopathology	Mental disorders affect people's ability to work and so addressing these will likely have benefits for the economy. Further, psychologically healthy people are less likely to need use of health services or end up in prison, so psychological research may help save money in these areas. For example, psychological research has found effective therapies for treating depression (see page 29). The economic benefits of such therapies are likely to outweigh the costs because they enable the person to return to work and pay taxes, as well avoiding long-term costs to the health service.
Memory	Public money is required to fund police investigations. And psychological tools, such as the cognitive interview (see page 16), have improved the accuracy of eyewitness testimonies, which equates to more efficient use of police time and resources.

RESEARCH METHODS – SCIENTIFIC REPORTING

A **scientific report** will have the following features:

Title	A short and clear description of the research.
Abstract	A summary of the research (e.g. aim, hypothesis, methods, results, conclusion).
Introduction	Funnel technique: Broad overview of context (e.g. current theories, previous studies, etc.) before focusing on this particular study's aims and hypothesis.
Method	A detailed description of the procedure used in the study, so that the study can be evaluated and replicated. Includes: Study design, participant details (e.g. sampling methods), equipment used, the procedure, and control of variables.
Results	A presentation of the key findings from the data collected. This is typically written summaries of the raw data (descriptive statistics), which may also be presented in tables, charts, graphs, etc. Raw data goes in the appendices.
Discussion	An explanation of what the results mean and how they relate to the experimental hypothesis, any issues with how results were generated, how the results fit with other research, and suggestions for future research.
Conclusion	A short summary of the key findings from the study.
References	A list of all the sources (i.e. books and published articles) used in the study. These are listed using standard formats – see the back of this book for examples.
Appendices	Any supporting materials that are too detailed or long to include in the main report. For example, the complete list of questions in a questionnaire.

The completed scientific report gets submitted to journals for **peer review**

Peer review is a way of assessing a research paper's **scientific credibility** before it is published. The researchers submit their paper to the journal they want it to be published in, and the editor then sends the paper to expert reviewers (i.e. psychologists who are experts in that area) who evaluate the paper's scientific validity. The reviewers may accept the paper as is, accept it with changes, reject it and suggest revisions for resubmission at a later date, or reject it completely.

Strengths:	• **Prevents false ideas and bad research:** Having an experienced scientist double-check research *should* ensure only good science is accepted as true.
Weaknesses:	• **Bias:** Many academics are funded by organisations and companies that may prefer certain ideas to be accepted as scientifically legitimate, and so this funding may produce conflicts of interest. Further, academics often know each other and so these relationships may affect publication decisions. • **Prevents progress:** Since reviewers are typically older established academics who have made their careers *within the current scientific paradigm*, they may reject new or controversial ideas simply because they go against the current paradigm (see page 53) rather than because they are unscientific. • **Doesn't work:** There are many examples of fraudulent research passing peer review and being published (e.g. the "Grievance Studies" affair).

Research Methods

RESEARCH METHODS – THE EXPERIMENTAL METHOD

There are many **types of experiment**, but they all look at how **variables** affect **outcomes**.

Independent variable (IV): Something *changed* by researchers in an experiment.
Dependent variable (DV): Something *measured* by researchers in an experiment.
Example: In Bickman's study of the effect of uniforms on obedience (page 8), the IV was the uniform of the person giving orders and the researchers looked at how changing this IV affected the DV of how many people followed the orders.

Laboratory vs. field experiment

A **laboratory experiment** is carried out in an artificial, **controlled**, environment deliberately set up for the purposes of the experiment.
Example: Bandura's Bobo experiments (page 34) were all done in the same room, same toys, etc.

Strengths:	The controlled environment minimises the risk of extraneous variables (see page 56) from skewing the results of the experiment. So, changes in the dependent variable are likely to be a result of a change in the independent variable. The controlled environment also means the experiment can easily be replicated.
Weaknesses:	Results obtained in an artificial environment might not translate to real-life and so laboratory experiments may lack ecological validity (see page 61). For example, participants in a laboratory experiment will know they're taking part in an experiment, which might induce demand characteristics (see page 56).

Whereas a **field experiment** is carried out in a natural, **real-world**, environment.
Example: In Bickman's study of the effect of uniforms on obedience (page 8), the person wearing the uniform went up to people on the street and gave them orders.

Strengths:	Field experiments are likely to have better ecological validity (see page 61) than laboratory experiments because they're carried out in real-world settings.
Weaknesses:	Extraneous variables in the environment may skew the results.

Natural vs. quasi experiment

Natural experiments are where the independent variable varies *naturally*. In other words, the researcher can't or doesn't manipulate the variables. There are two types of natural experiment:
- **Natural experiment:** An experiment where the independent variable changes naturally and the researcher seizes the opportunity to study the effects.
    - *Example:* Studying the effect a change in drug laws (IV) has on addiction (DV).
- **Quasi experiment:** Compares between independent variables that can't be changed.
    - *Example:* Studying differences between men and women (IV) in how many words they can remember from a list (DV).

RESEARCH METHODS – THE EXPERIMENTAL METHOD

Experimental designs: **Independent groups** vs. **repeated measures**

Independent groups: Participants are divided into two groups. One group does the experiment with variable 1, the other group does the experiment with variable 2. Results are compared.
A **matched pairs** design is another form of independent groups design. Participants are selected and then the researchers recruit *another group* of participants one-by-one to match the characteristics of each member of the original group.

AO3: With independent groups, participants must be carefully assigned to groups to prevent **participant variables** from skewing results. A matched pairs design should avoid this problem.

Repeated measures: Participants are *not* divided into groups. Instead, all participants do the experiment with variable 1, then afterwards the same participants do the experiment with variable 2. Results are compared.

Extraneous variables are additional (unwanted) variables

If extraneous variables are not properly **controlled** for, they are known as **confounding variables** and may skew a study's results, leading to invalid conclusions.

	Description	**How to control**
Participant variables	E.g. If you're doing an *independent groups* study of the effect of caffeine on memory and decide the caffeine group will be all male and the non-caffeine group female, then gender might skew the results.	**Random allocation**: Participants are *randomly* assigned to either the caffeine group or the non-caffeine group.
Task order	E.g. if you're doing a *repeated measures* study of the effect of caffeine on memory, then participants may find the task easier second time around.	**Counterbalancing**: Half the participants do the experiment with caffeine first and the other half do it without caffeine first.
Situational variables	E.g. if you're doing a study of the effect of caffeine on memory but some participants do the experiment in a quiet room and the others do it in a nightclub, the different *environments* may skew the results.	**Control** the location, time of day, equipment, etc. so it's the same for all participants. The easiest way to do this is with a *laboratory experiment*.
Demand characteristics	Where participants know they're in a study and so behave differently. E.g. in a drug trial, participants may suffer imagined side effects.	In a **single-blind** drug trial, half the participants get the drug and half get a *placebo*.
Investigator effects	Where characteristics of the researcher affect the participant's behaviour. E.g. in a drug trial for an antidepressant, the researcher may *expect* the group taking the drug to be less depressed and so treat them differently.	In a **double-blind** drug trial, neither the participants *nor the researcher* know which participants got the drug and which got the placebo.

Research Methods

RESEARCH METHODS – THE OBSERVATIONAL METHOD

Whereas experiments are about *changing* variables, **observations** just… **observe**.

Naturalistic vs. controlled observation is about the *setting*

- **Naturalistic:** Observations made in a **real-life** setting.
  - *Example:* Setting up cameras in an office to observe interactions in that environment.
- **Controlled:** Observations made in an **artificial** setting set up for the purposes of observation.
  - *Example:* Zimbardo's prison study (page 6).

AO3: Naturalistic observations are likely to have higher ecological validity (see page 61).

Covert vs. overt is about *whether the participants know they're being observed*

- **Covert:** Participants are **not aware** they are being observed as part of a study.
- **Overt:** Participants are **aware** they are being observed as part of a study.
  - *Example:* Zimbardo's prison study (page 6).

AO3: Overt observations may induce demand characteristics (see page 56), but covert observations may be unethical if the researcher does not get participants' consent.

Participant vs. non-participant is about *whether the researcher gets involved*

- **Participant:** Where the researcher/observer is actively involved in the situation being observed.
  - *Example:* In Zimbardo's prison study (page 6), Zimbardo played the role of prison superintendent himself.
- **Non-participant:** When the researcher/observer is not involved in the situation being observed.
  - *Example:* In Ainsworth's strange situation (page 21), the observer does not interact with the child when they're being observed.

Observational design: Behavioural categories and event vs. time sampling

	Participant	Observation	Anxiety
An observational study will use **behavioural categories** to prioritise which behaviours are recorded and ensure the different observers are consistent in what they are looking for. E.g. An observation of how infants behave with a stranger could use the behavioural categories in the table opposite (anxiety is *quantified* from 1-5).	A	Interacted	2
	B	Avoided	4
	C	Interacted	1
	D	Avoided	2

It may not be possible to record *every single behaviour* during the observation period. So, study designers will also decide *when* to record a behaviour:

- **Event sampling:** Counting *how many times* the participant behaves in a certain way.
- **Time sampling:** Recording participant behaviour at regular time intervals. For example, making notes of the participant's behaviour at scheduled 15 minute intervals.

RESEARCH METHODS – THE SELF REPORT METHOD

Self-report methods get participants to provide information about themselves.

A **questionnaire** is a standardised list of questions...

...that all participants in a study answer. For example, Hazan and Shaver's love quiz (page 23). Questions in a questionnaire can be either closed or open:
- **Closed:** Have a **fixed set of responses**, such as "yes" or "no", or multiple choice questions.
- **Open:** Do not have a fixed set of responses, instead enabling participants to provide responses in their own words (e.g. "what do you look for in a romantic partner and why?")

Strengths	• **Quantifiable:** Closed questions provide quantifiable data in a consistent format, which enables to statistically analyse information in an objective way.
Weaknesses	• **Biased samples:** Questionnaires will select for participants who actually have the time and are willing to complete a questionnaire. As such, the responses may be biased towards those of people who e.g. have a lot of spare time. • **Less detail:** Interviews may be better suited for detailed qualitative information.

With **interviews**, participants are asked questions in-person

Interviews can either be structured or unstructured:
- **Structured:** Questions are standardised and pre-set. The interviewer asks all participants the same questions in the same order.
- **Unstructured:** The interviewer discusses a topic with the participant in a less structured and more spontaneous way, pursuing avenues of discussion as they come up.

Strengths	• **Rich qualitative detail:** Unstructured interviews enable researchers to delve deeper into topics of interest, for example by asking follow-up questions.
Weaknesses	• **Investigator effects** (page 56): For example, a female participant may be less comfortable answering questions on sex asked by a male interviewer and and thus give different answers than if she were asked by a female interviewer.

Content analysis is a way of making qualitative data *quantifiable*

Although the **qualitative data** from interviews and questionnaires may be valuable, this level of detail can make it hard to mathematically analyse. That's where **content analysis** comes in:
- A sample of qualitative data is collected (e.g. unstructured interviews about childhood)
- Relevant **coding units** are identified and operationalised (e.g. traumatic events, happy memories, births, and deaths)
- The data is analysed according to these coding units to produce quantitative metrics (e.g. researchers listen to the interviews and *count* how often traumatic events are mentioned)
- Statistical/**mathematical analysis** is carried out on this data.

Research Methods

RESEARCH METHODS – CASE STUDIES AND CORRELATIONS

Case studies are detailed investigations into an individual, a group of people, or an event.

Most **cases studies** focus on **unusual** cases

For example, page 49 describes Danelli et al (2013), which was a case study of a boy who had the entire left hemisphere of his brain removed aged 2 and a half. This case study was **longitudinal:** The researchers collected data on the boy at ages 2.5, 4, and 14 to see how he progressed.

Strengths:	• **Rich qualitative detail:** Case studies produce detailed qualitative data (rather than just one or two aspects of behaviour at a single point in time). • **Only option:** Case studies allow for investigation into issues that may be impractical or unethical to study otherwise. For example, it would be unethical to remove half a toddler's brain just to *experiment*, but if such a procedure is medically necessary then a case study is an opportunity to learn the effects.
Weaknesses:	• **Unscientific:** Because case studies are often single examples that cannot be replicated, the results may not be valid when applied to the general population. • **Researcher bias:** The small sample size of case studies means researchers need to apply their own *subjective* interpretation when drawing conclusions. As such, these conclusions may be skewed by the researcher's own bias and invalid when applied more generally. This criticism is often directed at Freud's psychoanalytic theory (page 40) because it draws heavily on isolated case studies of individuals.

Correlational studies look for relationships – *correlations* – between two or more variables.

Unlike an *experiment,* the variables in a **correlational study** are not manipulated

For example, page 30 describes Davis et al (2013), where researchers looked for **correlations** between genetic patterns and OCD.

The variables in a correlational study are called **co-variables**. If two co-variables are **positively correlated**, it means that when one goes *up*, the other goes *up* as well. If they're **negatively correlated**, it means that when one goes *up*, the other goes *down*.

Strengths:	• **Only ethical option:** Some things might be unethical to study an experiment. For example, getting 50 people to smoke cigarettes for 10 years to study the effects on lung cancer would unethical. But correlational studies can look at the relationship between lung cancer rates among people who smoke anyway.
Weaknesses:	• **Correlation does not guarantee causation:** For example, ice cream sales are (probably) correlated with cases of heatstroke. But it's not like the increased consumption of ice creams *causes* people to develop heatstroke – they're both caused by something else: Hot weather. As such, correlational studies cannot prove causal relationships (although correlational studies are often a good starting point for an investigation into a causal relationship).

Research Methods

RESEARCH METHODS – OPERATIONALISATION AND SAMPLING

Operationalisation of variables means *clearly* and *measurably* defining them

For example, an experiment on the effects of sleep (IV) on anxiety (DV) would need to clearly **operationalise** each variable. Sleep could be defined by **number of hours spent in bed**, and anxiety could be defined based on measurements such as **blood pressure and cortisol levels**. If variables are not properly operationalised, the experiment cannot be properly replicated, experimenters' subjective interpretations may skew results, and the findings may not be *valid*.

Sampling means choosing participants from the population for your study

Random sampling involves selecting participants from a target population at random – such as by drawing names from a hat or using a computer program to select them.

Strengths:	• **No bias:** Each member of the population has an equal chance of being selected and thus is not subject to any bias.
Weaknesses:	• **Impractical:** For example, a study of women (population) couldn't randomly sample all the women on the planet!

Systematic sampling involves selecting participants from a target population by selecting them at pre-set intervals. For example, selecting every 50th person from a list, or every 7th, etc.

Strengths:	• **No bias:** A person's order in a list is arbitrary, so shouldn't bias the sample.
Weaknesses:	• **Unexpected bias:** For example, houses tend to be have *even* numbers on one side of a road and *odd* numbers on the other. If houses on one side are more expensive, say, this could introduce an unexpected bias in the sample.

Stratified sampling involves dividing the population into relevant groups for study, working out what percentage of the population is in each group, and then randomly sampling the population according to these percentages. For example, if 20% of the population being studied is aged 0-18, then 20 out of 100 participants you select for your study will be aged 0-18.

Strengths:	• **Representative:** People with certain characteristics won't be over- or under-represented within the sample, so the sample fairly represents the population.
Weaknesses:	• **Requires accurate data:** If population data is wrong, the sample will be biased.

Opportunity sampling: *Approaching* participants and asking them to take part (e.g. approaching people in the street and asking them to complete a questionnaire).
Volunteer sampling: Participants *offer* to take part (e.g. placing an advert online inviting people to complete a questionnaire). Volunteer sampling is sometimes called *self-selected sampling*.

Strengths:	• **Quick and easy:** No random sampling, population lists, or stratification needed!
Weaknesses:	• **Unrepresentative and biased:** For example, if you conduct *opportunity sampling* on a weekday at 10am, this sample will likely exclude people who are at work. Similarly, *volunteer sampling* is likely to exclude people who are too busy to take part in the study.

Research Methods

RESEARCH METHODS – VALIDITY AND RELIABILITY

	A study is **valid** if it *accurately* measures what it's supposed to
Face validity	The study just looks like it measures what it's supposed to at face value. *Example:* A study that measures participants' intelligence levels by asking them when their birthday is would have *low* ecological validity.
Ecological validity	The a study's findings apply outside of the environment it was conducted in (i.e. in real life or other contexts). *Example:* If you conducted a *laboratory experiment* (page 55) to see how angry people get in response to an annoying person, the results would probably have *low* ecological validity because participants would know it was just an experiment.
Temporal validity	The study's results stay true over time. *Example:* A 1920 study of participants' attitudes towards social issues may have *low* temporal validity because societal attitudes have changed since 1920.
Concurrent validity	A test's results are correlated with (i.e. similar to) the results of a similar test. *Example:* Participants who score highly on a new intelligence test also score highly on a standardised IQ test, so the new test has *high* concurrent validity.

	A study is **reliable** if the results can be *replicated* in the same circumstances
	Note: A *reliable* study is not automatically *valid*. For example, a broken tape measure may *reliably* (i.e. consistently) record a person's height as 250 miles, but that doesn't make it an accurate (i.e. valid) measure of the person's height.
Test-retest reliability	If you give the **same test** to the same person on **two different occasions** and the results are the same or similar both times, this suggests they are reliable. *Example:* If your study used scales to measure participants' weight, you would expect the scales to record the same (or a very similar) weight for the same person in the morning as in the evening. If the scales said the person weighed 100kg more later that same day, the scales (and therefore the results of the study) would be *unreliable*.
Inter-observer reliability	Inter-observer reliability is a way to test the reliability of **observational studies** (see page 57). It can be assessed mathematically – e.g. by using chi-squared (see page 69) – by calculating the **correlation** between different observers' scores. *Example:* If your study required observers to assess participants' anxiety levels, you would expect different observers to grade the same behaviour in the same way. If one observer rated a participant's behaviour a 3 for anxiety, and another observer rated the exact same behaviour an 8, the results would be *unreliable*. Inter-observer reliability can be improved by setting clearly defined **behavioural categories** (see page 57).

RESEARCH METHODS – ETHICAL ISSUES

The British Psychological Association has a **code of human research ethics**

In psychological studies, **ethical issues** are questions of what is morally **right** and **wrong**.

An ethically-conducted study will protect the health and safety of the participants involved and uphold their dignity, privacy, and rights.

Participants must give **valid consent**

- Participants are told the project's **aims**, the **data being collected**, and **any risks** associated with participation.
- Participants have the **right to withdraw** or modify their consent at any time.
- Researchers *can* use incentives (e.g. money) to encourage participation, but these incentives can't be so big that they would compromise a participant's **freedom of choice**.
- Researchers must consider the participant's **ability to consent** (e.g. age, mental ability, etc.).

There must be **no deception**

Researchers should avoid misleading participants about the nature of the study **where possible**. However, some studies *require* a degree of deception. For example, Asch's experiments (page 5) wouldn't have worked if participants were told the *true* nature of the test. So, in such cases, the **deception must be scientifically justified** and researchers must use **risk management**:

- **Prior (general) consent:** Informing participants they will be deceived without telling them *how*. However, this may affect their behaviour as they try to guess the real nature of the study.
- **Retrospective consent:** Informing participants that they were deceived *after* the study is completed and asking for their consent. However, if they don't consent then it's too late!
- **Presumptive consent:** Asking people who *aren't* participating in the study if they would be willing to participate in the study. If these people say they'd be willing to give consent, then it's reasonable to assume those taking part in the study would also give consent.

Researchers must respect participant **confidentiality**

Personal data obtained about participants should not be disclosed (unless the participant agreed to this in advance). Any data that is published will not be publicly identifiable as the participant's.

Participants must be appropriately **debriefed** after the study

Once data gathering is complete, researchers must explain all relevant details of the study to participants – especially if deception was involved. If a study might have harmed the individual (e.g. its purpose was to induce a negative mood), it is ethical for the debrief to address this harm (e.g. by inducing a happy mood) so that **the participant does not leave the study in a worse state than when they entered**.

RESEARCH METHODS – DATA HANDLING AND ANALYSIS

Data collected will be either **qualitative** or **quantitative**

- **Quantitative:** Numerical.
    - *Example:* **How many** subjects delivered a lethal shock in Milgram's experiments.
- **Qualitative:** Non-numerical.
    - *Example:* asking subjects in Milgram's experiments to describe **how they felt** about delivering the lethal shock.

AO3: *Quantitative* data enables researchers to mathematically and objectively analyse data. For example, mood ratings of 7 and 6 can be compared objectively, whereas *qualitative* assessments such as 'sad' and 'unhappy' are hard to compare scientifically. However, in reducing data to numbers and narrow definitions, quantitative data may miss important details and context.

Researchers can produce **primary data** or use **secondary data**

- **Primary data:** *Original data* collected for the study.
- **Secondary data:** *Data from another study* previously conducted (e.g. a *meta-analysis*).

A **meta-analysis** is a study of studies. It involves taking several smaller studies within a certain research area and using statistics to identify similarities and trends within those studies to create a larger study. We have looked at some examples of meta-analyses elsewhere in the course such as Van Ijzendoorn's meta-analysis of several strange situation studies (page 21).

AO3: A good meta-analysis is often more reliable than a regular study because it is based on a larger data set, and any issues with any single study will be balanced out by the other studies.

How to calculate **percentages** and **percentage change**

A **percentage (%)** describes how much out of 100 something occurs. It is calculated as follows:

- *Example:* **63** out of a total of **82** participants passed the test
- 63/82 = 0.768
- 0.768*100 = 76.8
- **76.8%** of participants passed the test.

To calculate a **percentage** *change*, work out the difference between the original number and the after number, divide that difference by the original number, then multiply the result by 100.
For example:

- *Example:* He got **80** marks on the test but *after studying* he got **88** marks on the test
- 88-80=8
- 8/80=0.1
- 0.1*100=10
- His test score **increased by 10% after studying**.

RESEARCH METHODS – MEASURES OF CENTRAL TENDENCY

Measures of central tendency are ways of reducing data sets to *averages*

The **mean** is calculated by adding all the numbers in a set together and dividing the total by the number of numbers. For example:
- *Example data set:* 22, 78, 3, 33, 90
- 22+78+3+33+90=226
- 226/5=45.2
- The mean is **45.2**

Strengths:	• **Uses all data in the set** • **Accurate:** Provides a precise number (to as many *significant figures* as needed) based on all the data in a set.
Weaknesses:	• **Can be skewed by freak scores:** E.g.: 1, 3, 2, 5, 9, 4, 913 ← the mean is 133.9, but the 913 could be a measurement error or something and thus the mean would not be representative of the data set.

The **median** is calculated by arranging all the numbers in a set from smallest to biggest and then **finding the number in the middle**. For example:
- *Example data set:* 20, 66, 85, 45, 18, 13, 90, 28, 9, 17
- 9, 13, 17, 18, **20, 28,** 45, 66, 85, 90
- (20+28)/2 = 24
- The median is **24**

Note: If the total number of numbers is odd, you just pick the middle one. But if the total number of numbers is even (like this example), you take the mean of the two numbers in the middle.

Strengths:	• **Won't be skewed by freak scores:** Unlike the mean.
Weaknesses:	• **May not be representative:** E.g.: 1, 1, 3, 9865, 67914 ← the median of *3* is not really representative of the larger numbers in the set. • **Less accurate/sensitive:** Compared to the mean.

The **mode** is calculated by counting which is the **most commonly occurring** number in a set. For example:
- *Example data set:* 7, 7, **20**, 16, 1, **20**, 25, 16, **20**, 9
- There are two 7's, but *three* 20's
- The mode is **20**

Strengths:	• **Won't be skewed by freak scores:** Unlike the mean. • **Makes more sense for certain applications:** Sometimes it makes more sense to represent the average as a whole number. E.g. the *average number of limbs* for a human being will have a *mean* of something like 3.99, but a *mode* of 4.
Weaknesses:	• **Does not use all data in a set** • **A data set may have more than one mode**

Research Methods

RESEARCH METHODS – MEASURES OF DISPERSION

Measures of dispersion are ways to quantify how much scores in a data set *vary*

The **range** is calculated by subtracting the smallest number in a data set from the largest number:
- *Example data set:* 59, 8, 7, 84, 9, 49, 14, 75, 88, 11
- The largest number is 88 and the smallest number is 7
- 88-7=81
- The range is **81**

Strengths:	• **Quick and easy:** You just subtract one number from another.
Weaknesses:	• **Can be skewed by freak scores:** The difference between the biggest and smallest can be skewed by a single anomalous result or error, which may give an exaggerated impression of the data distribution. • **Does not account for how common scores are**.

The **standard deviation** (σ) is a measure of how much numbers in a data set deviate from the mean (average). It is calculated as follows:

- *Example data set:* 59, 179, 43, 42, 81, 196
- Calculate the mean (see page 64). In this case, it's 100.
- Subtract the mean from each number: • And square these numbers:

59 – 100 = -41	→	$-41^2 = 1681$
179 – 100 = 79	→	$79^2 = 6241$
43 – 100 = -57	→	$-57^2 = 3249$
42 – 100 = -58	→	$-58^2 = 3364$
81 – 100 = -19	→	$-19^2 = 361$
196 – 100 = 96	→	$96^2 = 9216$

- Add all the squared numbers together:

1681 + 6241 + 3249 + 3364 + 361 + 9216 = 24112

- And divide the result by the number of numbers :

24112/6 = 4018.666666667

- The square root of this number is the standard deviation :

$\sqrt{4018.666666667}$ = The standard deviation is **63.392954393**

Note: This method is based on the entire *population*. For calculating standard deviation based on a *sample* of a population, you instead divide by the *number of numbers-1* in the second to last step (in this case 24112/5=4822.4). This gives a standard deviation of 69.44 (because $\sqrt{4822.4}$ = 69.44).

Strengths:	• **Won't be skewed by freak scores:** Standard deviation measures the *average* difference from the mean so is less likely to be skewed by a single freak score.
Weaknesses:	• **Takes much longer to calculate.**

RESEARCH METHODS – MORE DESCRIPTIVE STATISTICS

Normal and skewed distributions

A data set that has a **normal distribution** will be **symmetrical:** There will be an equal number of scores *above* the mean as *below* it. The mode and the median will also be similar to the mean. Scores become rarer the more they deviate from the mean. *Examples:* IQ scores and human heights.	Normal	*(bell curve with Mean, Median, Mode at centre)*
A data set that has a **skewed distribution** will *not* be symmetrical. This skew can be either **positive** or **negative**: • **Positive skew:** A single freakishly *high* score (or a cluster of low scores) makes the mean higher than most of the scores, so *most scores are below the mean*. ○ Mean > Median > Mode	Positive skew	*(right-skewed curve: Mode, Median, Mean)*
• **Negative skew:** A single freakishly *low* score (or a cluster of high scores) makes the mean lower than most of the scores, so *most scores are above the mean*. ○ Mean < Median < Mode	Negative skew	*(left-skewed curve: Mean, Median, Mode)*

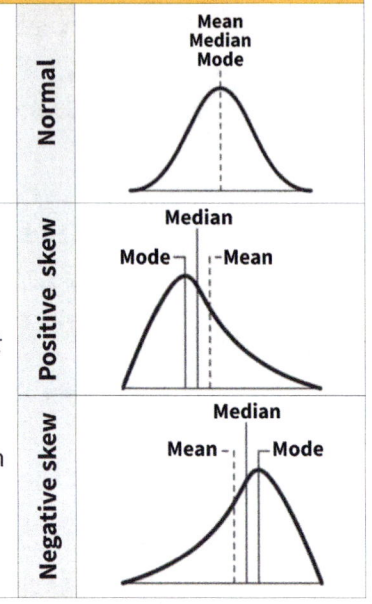

Correlation and scattergrams

Correlations are measured mathematically using **correlation coefficients** (r).

A correlation coefficient will be anywhere between **+1** and **-1**:

- **r = + 1** means two things are perfectly *positively* correlated: When one goes up, the other also goes up by the same amount.
- **r = -1** means two things perfectly *negatively* correlated: When one goes *up*, the other goes *down* by the same amount.
- **r = 0** means two things are **not correlated** at all: A change in one is totally independent of a change in the other

Correlations can be illustrated visually using **scattergrams,** which are ways of visually illustrating two variables for various data points.

For example, each dot on the scattergram at the bottom could represent a student. The x-axis could represent the **number of hours the student studied**, and the y-axis could represent the **student's test score**. In this case, the correlation coefficient is around +0.7, which suggests a strong (but not perfect) positive correlation.

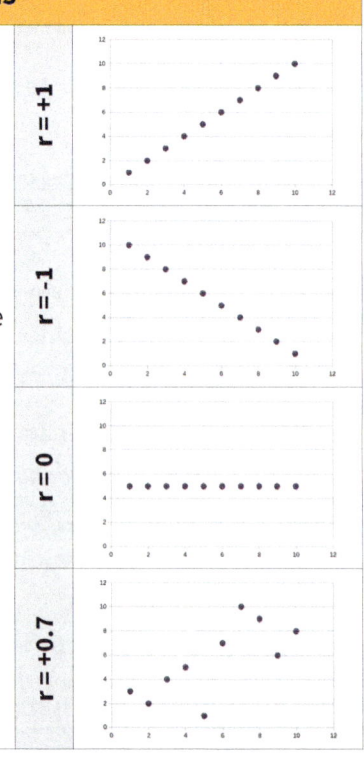

Research Methods

66

RESEARCH METHODS – VISUALLY PRESENTING DATA

A **bar chart** represents *discrete data categories* for comparison

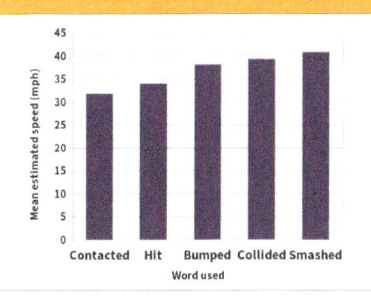

The x-axis lists the categories and the y-axis illustrates the different results between the categories. For example, the results of Loftus and Palmer's study into the effects of leading questions on EWT (page 16) could be presented using the bar chart opposite. It's not like there are categories *in-between* 'contacted' and 'hit', so **the bars have gaps between them** (unlike a histogram).

Histograms are like bar charts – *with an important difference*

It's used to illustrate **continuous**, rather than discrete, data. For example, it's not like you can only weigh 100kg or 101kg – there are many intervals in between. The x axis on a histogram organises this continuous data (i.e. the in-between scores) into categories. The y axis illustrates the frequency of scores within each category. Because the data on the x axis is continuous, there are **no gaps between the bars**.

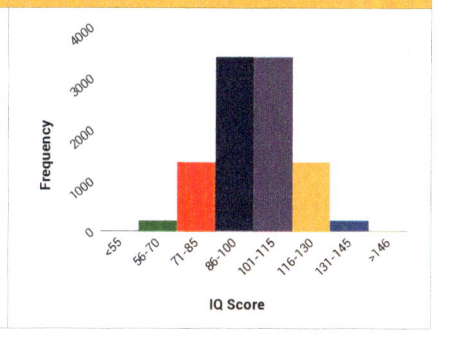

Line graphs can illustrate multiple data categories

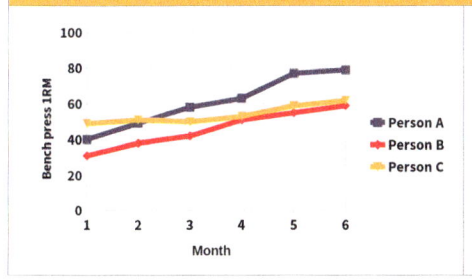

Like a histogram, a line graph (sometimes called a *frequency polygon*) also illustrates continuous data. But whereas a histogram can only represent *one* data category, a line graph can illustrate **multiple data categories**. For example, the line graph opposite illustrates **3 different people's** progression in a strength training program over time.

Pie charts are the best way to illustrate percentages

Pie charts illustrate how commonly different things occur relative to each other.

In other words, they provide a visual representation of **percentages** and **proportions**.

For example, the frequency with which different attachment styles occurred in Ainsworth's original strange situation study (see page 21) could be represented by the pie chart opposite.

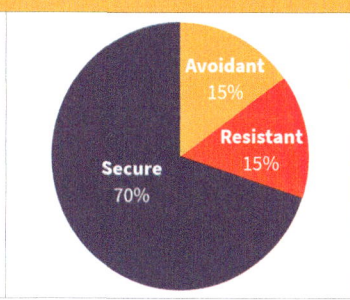

Research Methods

RESEARCH METHODS – PROBABILITY AND SIGNIFICANCE

Inferential testing is to see whether results are **statistically significant**...

...i.e. whether any observed effects are a result of whatever is being studied or whether they are just due to **luck**.

Example: You conduct an experiment to see whether flipping a coin *outdoors* (IV) increases the likelihood of getting tails (DV). Your null hypothesis (see page 52) is that there is no effect and the ratio of heads:tails will be **50:50**. So you flip the coin 100 times and get **48** heads and **52** tails. Does this experiment show that flipping a coin outdoors makes you more likely to get tails? No, because a ratio of 48:52 isn't very significant and **could have occurred due to luck**. So, the **probability** that this effect occurred *because* you flipped the coin *outside* is low.

Probability is denoted by the symbol p. The lower the p value, the more **statistically significant** your results are. You can never get a p value of 0, though, so researchers will set a threshold at which point the results are considered statistically significant enough to reject the null hypothesis and accept the experimental hypothesis. In psychology, this threshold is usually **<0.05**, which means there is a less than **5% chance** the observed effect is due to luck and a >95% chance it is a real effect.

Type 1 (false *positive*) and type 2 (false *negative*) errors

When interpreting statistical significance, there are **2 types of errors**:

- **Type 1 error:** When researchers conclude an effect is real (i.e. they reject the null hypothesis), but it's actually not. This is sometimes called a *false positive*.
    - *Example:* The p threshold is <0.05, but the researchers' results are among the 5% of fluke outcomes that look significant but are just due to luck.
- **Type 2 error:** When researchers conclude there is no effect (i.e. they accept the null hypothesis), but there actually is a real effect. This is sometimes called a *false negative*.
    - *Example:* The p threshold is set too low (e.g. <0.01), and the data falls short (e.g. p=<0.02).

AO3: If you set the p value too low, this increases the likelihood of a type 2 error, but if you set the p value too high, this increases the likelihood of a type 1 error.

Which p value is appropriate will depend on the context. Psychology typically uses a p value of <0.05 because there's a low chance of a type 2 error and there's unlikely to be any serious consequences if the researchers have made a type 1 error (i.e. if they are among the 5% of false positives). However, with something like a clinical drug trial, a p value of <0.05 is too high because you need to be very sure that the drug works – it's not good enough to be just 95% sure.

A good way to reduce the likelihood of both type 1 and type 2 errors is to increase the sample size (e.g. the number of people in your drug trial, or the number of participants in your experiment).

Research Methods

RESEARCH METHODS – INFERENTIAL TESTING

Which inferential test is appropriate will depend on **3 things:**

1. Whether you are looking for a **difference** or a **correlation**.

2. Whether your data is **nominal**, **ordinal**, or **interval**.
- **Nominal:** A basic tally of how many people fall into *discrete* categories.
    - *Example:* At the competition there were 8 runners, 12 swimmers, and 6 long jumpers. It's not like there's any categories *in-between* 'swimmer' and 'runner', for example.
- **Ordinal:** *Whole numbers* that can be ordered (but are not necessarily equal units).
    - *Example:* Anxiety scores on a scale of 1-10. It's not like a score of '4' is exactly twice as anxious as a score of '2', but the two numbers can be ranked against each other.
- **Interval:** Precise and *standardised units of measurement* (think decimal point).
    - *Examples:* Weights in kilograms, heights in metres, times in seconds/milliseconds.

3. Whether the data is **related** or **unrelated**.
- **Related:** A *repeated measures* experimental design (see page 56).
- **Unrelated:** An independent groups experimental design (see page 56).

You often get questions asking **which statistical test** to use – here's the answers:

	Test of difference		Test of correlation
	Unrelated	**Related**	
Nominal	Chi-squared	Sign test	Chi-squared
Ordinal	Mann-Whitney	Wilcoxon	Spearman's rho
Interval	Unrelated *t*-test	Related *t*-test	Pearson's *r*

You don't have to be able to do *all* these tests – but you need to know…

…how to use a **critical values table**. They're all quite similar. Here's one for the unrelated *t*-test:

Level of significance for a one-tailed test		
	0.05	0.025
Level of significance for a two-tailed test		
df	0.1	0.05
17	1.74	2.110
18	1.734	2.101
19	1.729	2.093

Significance is shown if the calculated value of *t* is **equal to or greater than** the critical value (cv).

The question will tell you the value of *t*, the level of significance, and the degrees of freedom (*df*). Your job is to use this data to say whether the result (in this case *t*) is statistically significant.

Example: df=18 and it's a one-tailed test with a 0.05 level of significance, so the cv = 1.734. Let's say *t*=0.7. Then *t* (0.7) is less than cv (1.734), so the results are **not statistically significant**.

RESEARCH METHODS – THE SIGN TEST

Here's how to use the **sign test** to tell if a result is statistically significant

The sign test is a way to calculate the statistical significance of **differences** between **related** pairs of **nominal data** (see the table for which statistical test to use on page 69).

Example: Participant depression scores before and after taking a new antidepressant drug. We expect the drug to *reduce* depression, so our hypothesis is one-tailed.

Participant	Before	After	Sign
A	4	3	-
B	3	3	n/a
C	4	3	-
D	5	4	-
E	3	4	+
F	4	3	-

- The most important thing in the sign test is not the actual amount (e.g. 4, 5, etc.), but the *sign* – i.e. whether the difference between the pairs is positive (+) or negative (-). You exclude any results that are the same between the pairs:
    - **n = 5** (because even though we have 6 participants, we exclude participant B because there was no change)
    - We have 4 '-' signs and 1 '+' sign
- *S* = count how many instances of the less frequently occurring sign. We only have 1 '+', so **S = 1**
- Read the question and make a note of the *p* value, if the experimental hypothesis is two-tailed (i.e. a change is expected in either direction) or one-tailed (i.e. change is expected to go in one direction), and the sample size (i.e. the number of participants)
    - *p* = **0.05** (let's say), the experimental hypothesis is **one-tailed**, and **n = 5**
- Use the information above to look up the critical value in the **critical values table**

	Level of significance for a one-tailed test		
	0.1	0.05	0.025
	Level of significance for a two-tailed test		
Sample size (n)	0.2	0.1	0.05
5	0	0	-
6	1	0	0
7	1	0	0

Significance is shown if the calculated value of *S* is **equal to or less than** the critical value.

- As it says, significance is shown if the S is **equal to or less than** the critical value
    - **S = 1**
    - **Critical value = 0**
- 1 is greater than 0, so the results are **not statistically significant**.

Research Methods

ISSUES AND DEBATES – GENDER AND CULTURAL BIAS

Gender bias may lead to invalid conclusions about men and women

- **Alpha bias:** When a theory *exaggerates* differences between genders.
  - *Example:* Freud's psychoanalytic theory (see page 40) argues that women develop weaker superegos than men and suffer from 'penis envy' (see page 90).
- **Beta bias:** When a theory *ignores* differences between genders.
  - *Example:* The behavioural response to stress is typically characterised as *fight or flight* (see page 46). However, this research was based solely on *males* and assumed these behavioural responses were the same across genders. However, Taylor et al (2000) looked at *female* responses to stress and found that female stress behaviour is better characterised as *tend and befriend* than fight or flight.

Beta bias within psychology can lead to **androcentrism**: A perspective where male psychology and behaviours are viewed as the default. For example, in the stress example above, female tend and befriend behaviours could be falsely viewed as *abnormal* (even though they're perfectly normal *for females*) because they deviate from typical *male* (fight or flight) behaviours.

AO3: Gender bias can occur for a variety of reasons. For example, researchers may have pre-conceived gender stereotypes that affect how they treat participants, resulting in investigator effects (see page 56). Further, publication bias could cause alpha bias: Studies that find no differences between genders may be seen as less interesting and be less likely to get published.

Cultural bias is when research from one culture is applied to all cultures

Berry (1969) distinguishes between **emic** and **etic** research:
- **Emic:** Researching a culture from within to understand *that culture* specifically (and not applying the findings to other cultures).
- **Etic:** Conducting research from an outside perspective to understand *universal truths* about human psychology (i.e. applying the findings to all people in all cultures).

An *imposed* etic can lead to **ethnocentrism**: A perspective where the behaviours of a certain ethnicity or culture are seen as the default and normal. As such, any behaviour that deviates from the norms of that culture may be seen as *abnormal*.

For example, Ainsworth's studies (see page 21) only looked at *American* infants and concluded that secure attachment styles are best. From this perspective, child-rearing practices in other countries may be seen as psychologically abnormal. For example, the American perspective might see German parents as cold and rejecting. However, *from the German perspective*, American parents may seem overly coddling, preventing infants from becoming independent.

AO3: Given that all humans in all cultures have very similar biology, there are likely to be many universal psychological truths, so etic research is not automatically bad. But if researchers *assume* their culture is the default, that's where the bias comes in. Psychological research can avoid cultural bias by being conscious of **cultural relativism**, i.e. differences between cultures.

ISSUES AND DEBATES – SOCIALLY SENSITIVE RESEARCH

Socially sensitive research may affect people beyond those directly involved

On page 62, we looked at ethical issues involved in the study *itself* – like harm to participants. But **socially sensitive research** may have ethical implications for wider society – affecting certain social groups, the participants' friends and family, or the researcher's institution.

For example, if a study that found differences in skills between genders, this could bias company hiring practices. Or if a participant in a study found out they have genes associated with OCD, this may lead their children to wonder if they too have inherited the OCD genes.

Sieber and Stanley (1988) outline various ethical concerns that researchers should consider before conducting socially sensitive research. These include:

- **Implications:** What harmful effects could the study have on society? For example, could it be used to legitimise discrimination (e.g. Raine's brain scans described below)?
- **Public policy:** Could the study be used by governments to support or inform policies (e.g. Burt's (1955) research described below)?
- **Validity:** Are the study's results accurate? There are many cases where research findings have turned out to be inaccurate or fraudulent (e.g. Burt (1955)).

AO3: Researchers must weigh up ethical concerns against the potential benefits.

Socially sensitive research findings may have positive and negative effects. For example, the 1909 Asexualisation Act in California allowed for the sterilisation of people on the basis of psychological traits such as low intelligence or mental illness. On the other hand, Scarr (1988) argues that research into differences between groups (e.g. genders, races, sexual orientations) can lead to greater understanding, which is likely to *reduce* discrimination.

Examples of **ethical implications** of socially sensitive research include:

Study	Description	Ethical implications
Burt (1955)	Research supporting a genetic basis of intelligence.	Burt's research led to the 11+ exam in the UK, which tested for 'natural' intelligence. This exam decided if a child went to grammar school or not, which affected the child's life opportunities. Later, it emerged some data in Burt's study was made up, but the 11+ exam remained.
Raine (1996) and Raine et al (1997)	Brain scans suggesting antisocial, violent, and murderous people have particular brain structures.	Raine suggested brain scans in childhood could be used to identify potentially violent criminals of the future. This policy, if enacted, could potentially reduce crime but would also likely lead to discrimination against people with these brain structures.
Milgram's experiments (page 7)	Research into the effects of authority on obedience.	Milgram's experiments deceived participants and caused distress. Although this may be seen as unethical, some argue that the value of the knowledge gained from these experiments outweighs the harm done.

Issues and Debates in Psychology

ISSUES AND DEBATES – FREE WILL VS. DETERMINISM

There are differing opinions on whether humans have **free will**

Free will means humans are able to freely *choose* their behaviours.

The opposite of free will is **determinism**, which says that human behaviours are caused by physical processes and that these physical processes cannot be overruled.

The various approaches to psychology (see page 32) fall on different sides of the debate. For example, the *humanistic* **approach** believes humans *do* have free will. While it acknowledges that physical factors – e.g. genetics and environment – *influence* our behaviours, humanistic psychologists believe humans are able to transcend these physical factors and make free choices.

There are different kinds of **determinism**

Hard vs. **soft** determinism	• **Hard determinism:** Human behaviour is *entirely* caused by physical processes that are beyond our control. So, free choices are impossible. • **Soft determinism:** Human behaviour is largely determined by physical processes (e.g. biology, upbringing, etc.) but humans are able to overrule these processes and exert their free will in some circumstances.
Biological determinism	The *biological* **approach:** Behaviour is determined entirely by biological processes beyond our control, such as genetics, hormones, brain structure, and physiological processes. For example, brain scans show that people with OCD often have increased activity in the prefrontal cortex of the brain.
Environmental determinism	The *behaviourist* **approach:** Behaviour is determined by conditioning from our environment. For example, being rewarded for working hard as a child, positively reinforces hard-working behaviours and makes you a hard worker.
Psychic determinism	The *psychodynamic* **approach:** Behaviour is governed by desires and conflicts below the level of conscious control.

AO3: **Strengths** of free will (i.e. *weaknesses* of determinism)

- **Consistent with our moral and legal intuitions:** If determinism is correct, then we couldn't hold people morally responsible for their actions (because they're not freely chosen). This would make it unfair to, for example, send murderers to prison.
- **Subjective validity:** When we make decisions, it *feels* like we have free will.

AO3: **Weaknesses** of free will (i.e. *strengths* of determinism)

- **Conflicting evidence:** Some experiments suggest humans do *not* have free will. For example, Soon et al (2008) used brain scans to measure brain activity as participants made a decision to press a button with either their left or right hand. The brain scans showed activity in the prefrontal and parietal cortices (areas associated with decision making) up to 10 seconds before the participants were consciously aware of their decision.

ISSUES AND DEBATES – NATURE VS. NURTURE

People on the **nature** side of the debate are called *nativists*

Nativists believe our behaviour is explained by **heredity** – i.e. genetics. The ***biological*** **approach** tends to fall on this side of the debate.

The **heritability coefficient** is a way to *quantify* the extent to which a characteristic is determined by genetics. A heritability coefficient of 1 means the characteristic is 100% genetic, whereas 0 means the characteristic has nothing to do with genetics. For example:

Trait	Heritability coefficient	Study
Intelligence (IQ)	0.8	Bouchard (2013)
Schizophrenia	0.79	Hilker et al (2018)
OCD	0.45 – 0.65	Grootheest et al (2005)

People on the **nurture** side of the debate are called *empiricists*

They believe the mind is a **blank slate** at birth, so all behaviour is learned from **environment**. The ***learning*** **approach** leans towards the nurture side of the debate. Skinner, for example, explained behaviours as a result of operant conditioning and so different conditioning leads to different behaviour (regardless of genetics). For example, if someone who became a hard worker because of positive reinforcement *did not receive that positive reinforcement*, then they wouldn't be a hard worker (because different conditioning = different person).

In reality, most people are **interactionists** – i.e. *somewhere in the middle*

The distinction between **genotype** and **phenotype** (page 38) shows how genes can present differently in response to environment. For example, even though OCD has a strong genetic component, some people with 'OCD genes' may never experience events that trigger these genes.

One mechanism through which environment interacts with genetics is **epigenetics**. Lifestyle choices (e.g. smoking) and environmental effects (e.g. living in an area with air pollution) 'switch on' certain genes and 'switch off' others, showing how genes and environment interact.

AO3: **Strengths** of nativism (i.e. *weaknesses* of empiricism)

- **Supporting evidence:** Twin studies, family studies, adoption studies, and gene mapping all show genetics play an important role in psychological disorders and behaviour.

AO3: **Weaknesses** of nativism (i.e. *strengths* of empiricism)

- **Conflicting evidence:** Even among identical twins (who share *100%* of their genes), concordance rates for psychological disorders and behaviours are much less than 100%.
- **Confounding variables:** Sibling and non-identical twin studies assume the environments of siblings and twins are identical and so all differences are due to genetics. But this is unlikely. E.g. Siblings who both experience parental divorce will experience it at different *ages*.

Issues and Debates in Psychology

ISSUES AND DEBATES – HOLISM VS. REDUCTIONISM

Holism vs. reductionism is about **levels of explanation**

The same phenomena (e.g. depression) be explained at *different levels*. For example:

- Depression can be explained at a *psychological* level, such as sustained negative thoughts and low mood.
- But these thoughts and emotions can also be explained *biologically*, by referring to things like neurons firing and neurotransmitters (e.g. serotonin) binding to receptors.
- You can go even lower, though, such as by breaking down your description of neurons and neurotransmitters into *basic physical components* such as atoms.

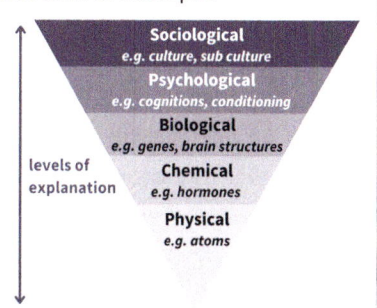

levels of explanation:
- Sociological (e.g. culture, sub culture)
- Psychological (e.g. cognitions, conditioning)
- Biological (e.g. genes, brain structures)
- Chemical (e.g. hormones)
- Physical (e.g. atoms)

Reductionists want to break things down to a *single* level of explanation

The **biological** approach leans heavily towards reductionism (**biological reductionism**). For example, a proponent of this approach might argue that behaviour can be explained entirely in terms of physical/biological causes *without reference to higher levels of explanation*, such as a person's upbringing or cognitions.

Similarly, the **behaviourist approach** can be reductionist (**environmental reductionism**). For example, an extreme behaviourist might explain behaviour *solely* in terms of conditioning without reference to lower levels of explanation such as the underlying biology.

Whereas **holism** thinks psychology must take account of *all* levels of explanation

The **humanistic** approach is arguably the most holistic approach. It treats every person as a unique individual that *cannot be reduced* to simple explanations. For example, in explaining a person's depression, humanistic psychologists would consider their genetics and biology but also the person's experiences, upbringing, and general social context and culture in which they live.

AO3: **Strengths** of reductionism (i.e. *weaknesses* of holism)

- **More scientific:** *Reducing* variables and behaviour enables psychology to be conducted in a scientific – i.e. repeatable, quantifiable, and objective – way. For example, reducing schizophrenia to dopamine activity enables researchers to objectively determine whether someone has schizophrenia and reliably measure whether a treatment is effective or not.
- **Practical applications:** E.g. biological reductionism resulted in SSRIs for depression.

AO3: **Weaknesses** of reductionism (i.e. *strengths* of holism)

- **Overly simplistic:** Reductionism may overly simplify behaviour and miss out important details. For example, behaviour in the Stanford prison experiment (page 6) couldn't just be explained biologically – the full explanation would need to include the social context.

Issues and Debates in Psychology

ISSUES AND DEBATES – NOMOTHETIC VS. IDIOGRAPHIC

The **nomothetic approach** looks at what makes humans *similar*

The **nomothetic approach** (*'nomos'* = *'law'*) to psychology seeks to identify *general laws* of human behaviour by looking at similarities between people and groups of people.

- It derives **general laws** by looking at *similarities* between multiple people.
- It emphasises **quantiative**, rather than qualitative, data.
- It prefers experiments with **large sample sizes** to individual case studies.
- It tends to be more **objective** and less subjective than the idiographic approach.

The *behaviourist*, *cognitive*, and *biological* **approaches** are all highly nomothetic: They want to identify general laws of human behaviour and use experiments and quantitative data to do so.

Whereas the **idiographic approach** looks at what makes individuals *different*

Advocates of the **idiographic approach** (*'idios'* = *'distinct self'*) believe the uniqueness of each person makes it difficult/impossible to identify general laws that apply across populations.

- It looks at individuals as **unique cases** and describes them rather than identifying general laws.
- It emphasises **qualitative data** over quantitative data.
- It prefers **individual case studies** and **self-report methods** over large-scale experiments.
- It tends to be more **subjective** and less objective than the nomothetic approach.

The **humanistic approach** is highly idiographic: It treats each individual as a unique case. The **psychodynamic approach** has idiographic *elements* (e.g. Freud sought to understand individuals through *case studies*), but also nomothetic *elements* (e.g. the psychosexual stages are universal).

AO3: **Strengths** of nomothetic approach (*weaknesses* of idiographic approach)

- **More scientific:** Science is all about what can be objectively measured and repeated. By using these tools, the nomothetic approach is able to identify general scientific laws of human behaviour (similar to how physics identifies the general scientific laws that govern physical matter). These psychological laws have predictive power. For example, Milgram's experiments tell you how likely someone is to obey an authority figure.
- **Practical applications:** E.g. identifying *similarities* in brain chemistry across individuals with depression could yield new treatments that treat depression by addressing this brain chemistry. Or, identifying *common* thought patterns among gambling addicts could lead to cognitive therapies that target these thought patterns and reduce gambling addiction.

AO3: **Weaknesses** of nomothetic approach (*strengths* of idiographic approach)

- **Exceptions:** For example, operant conditioning (a nomothetic explanation) may be able to explain why *some* people get addicted to cigarettes – but another person may smoke exactly the same amount and not get addicted. Exceptions like this highlight the limitations of the nomothetic approach: Universal nomothetic laws never apply to *all* people.

RELATIONSHIPS – EVOLUTIONARY EXPLANATIONS

Evolution is the process by which species adapt to their environment

Random mutations in genes that are advantageous to the animal become more common:
- Either because the mutation increases the animal's chances of **survival** (which increases the likelihood the animal will live long enough to reproduce and pass on its genes)
- Or the mutation increases the animal's **attractiveness** to potential mates (which also increases the likelihood the animal will reproduce and pass on its genes)

This second way is known as **sexual selection**. Evolutionary (socio-biological) explanations of relationships are based on the different sexual selection pressures between men and women.

Anisogamy is the differences between male and female sex cells

Female (ova/eggs)	Male (sperm)
Finite number of eggs	Continuously produce sperm
Approximately 25 years of fertility after puberty	Continuously fertile after puberty into old age
Fewer reproductive opportunities (~300 monthly ovulations over reproductive life)	Greater reproductive opportunities (~100,000,000 sperm per ejaculation)
Each child is a significant investment of resources (e.g. the mother has to bear the child for 9 months during pregnancy)	Little investment of resources (i.e. sperm is reproductively 'cheap' – it doesn't take a lot of time or energy to produce)
Can produce at most 1 child every 9 months	Could produce multiple children per day

Anisogamy means the optimal breeding strategy differs between men and women (from an evolutionary standpoint of passing on genes). This results in **different reproductive behaviours**.

Male reproductive behaviour is all about *quantity* over *quality*

That's a bit of a generalisation, but it's what evolution would suggest. Men can produce children with very little investment of time and resources – they just need to have sex. For a man, getting as many women pregnant as possible produces the most amount of his children, which increases the amount of his genes that survive. There are several strategies males may use to achieve this:
- **Signs of fertility:** Men value signs of youth and beauty in women as these indicate the woman is fertile. The more fertile a woman is, the more likely she is to fall pregnant with his child.
- **Fighting:** Males compete with other males for women. For example, some species of deer use their antlers to fight with each other.
- **Sneak copulation:** Men may secretly cheat on their partners in order to maximise the number of children they have.
- **Mate-guarding:** Men stay close to their partners to ensure they are not having sex with other males behind their back. This is to prevent getting cuckolded: Where the man ends up raising a child that is not his own.

RELATIONSHIPS – EVOLUTIONARY EXPLANATIONS

Whereas **female reproductive behaviour** is all about *quality* over *quantity*

Each child is a significant investment of time and resources for a woman. For example, she has to carry the baby for 9 months in her womb. This results in a different optimal strategy for ensuring the survival of her genes compared to men. Rather than trying to have as many children as possible, women focus more on ensuring the children they do have are healthy and provided-for. There are several strategies females may use to achieve this:

- **Signs of resources:** Women value signs of resources and wealth as these indicate that the man is able to provide for and raise the child. Sufficient resources (e.g. food and shelter) increase the likelihood that the child will survive and thrive.
- **Courtship (dating):** Women use courtship to get to know a man and work out whether he would be a suitable partner and father. Courtship has the additional benefit of making the man invest time and effort into the woman (and maybe fall in love with her), which makes the man more likely to stick around after she falls pregnant.
- **Sneak copulation:** Women may also secretly cheat on their partners as this increases the genetic diversity of their children. The risk of this strategy is the woman getting found out and losing access to her partner's resources. The potential reward, however, is that she can have children with a genetically desirable 'stud' while maintaining access to her partner's resources.

AO3: **Strengths** of evolutionary explanations of relationships

- **Evidence supporting evolutionary explanations of human reproductive *behaviour*:** E.g. in Clark and Hatfield (1989) student participants were asked to approach other students of the opposite sex and ask questions like: "Would you go to bed with me?". The *vast majority of men said yes* to the women, whereas *zero women said yes* when the men asked them.
- **Evidence supporting evolutionary explanations of *partner preferences*:** For example, Buss (1989) surveyed 10,000+ adults from *all over the world* on partner preferences. He found that males valued signs of fertility (i.e. physical attractiveness and youth) more than females, and that females valued signs of resources (i.e. financial capacity, ambition) more than males. These preferences were common across all countries and cultures, which suggests that evolutionary explanations of partner preferences have cross-cultural validity.

AO3: **Weaknesses** of evolutionary explanations of relationships

- **Cannot explain all relationships:** Evolutionary explanations explain male and female relationships on the basis that they are necessary for reproduction and passing on genes. But this explanation is less able to explain other forms of relationships, such as homosexual couples or couples who choose not to have children.
- **Ignores social and cultural factors:** Bovet and Raymond (2015) found the ideal waist-to-hip ratio of women (as depicted in art and media over many centuries) *changed significantly* over time. These changes occurred too quickly to be explained evolutionarily, suggesting cultural influences are also important in explaining partner preferences.

Relationships

RELATIONSHIPS – FACTORS AFFECTING ATTRACTION

Physical attractiveness is an immediate way to select potential partners

Men are typically attracted to physical characteristics that indicate **fertility** in females, such as youth and a **low waist-to-hip ratio**. Evidence suggests physical attractiveness is less important to women than men, but women are also attracted to physical features that indicate **genetic fitness**, such as **high shoulder-to-hip ratio**. A physical attribute attractive to *both* males and females is **facial symmetry**. Shackelford and Larsen (1997) found that people with symmetrical faces are consistently rated as more attractive than people with asymmetric faces.

AO3: There is some evidence of cross-cultural similarity in what is considered physically attractive. For example, Cunningham et al (1995) found that White, Asian, and Hispanic males *all* rated high cheekbones, large eyes, and small noses as attractive in females. These similarities in what's considered physically attractive suggest an evolutionary (biological) basis to physical attraction.

Walster et al's (1966) **matching hypothesis** says we choose partners who are **similar** in physical attractiveness to ourselves. E.g. if you rate yourself 7/10, you'll go for a partner who is also 7/10.

There's an evolutionary element to the matching hypothesis: While it might be *desirable* to form relationships with the most attractive people, it is not always *realistic*. If people only went for partners out of their league, they might never find a partner and thus never pass on their genes.

AO3: Walster et al's *own study* did not support the matching hypothesis, as participants in the study preferred partners who were *more attractive* than them rather than equally attractive. More recently, Taylor et al (2011) found participants using online dating services did not consider their own attractiveness but instead sought partners more attractive than themselves.

Self-disclosure is revealing personal and intimate information about yourself

Altman and Taylor's (1973) **social penetration theory** describes the process of self-disclosure in relationships. Both the *breadth* (i.e. the range of topics) and the *depth* of self-disclosures is important. They compare it to peeling back the **layers of an onion**: Initially, disclosures will cover a narrow range of basic topics in a shallow way – you talk about what you do for a living, your hobbies, etc. As the relationship develops, the breadth of topics and depth of disclosure increases. For example, you talk about more controversial or intimate topics, share painful or embarrassing memories, and maybe reveal some secrets.

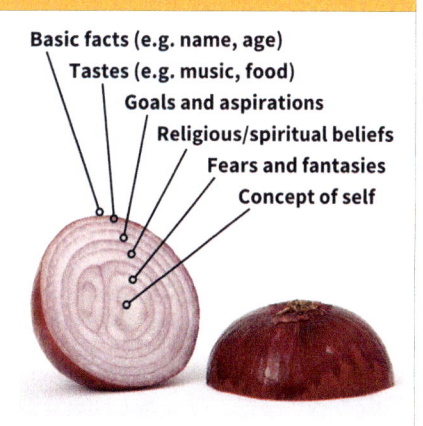

Basic facts (e.g. name, age)
Tastes (e.g. music, food)
Goals and aspirations
Religious/spiritual beliefs
Fears and fantasies
Concept of self

Self-disclosure is important in the development of a relationship as it establishes **trust** and **intimacy**. However, too much self-disclosure too quickly tends to have the opposite effect: Altman and Taylor found that revealing intimate details too early on (e.g. talking about childhood trauma on a first date) is unattractive.

RELATIONSHIPS – FACTORS AFFECTING ATTRACTION

AO3: **Strengths** of self-disclosure as a factor affecting attraction

- **Supporting evidence:** Sprecher and Hendrick (2004) found self-disclosure between couples to be strongly *correlated* with relationship satisfaction, supporting self-disclosure as an important factor in attraction. However, correlation does not necessarily equal causation – it could be that being in a good relationship in the first place causes couples to self-disclose to each other rather than that self-disclosure causes the relationship to be a good one.

AO3: **Weaknesses** of self-disclosure as a factor affecting attraction

- **Other factors:** Although self-disclosure seems to be a factor in attraction, it is unlikely that self-disclosure alone is enough. Instead, self-disclosure likely interacts with other aspects of attraction, such as physical attractiveness and similarity of attitudes.
- **Cultural differences:** Tang et al (2013) found that sexual self-disclosure among US couples was far higher than among Chinese couples, yet relationship satisfaction was equal among both groups. This suggests there may be cultural differences in self-disclosure and attraction.

Kerckhoff and Davis' (1962) **filter theory** says there are *3 filters* we use…

…to narrow down the range of available options:

- **Social demography:** These are the basic facts that determine whether a relationship is even practical. For example, if someone lives really far away it is likely to decrease the attractiveness of a relationship with them because you will never see them. Similarly, if someone is from a different religion or social class, these basic facts make a relationship unrealistic.
- **Similarity of attitudes:** People tend to be attracted to people with similar values to them. Within the first 18 months of a relationship, partners self-disclose information that enables them to suss out each others' values and attitudes. If there are few similarities in attitudes, relationships tend not to last beyond 18 months.
- **Complemetarity:** When each partner has traits that the other lacks. This makes couples feel like they 'complete' each other, and that they fulfil each other's needs. For example, if one partner has a caring nature and the other likes to be cared for, these traits complement each other.

Strengths:	- **Supporting evidence:** Winch (1959) found that similarity of attitudes was important for couples in the early stages of a relationship and that complementarity becomes more important in long-term relationships. This supports 2 of the 3 filters (similarity of attitudes and complementarity).
Weaknesses:	- **Cause or effect?:** Davis and Rusbult (2001) found that partners' attitudes *change* over time to become more aligned rather than that partners select each other *because* their attitudes align (as filter theory claims). - **Questions of temporal validity:** The growth of online dating may have reduced the importance of social demography as a filter. For example, people may be more likely to interact with and date people outside their social class or religion.

Relationships

RELATIONSHIPS – THEORIES OF ROMANTIC RELATIONSHIPS

Social exchange theory (SET) sees relationships as a *cost:benefit* analysis

According to SET, humans are selfish and so engage in romantic relationships in order to get some benefit. Partners **weigh the costs** of being in the relationship (e.g. time, effort, loss of freedom, stress) **against the benefits** (e.g. companionship, help, gifts, sex). If the benefits outweigh the costs, the relationship is **profitable** and there is a desire to maintain it. However, if the costs outweigh the benefits for one partner, they'll end the relationship as it's **unprofitable**.

In addition to the 'profitability' of the *current* relationship (comparison level), there is the potential profitability of *alternative relationships* (comparison level for alternatives). If a partner judges an alternative relationship to be more profitable than the current one, they may break off the current relationship – even if it is profitable – to pursue the *more profitable* one.

Strengths:	• **Supporting evidence:** A longitudinal study by Rusbult (1983) found a correlation between perceived benefits and relationship satisfaction. However, Rusbult also found that increases in the costs associated with a relationship did not decrease relationship satisfaction, weakening support for SET.
Weaknesses:	• **Other factors:** Other theories (see below) suggest factors beyond profitability – such as commitment and equity – are important for successful relationships. • **Questions of external validity:** Much of the data supporting SET comes from artificial tasks (e.g. two random people are put together for an experiment to see how they act in a game with rewards and costs) and so the findings may not be valid when applied to real-life relationships.

Equity theory says *fairness* is what makes relationship succeed

Whereas SET sees people as selfishly trying to maximise *their own benefits* in a relationship, equity theory sees people as trying to maximise **equity** (fairness) in a relationship.

If one partner is benefiting from the relationship more than the other, this leads to relationship dissatisfaction *on both sides:* The underbenefiting partner may feel angry they're making all this effort and getting little in return, whereas the overbenefiting partner may feel shame and guilt. Equity theory predicts that inequity (unfairness) is correlated with relationship dissatisfaction.

Strengths:	• **Supporting evidence:** Hatfield et al (1984) conducted surveys of newlywed couples. They found couples in equitable relationships were more likely to be happy with their relationship compared to couples in inequitable relationships.
Weaknesses:	• **Conflicting evidence:** Huseman et al (1987) found that equity is not an important factor in *all* relationships because some partners are less sensitive to equity than others. Some people getting more than they give, for example. • **Cultural differences:** Aumer-Ryan et al (2007) found equity was important to couples in *individualist* cultures, but partners from collectivist cultures had greater relationship satisfaction when they were *overbenefitting*.

RELATIONSHIPS – THEORIES OF ROMANTIC RELATIONSHIPS

Rusbult's (1980) **investment model** is about how *committed* partners are...

...to their relationship – i.e. how much they've *invested* in it. **Commitment** has 3 components:

- **Satisfaction level:** This is similar to social exchange theory in that it is the weighing of costs vs. benefits of being in the relationship. If benefits outweigh costs and the partner's needs are being met, then satisfaction is high. Satisfaction increases commitment to the relationship.
- **Comparison with alternatives:** Also similar to SET, this is the weighing of benefits of the current relationship vs. the best possible alternative. If the benefits of the current relationship are greater than alternatives, this increases commitment to the relationship.
- **Investment size:** The amount of resources – time, money, effort, etc. – invested into the relationship. Investment also covers things like children, shared friends, shared possessions. High investment in a relationship increases commitment to it.

Strengths:	• **Supporting evidence:** A meta-analysis of 52 studies conducted by Le and Agnew (2003) found relationship commitment was positively correlated with all 3 elements of Rusbult's investment model, supporting the theory.
Weaknesses:	• **Methodological concerns:** Much of the data supporting Rusbult's model comes from questionnaires. But such self-report methods may not produce valid findings as participants often give socially desirable rather than honest answers. Further, many studies supporting Rusbult's model are *correlational* and so do not prove that the 3 components above *cause* relationship commitment.

Duck's phase model is a 4-stage model of relationship *breakdown*

Intrapsychic	**Thinking** you are dissatisfied with the relationship. Consider the costs of ending the relationship. Weigh up whether to express the dissatisfaction or repress it.
Dyadic	**Discussing** your dissatisfaction with the relationship with your partner. Possible attempts to resolve the problem and repair the relationship.
Social	Discussing the relationship **with other people** outside the relationship. Seek support from friends, family, etc. Negotiate terms of the break-up with partner.
Grave-dressing	**Break up and move on**. Come up with stories/explanations of the break-up to tell other people that place blame on the partner and make you look good.

Each stage marks a '**threshold**' at which the *perception* of the relationship changes. If the partner does not feel there has been enough change at that stage, they may move on to the next stage.

Strengths:	• **Practical applications:** Rollie and Duck (2006) describe how communication at each of the four stages of the model can revert the relationship to a previous stage and avoid progression towards relationship breakdown.
Weaknesses:	• **Describes, but doesn't explain:** A complete psychological model of relationship breakdown would explain *why* relationships break down in the first place – but Duck's phase model just *describes* the process without explaining it.

RELATIONSHIPS – VIRTUAL RELATIONSHIPS

Virtual relationships may lead to greater levels of **self-disclosure**

Anonymity in virtual relationships may increase self-disclosure. Unlike face-to-face interactions, virtual relationships can be conducted anonymously (e.g. via anonymous forums and burner accounts). This may increase self-disclosure compared to real-life, as anonymity protects people from potential negative social consequences of self-disclosing private or intimate information.

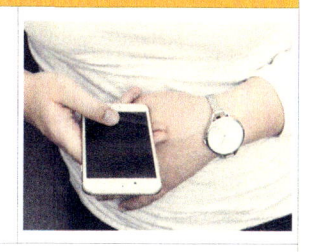

Further, **verbal cues** that are ordinarily there in face-to-face interactions, such as body language and tone of voice, are not present in many virtual interactions. This may affect self-disclosure too. Walther's (1996) *hyperpersonal model* argues that non-verbal cues distract from the content of the communication. By removing them in virtual contexts, the sender is able to focus more on how they present themselves, enabling superior ('hyperpersonal') communication. The hyperpersonal model is further supported by Jiang et al (2010), who found that disclosure and intimacy were higher in text-based virtual interactions than in face-to-face ones.

AO3: Self-disclosure is likely to differ depending on the online context. For example, a post on a public profile linked to your real name and photos (e.g. Instagram) is likely to be curated to present the best version of yourself and not disclose embarrassing or intimate information. In contrast, a post to an anonymous forum is likely to involve more self-disclosure because anonymity protects the person from the negative social effects of self-disclosure.

Things that might prevent a relationship in real life may not be present online

This is called **absence of gating**. McKenna and Bargh (1999) give several examples of potential '**gates**' that might prevent a person from forming face-to-face relationships. Such gates include facial disfigurement, a stammer, or extreme shyness of social anxiety. In the virtual context, these gates don't exist and so a person may be able to form relationships with people who might otherwise reject them because of these reasons.

On the internet, no one knows you're a goblin

Similarly, the social demography filter of filter theory (page 80) is less likely to serve as a gate in virtual relationships. For example, the internet means people can communicate and maintain relationships over large distances, and with people outside their social class or ethnicity.

AO3: Absence of gating has both positives and negatives. A positive is that people are able to overcome barriers that might otherwise prevent them from forming close relationships. For example, McKenna (2002) found that people who are socially anxious in face-to-face settings are better able to express their true selves online, leading to close relationships online. However, the absence of gates in virtual settings means people can lie about themselves or create fake personas in order to deceive people into relationships (catfishing).

RELATIONSHIPS – PARASOCIAL RELATIONSHIPS

Parasocial relationships are *one-sided* relationships...

...where a person gets *attached* to someone they **don't know in real life**, e.g. a celebrity. McCutcheon et al's (2002) **celebrity attitude scale** can identify **3 levels** of parasocial relationship:

- **Entertainment-social:** The *least extreme* form of parasocial relationship. The person sees the celebrity as a source of entertainment and something to discuss socially.
- **Intense-personal:** More intense. The person is personally invested in the celebrity's life and may have obsessive thoughts about them.
- **Borderline-pathological:** The *most extreme* form of parasocial relationship. The person has delusional fantasies about a celebrity and may exhibit irrational behaviour that prevents them living a normal life. E.g. *"Celebrity X is my soulmate, I'm going to marry them."*

The **absorption-addiction model** is one explanation of parasocial relationships

McCutcheon et al's (2002) **absorption-addiction model** says people engage in parasocial relationships to compensate for deficiencies in their lives. For example, a person whose life is *boring* may follow a celebrity's life in order to '**absorb**' some of the *fun* they experience. Or a person who feels *unsuccessful* may try to absorb some of the celebrity's *success*. However, the person may become **addicted** to these vicarious feelings. When this happens, they may need to increase the 'dose' in a way similar to physical addiction in order to get the same positive feelings as before. This may increase to the borderline-pathological level of parasocial relationship.

And **attachment theory** also provides an explanation of parasocial relationships

Remember Ainsworth's attachment styles (page 21)? According to the **attachment explanation** of parasocial relationships, individuals with **insecure-resistant** attachment styles in infancy are most likely to engage in parasocial relationships when they grow up. The reasoning behind this is that insecure-resistant infants still *desire* to form emotional connections (unlike insecure-avoidant infants) but don't want to risk the possibility of rejection. Parasocial relationships thus provide a way for insecure-resistant individuals to experience the positive emotions of a relationship without the risk of rejection that comes with typical social relationships.

Weakness:	• **Conflicting evidence:** McCutcheon et al (2006) measured attraction to celebrities and attachment styles in 299 students. They found no correlation between insecure attachment styles and attraction to celebrities – although insecure-resistant types *were* more likely to condone stalking and obsessive behaviours.

AO3: Much of the research into parasocial relationships uses self-report techniques such as questionnaires (see page 58). But these methods may not produce valid findings, as participants may give answers that are socially desirable rather than honest. For example, someone who has thoughts about stalking a celebrity may be embarrassed to admit so in a questionnaire.

Relationships

GENDER – SEX, GENDER, AND ANDROGYNY

Sex: Whether a person is *biologically* male or female (i.e. what sex organs and chromosomes they have).

Gender: Whether a person is *psychologically* masculine and/or feminine.

Sex-role stereotypes are social expectations of male and female behaviour

Examples of **sex-role stereotypes** include:
- Women are more nurturing than men
- Men are more aggressive than women
- Caring for children is women's work, men do the DIY
- Pink is a girl's colour, blue is a boy's colour

Some sex-role stereotypes are *valid*. For example, the stereotype that men are more aggressive than women may reflect a valid biological difference between the sexes. But many stereotypes, such as women wearing skirts and men wearing trousers, are entirely **created by culture**.

Androgyny is when someone has a mix of both feminine and masculine traits

Psychological androgyny can be *measured* using the **Bem (1974) sex-role inventory** (BSRI): A self-report method that asks participants to rate themselves on a scale of 1-7 for 60 items. 20 of these items are considered 'masculine', 20 items are 'feminine', and 20 are neutral. For example:

Item	1	2	3	4	5	6	7
Aggressive							
Understanding							
Reliable							

Bem argues androgyny – scoring highly for both masculinity and femininity – is **psychologically healthy** and **advantageous**. One reason androgyny may be advantageous is that having a mix of masculine and feminine traits enables a person to adapt and excel in more situations, whereas a person who scores highly one way but not the other is likely to have a more limited skillset.

Strengths:	• **Test-restest reliability:** Bem (1974) re-administered the BSRI to a sample of participants 4 weeks after they originally completed the test. She found the participants' answers were consistent both times.
Weaknesses:	• **Overly simplistic:** The BSRI focuses solely on personality traits and reduces gender to a single number. However, Golombok and Fivush (1994) argue that gender identity also includes things like interests and abilities. • **Cultural and temporal validity:** The items in the Bem sex-role inventory were decided based on surveys of what American students in the 1970's considered to be desirable traits for each gender. However, American attitudes have likely changed since then and other cultures may have different ideas about gender.

GENDER – BIOLOGICAL INFLUENCES ON GENDER

Human cells have 46 **chromosomes** (23 pairs), which carry genetic information

The 23rd pair determines a person's **biological sex**:
- In **females**, this 23rd pair looks like **XX** under a microscope
- And in **males**, the 23rd pair looks like **XY** under a microscope

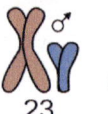

Females have two pairs of X chromosomes, whereas males have one X chromosome and one Y chromosome. It is genes in the Y chromosome that are responsible for male development, such as the formation of testes and higher levels of the hormone testosterone.

Some people have **atypical sex chromosome patterns**

Atypical sex chromosome patterns are when a person has a 23rd chromosome pair that is something **other** than the typical XX pattern for females or XY pattern for males.

	Physical characteristics	**Psychological characteristics**
Klinefelter's syndrome (also known as **47,XXY**) affects roughly 1 in 750 males.	• Less body hair than average males • Gynaecomastia (breast tissue) • Poorly functioning testicles (sterility) • Weaker muscles • Taller height than average males	• Low libido • Below average reading ability and poor language skills • Shyness and difficulties with social interaction
Turner's syndrome (also known as **45,X**) affects roughly 1 in 5000 females.	• No menstrual cycle (sterility) • Underdeveloped breasts • Webbed neck, broad chest, and narrow hips • Shorter than average females	• Above average reading abilities • Below average mathematics abilities • Social immaturity

Hormones, like **testosterone**, are an important biological influence on gender

Testosterone is the primary sex hormone in **males**. *On average,* men have around **10 times** as much testosterone as women.

During development in the womb, genes in the Y chromosome cause **testes**, rather than ovaries, to form. At around **8 weeks**, the testes start producing testosterone. This testosterone causes physical changes, such as the development of male sex organs, and also *psychological* changes by affecting **brain structure**. For example, men typically have greater spatial reasoning than women, and studies of females exposed to high levels of prenatal testosterone (e.g. Puts et al (2008)) suggest testosterone plays a role in developing these areas of the brain. *After birth*, testosterone is associated with stereotypical male behaviours, such as **aggression** and **competitiveness**. For example, Albert et al (1989) found that injecting female rats with testosterone made them *act more aggressively*. In humans, Dabbs et al (1995) studied a prison population and found prisoners with higher testosterone levels were more likely to have committed violent crimes.

GENDER – BIOLOGICAL INFLUENCES ON GENDER

Estrogen hormones, like estradiol, are associated with *female* gender

Females typically having **10 times** as much **estradiol** as men.
In the womb, having an X chromosome instead of Y means **ovaries**, rather than testes, form. This results in higher estrogen levels and lower testosterone levels. These higher estrogen levels have psychological effects by affecting **brain development**. For example, women generally have greater verbal fluency than men, with some studies (e.g. Schultheiss et al (2020)) suggesting this is a result of estrogen exposure in the womb. Estrogens are associated with stereotypical female behaviours, such as **compassion** and **sensitivity**. *After puberty*, estrogen also regulates the menstrual cycle in women. In some women, hormonal changes during the menstrual cycle cause pre-menstrual syndrome (PMS) – a condition with psychological symptoms that include stress, anxiety, and irritability. However, some researchers (e.g. Rodin (1992) and Offman and Kleinplatz (2004)) criticise the characterisation of PMS as a medical disorder.

Oxytocin is sometimes called the 'love hormone'...

...because it's associated with **bonding**, **nurturing**, **trust**, and **sociability**. Oxytocin levels are typically **higher in women** than men and the effects of oxytocin are amplified by estrogen, so oxytocin also contributes to gender differences.

An example of the role of oxytocin on gender-typical behaviours can be seen on page 71: Taylor et al (2000) suggest the female *tend and befriend* stress response is due to higher oxytocin levels.

AO3: **Strengths** of biological influences on gender

- **Supporting evidence:** The studies above are examples of how hormones influence gender development. Another useful example is Van Goozen et al (1995), who demonstrated that administering cross-sex hormones to transgender people results in gender-stereotypical behavioural changes. For example, FtMs given testosterone act *more aggressively* and MtFs given estrogen act *less aggressively*. Further, atypical sex chromosome patterns demonstrate how chromosomes also have important effects on gender development.

AO3: **Weaknesses** of biological influences on gender

- **Conflicting evidence:** For example, Tricker et al (1996) randomly assigned 43 men to receive either 600mg of testosterone per week or placebo but found no differences in aggression between the two groups. This weakens support for the effects of hormones on gender.
- **Socially sensitive:** Biological explanations of gender development could reinforce harmful stereotypes. For example, if males have a slight advantage in spatial reasoning on average, it might cause society to discriminate against women entering fields that require spatial reasoning (e.g. engineering) even if the woman is equally or more able than the average man.
- **Other factors:** Although there is strong evidence for a biological component to gender, other factors – such as cognitive factors and social learning – likely play a role as well.

COGNITIVE EXPLANATIONS OF GENDER DEVELOPMENT

Kohlberg's theory says gender development is part of *cognitive* development

In other words, **gender development** occurs alongside *general developments in thinking* that come with age. It's based on Piaget's theory of *cognitive* development (see page 94).
Kohlberg (1966) identifies **3 stages of gender development:**

Stage	Age	Description
Gender **identity**	18 months – 3 years	The child identifies *themself* as male or female and can categorise others as male or female. However, the child does not recognise the stability of gender, e.g. that girls grow up to become women, and so a girl might say something like "I'm going to be a daddy when I'm older".
Gender **stability**	3 – 5 years	The child realises that their gender is *stable*, i.e. that they will remain the same gender for life. However, they may not apply this same stability to others. For example, if a woman does some typically male activity or cuts her hair short, the child may think she is now a man.
Gender **constancy**	> 6 years	The child realises that theirs and other people's gender is permanent and *constant* over time and in different situations despite superficial changes. For example, if a woman cuts her hair short, the child understands that she is still a woman.

After gender constancy, children **seek out** and **imitate** role models who **match their gender**. E.g. a boy become interested in football if he identifies with his father who's also interested in football.

Strengths:	• **Supporting evidence:** Several studies support a pattern of gender development in line with Kohlberg's theory. For example, Thompson (1975) found that 76% of 2 year olds demonstrated gender identity but that this increased to 90% among 3 year olds, which is consistent with Kohlberg's timeline. Similarly, Slaby and Frey (1975) found that after children reach gender constancy they pay more attention to same-sex role models, which is in line with Kohlberg's predictions. • **Cross-cultural validity:** Munroe et al (1984) observed a pattern of gender development in line with Kohlberg's 3 stages across multiple different cultures.
Weaknesses:	• **Conflicting evidence:** For example, gender schema theory argues that children start behaving in gendered ways as early as 2 years old, long before Kohlberg's gender constancy stage. This earlier development described by gender schema theory has some reseach support – see page 89 for more. • **Methodological concerns:** Kohlberg's theory was based on interviews with children as young as 2 years old. However, children this young may have more sophisticated concepts of gender than they can express due to the fact that they are still learning to talk at that age. • **Other factors:** The fact that Munroe et al (1984) observed the same pattern of gender development across cultures suggests a common *biological* process.

Gender

COGNITIVE EXPLANATIONS OF GENDER DEVELOPMENT

Gender schema theory says gender development happens much earlier

Remember **schema** from the cognitive approach (page 36)? Martin and Halverson (1981) and Bem (1981) argue that children start developing **gender schema** – mental frameworks to understand men and women – at around 2-3 years old.

For example, a boy might develop the schema that *"dolls are a girl's toy"*. These schema are used to make sense of the world and also affect how the child behaves. For example, the boy will play with toy trucks and not dolls.

Gender schema theory differs from Kohlberg's theory in that it argues children behave in gendered ways from a much earlier age. Whereas Kohlberg argues that children start imitating gender-appropriate role models at around 6 years old (after reaching *gender constancy*), gender schema theory proposes that **children start developing gender schemas from around age 2.**

Over time, gender schemas *develop* alongside general cognitive development. For example, early schemas focus on the child's **own gender** only, but by around age 8 children develop schemas for the **opposite gender** as well. Later, by the time the child is a teenager, they realise that a lot of beliefs about boys and girls are just social customs and so gender schema become more **flexible**.

Strengths:	• **Supporting evidence:** Martin and Little (1990) observed that children aged 3-5 have stereotypical beliefs about which toys and clothes go with each gender, which suggests they have already developed gender schema by this age. • **Predictive power:** People are biased towards information that fits their pre-existing schema (see page 36). So, if gender schema theory is correct, you would expect children to be biased towards information that fits their gender schema. Martin and Halverson (1983) found that children aged 5-6 were more likely to accurately remember gender-typical pictures (e.g. a boy playing with a train) and more likely to misremember non-stereotypical pictures (e.g. a girl sawing wood), which is in line with the predictions of gender schema theory.
Weaknesses:	• **Conflicting evidence:** Several studies suggest children demonstrate gender-typical behaviour earlier still – *before* forming gender schema. For example, Alexander et al (2009) found boys aged 3-8 months looked at toy trucks more than toy dolls and that girls aged 3-8 months looked at toy dolls more than toy trucks. Similarly, Caldera et al (1989) found that children as young as 18 months display preferences for gender-typical toys. Finally, Hassett et al (2008) found that rhesus monkeys – animals who clearly do not have gender schema! – also display preferences for gender-typical toys. • **Other factors:** The studies above suggest that gender development happens much earlier than cognitive development. This suggests *biological* processes precede gender schema, suggesting a possible interactionist (see page 74) explanation.

PSYCHODYNAMIC EXPLANATIONS OF GENDER DEVELOPMENT

Freud's **psychodynamic explanation of gender development** is typically wacky

Remember the **5 psychosexual stages** (page 41)? Well, during the **phallic stage** (3 – 5 years old):
- The child develops a **sexual attraction to their opposite-sex parent** and a **dislike of their same-sex parent** (for women this is the *Electra* complex and for men the *Oedipus* complex).
- The child resolves this conflict by **identifying** with the same-sex parent.
- This involves **internalising** the same-sex parent's personality, which settles their gender.

Oedipus complex (male gender development)	**Electra complex** (female gender development)
• Prior to the phallic stage, a boy has no concept of gender. • During the phallic stage, the boy develops an unconscious sexual desire for his mother. • The boy's **id** wants to **kill the father** to **have the mother** • But the boy's **ego** realises his father is stronger than him. The boy fears his father will remove his penis *(castration anxiety)*. • So the boy abandons his desire for his mother and **identifies** with his father. By identifying with the father, the boy incorporates the father's personality into his **superego**. • The boy develops his gender by **displacing** the sexual desire for his mother onto *other women*.	• At the phallic stage, the girl thinks the reason she doesn't have a penis is because she's been castrated. The girl wants a penis *(penis envy)* and so develops a **desire for her father**, as he has what she wants. • The girl also develops a **dislike of her mother** for two reasons: Firstly, because she blames the mother for taking her penis, and secondly, because she sees the mother as competition. • But the girl also fears losing her mother's love. • So the girl represses her feelings of dislike for her mother and instead **identifies** with her. She incorporates and internalises the mother's personality into her **superego**. • The girl develops her gender by **substituting** her desire for a penis for a desire for a *baby*.

Strengths:	• **Supporting evidence:** Freud (1909) describes the case study of Little Hans. Hans initially had an intense phobia of horses, which Freud saw as a displaced fear of his *father*. In a later therapy session, Hans described a dream where a plumber replaced his penis with a bigger one, which Freud interpreted as Hans identifying with his father and overcoming his Oedipus complex.
Weaknesses:	• **Unscientific:** Freud's theories are based on unconscious concepts such as the id. These concepts are difficult, if not impossible, to observe and measure. However, science is concerned with what is observable, measurable, and repeatable, so by this standard Freud's explanation of gender is unscientific. • **Conflicting evidence:** Freud claims children have no concept of their gender prior to the phallic stage (3 - 5 years). However, several studies (e.g. those discussed in the gender schema theory and Kohlberg's theory sections above) demonstrate that children are aware of their own gender much earlier than this. • **Androcentric bias:** For example, both the Oedipus complex and the Electra complex assume the *male* perspective as the default and desirable: Male development focuses on the penis (and fear of losing it) whereas female development is characterised by a lack of and desire for a penis.

SOCIAL LEARNING EXPLANATIONS OF GENDER DEVELOPMENT

Social learning theory says we observe and imitate role models in the **media**

Bandura and Bussey (1999) argue that **TV shows** typically portray men as ambitious and having high-status jobs whereas women are typically portrayed as unambitious and occupying domestic roles or low-status jobs. Men are also portrayed as having greater agency (i.e. control over events) than women. These **stereotypes** also exist in **adverts**, with women typically promoting food and beauty products and men promoting things like computers and cars.

The social learning explanation of gender development would say: Children **observe** role models in the media, **identify** with those of the same gender, and **imitate** their gender-typical behaviour.

Strengths:	• **Supporting evidence:** McGhee and Frueh (1980) demonstrate correlations between stereotypical representations of gender in the media and stereotypical views on gender, supporting the idea that media teaches gender stereotypes.
Weaknesses:	• **Questions of temporal validity:** Modern portrayal of men and women in the media is much less gender-stereotypical than it was when the studies above were conducted. Further, the types of media that children consume have changed since these studies, with social media likely playing a bigger role than television. As such, the findings of these studies may lack temporal validity.

If gender comes from **culture**, there should be cultural variations in gender roles

And this is exactly what **Mead (1935)** found when she compared **gender roles** among **3 different tribes** in Papua New Guinea with stereotypical gender roles in Western cultures:

- **Arapesh:** Both the men and women were caring and peaceful (stereotypically *female*).
- **Mundugumor:** Both the men and women were aggressive and warlike (stereotypically *male*).
- **Tchambuli (Chambri):** Women were the workers (e.g. catching fish) and organised society, while men decorated themselves (opposite gender roles to those typical in Western cultures).

This supports the social learning explanation of gender development: Children *learn* gendered behaviour by **observing** and **imitating** the behaviours of **role models** of their own gender. If the males and females in the culture behave differently, the children learn different gender roles.

Strengths:	• **Explanatory power:** Cultural changes may explain changing gender roles. For example, more women work in stereotypically 'male' fields like engineering than in the past. SLT could say this is because there are more such role models today.
Weaknesses:	• **Conflicting evidence:** Errington and Gewertz (1987) also studied the Tchambuli (Chambri) tribe but found no evidence to support the gender roles described by Mead (1935). And further, several studies have found similar gender roles cross-culturally, contradicting Mead (1935). For example, Barry et al (1957) looked at 110 different cultures and found almost all saw obedience and nurturing as feminine traits and self-reliance and achievement-striving as masculine traits.

GENDER – ATYPICAL GENDER DEVELOPMENT

Gender dysphoria: Where a person's biological sex does not match their psychological gender (previously called *gender identity disorder*).

Biological explanations of gender dysphoria include genetics

As always, **twin studies** (page 38) are a useful way to determine the extent to which a condition is caused by **genetic factors**. Diamond (2013) combined a survey of transgender twins with a review of studies on transgender twins. **Concordance rates** for gender dysphoria among *identical* male and *identical* female twin pairs were **33.3%** and **22.8%** respectively. In contrast, the concordance rate among *non-identical* twins (male or female) was **only 2.6%**. This higher concordance among identical twins than non-identical twins supports a genetic explanation of gender dysphoria.

This genetic basis is further supported by **gene association studies**. For example, Hare et al (2009) analysed gene samples from 112 male-to-female transgender people and 258 controls, finding that gender dysphoria is correlated with differences in AR (androgen receptor) genes.

Hormones are another biological explanation of gender dysphoria

Hormonal explanations of gender dysphoria focus on **prenatal** (i.e. in the womb) **hormone levels**. It's difficult to measure (and unethical to alter) prenatal hormone levels, but some evidence suggests prenatal hormones contribute to gender dysphoria. For example:

- **Congenital adrenal hyperplasia** causes increased testosterone exposure in the womb. Erickson-Schroth (2013) found that at least 5.2% of biological females with congenital adrenal hyperplasia develop gender dysphoria, which is much higher than average. This suggests that prenatal testosterone exposure increases the incidence of gender dysphoria in biological females.
- Some studies suggest prenatal hormone levels affect **finger length ratios** (2D:4D digit ratio). And a meta-analysis by Siegmann et al (2020) found male-to-female transgender people had higher 2D:4D ratios than male controls, suggesting differences in prenatal hormone levels.

Transgender people may also have **brain structures** of the opposite sex

Several studies have found correlations between gender identity and **brain structure**, suggesting a role in gender dysphoria. In particular, research has focused on a brain area known as the bed nucleus of the stria terminalis (**BSTc**), which is typically **40% larger in males** than females:

- Zhou et al (1995) used post-mortems to compare the brains of 6 male-to-female transgender people with cisgender male and female controls. The BSTc regions of the MtFs were closer in size to cisgender females than males, suggesting they had female brain structures.
- Kruijver et al (2000) compared the number of neurons in the BSTc regions of transgender people with cisgender people. The researchers found that MtF trans people had similar numbers of neurons as cisgender females and that FtM trans people had similar numbers of neurons to cisgender males.

Gender

GENDER – ATYPICAL GENDER DEVELOPMENT

AO3: **Strengths** of biological explanations of gender dysphoria

- **Supporting evidence**: See studies above. In general, the studies above support a genetic and neural basis of gender dysphoria, but the exact role of hormones is less clear.

AO3: **Weaknesses** of biological explanations of gender dysphoria

- **Conflicting evidence:** The fact that concordance rates for gender dysphoria among identical twins are much less than 100% suggests that other factors besides genetics (e.g. social explanations) play a role too. Further, Hulshoff Pol et al (2006) conducted brain scans on transgender people before and after cross-sex hormone therapy. The researchers found that hormone therapy *changed* the size of the BSTc, which suggest differences in brain structures may be an *effect* of hormone therapy rather than a *cause* of gender dysphoria.
- **Other factors:** Reducing gender dysphoria to biology could be overly reductive and may ignore the importance of other factors such as cognitions and social explanations.

Social explanations of gender dysphoria say gender identity is *learned*

Social learning theory would say that gender dysphoria is caused by children **observing** and **imitating** role models of the **opposite sex**. For example, a young boy might observe his mother receiving compliments on her dress (vicarious reinforcement) and imitate this behaviour.

This cross-gender behaviour may also be reinforced via **operant conditioning**. For example, adults may encourage or praise the boy for wearing a dress. This creates a conflict between the boy's biological sex and psychological gender, leading to gender dysphoria.

AO3: **Strengths** of social explanations of gender dysphoria

- **Supporting evidence**: Earlier research focused on social explanations of gender dysphoria (e.g. Rekers and Lovaas (1974)), but the general consensus is that social explanations of gender dysphoria are less important than biological ones. However, social factors still likely play a role, as biological explanations of gender dysphoria are incomplete. For example, concordance rates for gender dysphoria among identical twins are much less than 100%, which opens the door for factors other than biology to explain gender dysphoria.

AO3: **Weaknesses** of social explanations of gender dysphoria

- **Conflicting evidence:** Transgender people often face many social difficulties (e.g. prejudice and bullying) and if social explanations of gender dysphoria are correct this should discourage cross-gender behaviour. However, the fact that many transgender people insist on living as their preferred gender despite these negative consequences suggests there is a deeper, biological, reason for gender dysphoria.
- **Other factors:** As always, you don't have to come down on one side – biological or social – perfectly. An interactionist approach (see page 74) would acknowledge both factors.

COGNITION AND DEVELOPMENT – PIAGET'S THEORY

Schema are a key part of Piaget's theory of cognitive development

Piaget's theory explains children's cognitive development in terms of continually challenging and updating their **schema** (see page 36) through interacting with the **environment**.

According to Piaget, development of schema involves **equilibration** and **adaptation**.

Equilibrium is when an experience fits within the child's *existing* schema

Equilibrium is a **pleasant** and **desirable** state because it means the child **understands** the world around them. When a new experience fits with existing schema, it's **assimilated** into that schema.

Example: A child might develop the gender schema (see page 89) that women have long hair. If the child meets a new woman and she has long hair, the child can include/**assimilate** this new person within their existing schema of 'woman'.

Disequilibrium is when an experience **does not fit** within the child's existing schema. This is an **unpleasant** state because it means the child does not understand what is going on, causing confusion. This creates a motivation to *learn* and return to the pleasant state of equilibrium. When a new experience doesn't fit within existing schema, the child must create new schema or update their existing schema in order to **accommodate** the new experience.

Example: If a child has developed the gender schema that women have long hair but then meets a woman with short hair, this causes disequilibrium. The child can **accommodate** this experience and return to equilibrium by *updating* their schema of 'woman' to include people with short hair.

Piaget argues that intellectual development happens in **4 stages**

Piaget observed that children of similar ages would give similar *wrong answers* to certain questions, and that they would learn to give the *right* answers at similar ages too. These changes were observed cross-culturally, suggesting biologically-determined **stages of development:**

Stage	Age	Key concepts
Sensorimotor	0 – 2 years	As well as basic language, the child learns **object permanence** – that physical things still exist even when they are no longer in sight – at around 8 months old.
Pre-operational	2 – 7 years	Thinking is **egocentric**: The child can only see things from their own perspective.
Concrete operational	7 – 11 years	The child learns **conservation**: That an object can maintain its mass/volume/quantity even if its appearance changes. The child also learns **class inclusion:** E.g. that 'dogs' are in the *class* 'animals'.
Formal operational	>11 years	The child learns to reason **abstractly** (rather than focusing on concrete examples).

Cognition and Development – Chapter 11

COGNITION AND DEVELOPMENT – PIAGET'S THEORY

Thinking at the pre-operational stage is **egocentric**

In other words, the child can only see things from **their own perspective** and can't understand the perspective of other people. For example, Piaget and Inhelder's (1956) **3 mountains task** let children examine a model of a Swiss mountain on a table. A doll was placed on top of one of the model mountains and the children were asked to select pictures of **what *the doll* could see**. However, the 4 year olds would consistently select the pictures of **what *they* saw** (not the doll), which suggests the children were unable to visualise things from another person's perspective.

Children in the pre-operational stage don't understand **conservation**

Conservation is the the understanding that changing the appearance of an object does not change its mass or quantity or volume. For example, Piaget (1952) showed 7 year olds **two equal beakers of water**: A and B. The children could see that A and B contained the same amount of water. But when the water from B was poured into a taller, thinner, beaker (C), the children thought beaker C contained *more* water.

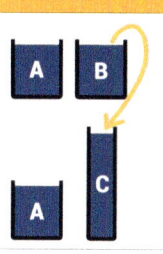

Class inclusion is the understanding of sets and subsets

For example, that *dogs* are part of the class of *animals*. Children learn class inclusion at the concrete operational stage. To illustrate this, Piaget and Inhelder (1956) showed children in the pre-operational stage a picture with **5 dogs and 2 cats** and then asked: *"Are there more dogs or more animals?"*. The children would answer that there are more dogs, because they were unable to comprehend that each dog was a member of the dog class *and* the animal class.

AO3: **Strengths** of Piaget's theory of cognitive development

- **Supporting evidence:** Piaget and Inhelder's studies above support the 4 stages of development. For example, that children learn conservation and class inclusion at set ages.

AO3: **Weaknesses** of Piaget's theory of cognitive development

- **Conflicting evidence:** For example, Siegler and Svetina (2006) found that 5 year-old children were able to learn class inclusion when it was explained to them, contradicting Piaget's claim that children don't learn class inclusion until at least 7 years old. Further, Hughes (1975) demonstrated that children aged 3 – 5 years old were able to see things from the perspective of a policeman doll, contradicting Piaget's claim that thinking in the pre-operational stage is egocentric. Finally, Baillargeon's violation of expectation research (see page 98) suggests infants understand object permanence before 8 months of age.
- **Methodological concerns:** Much of Piaget's theory was based on unstructured observations and interviews with children so it may be biased towards Piaget's subjective interpretations.

Cognition and Development

COGNITION AND DEVELOPMENT – VYGOTSKY'S THEORY

Vygotsky's theory emphasises social and cultural factors

Where Piaget emphasised interactions with *physical objects*, Vygotsky's theory of cognitive development emphasises *social interactions* (e.g. with **parents**, **teachers**, and other **children**). For Vygotsky, learning is first **intermental** (between 2 people) and then made **intramental** (internalised within the individual).

Language is crucial to cognitive development

According to Vygotsky, language develops according to the following timeline:

External	**Social speech** (0 – 3 years)	Infants learn language to communicate with caregivers (e.g. to say they're hungry).
	Self-speech (3 – 7 years)	The infant talks out loud to direct themself (i.e. thinking out loud).
Internal	**Inner speech** (>7 years)	The self-speech becomes internalised (i.e. thought) so that the infant can direct themself silently.

Vygotsky described 4 stages of development that are a bit like Piaget's

Vygotsky did experiments where he gave children of different ages objects with symbols on and then observed how they tried to work out what the symbols meant. Based on these experiments, Vygotsky argued that children develop **concept formation** according to the following sequence:

- **Vague syncretic:** Trial and error with no thought/reasoning of the underlying principles.
- **Complex:** Some use of reasoning/strategy but limited success.
- **Potential concept:** Successful use of a *single* strategy/reasoning process.
- **Mature concept:** Successful use of a *several* strategies/reasoning processes.

Zone of proximal development is the gap between *current* and *potential* ability

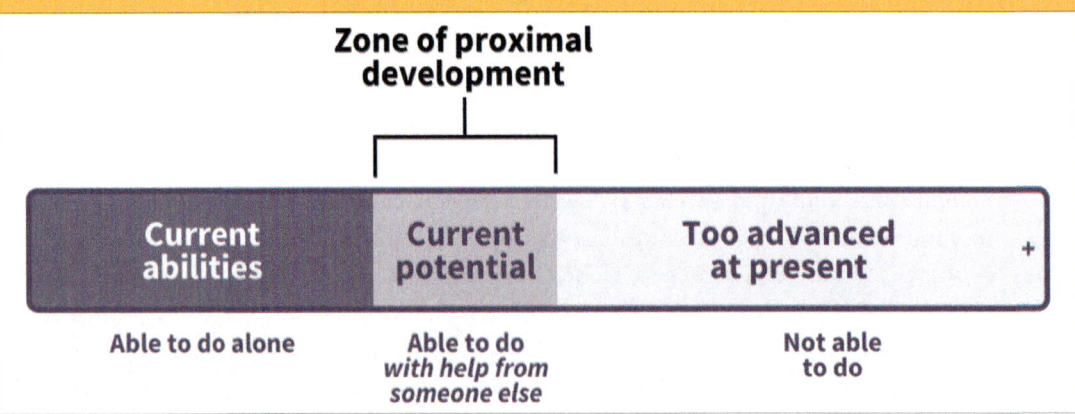

```
              Zone of proximal
                development
                   ┌──┴──┐
┌──────────────┬──────────┬────────────────────┐
│   Current    │ Current  │    Too advanced    │ +
│   abilities  │ potential│     at present     │
└──────────────┴──────────┴────────────────────┘
  Able to do alone   Able to do      Not able
                    with help from    to do
                    someone else
```

Cognition and Development

COGNITION AND DEVELOPMENT – PIAGET'S THEORY

> **Scaffolding** is when a teacher helps a learner by providing a *framework* to learn

According to Vygotsky, learning happens *within* the **zone of proximal development**. For example, a 3 year-old child may currently be able to write a few individual words but be unable to write a sentence. However, the 3 year-old child has the *potential* to be able to write a sentence *with help from a teacher* (e.g. a parent or older sibling) and so writing a sentence is within the child's zone of proximal development. The teacher's job is to guide the child through the zone of proximal development so that they can complete this task alone.

One way a teacher can help a child progress through the zone of proximal development is via **scaffolding**. Scaffolding is when a teacher (e.g. a parent or older sibling) helps an infant to learn by providing a framework – a scaffold – to help them solve a problem or complete a task. As the infant progresses, the scaffolding is gradually removed until the infant is capable of completing the task by itself.

For example, a parent may physically guide a young child's hand to show them how to write their name. Then, as the child attempts to write their name without the physical guidance, the parent may watch and provide verbal instructions to help. Eventually, this scaffolding is removed as well and the infant is able to write their name by itself.

AO3: **Strengths** of Vygotsky's theory of cognitive development

- **Supporting evidence:** Several studies support aspects of Vygotsky's theory. For example, Wood et al (1976) observed children aged 3 – 5 years old as they built a model pyramid from blocks with the help of a teacher. This task was too difficult for the children to complete *by themselves*, but simple enough that they could do it *with help* (i.e. it was in the subjects' zone of proximal development). The researchers found that scaffolding by the teacher (e.g. guiding children without telling them exactly what to do) enabled the children to complete the task.
- **Practical applications:** For example, teachers (e.g. adults or older/more able children) can employ scaffolding strategies – and there is evidence that this helps less-able infants learn. For example, in Van Keer and Verhaeghe (2005), 2nd grade children who were tutored by 5th grade children *in addition to normal teaching* saw greater reading improvement scores than a control group of 2nd grade children with normal teaching only.

AO3: **Weaknesses** of Vygotsky's theory of cognitive development

- **Other factors:** In focusing on cultural and social factors only, Vygotsky's theory may be too reductionist and ignore individual differences. Even within the same culture or social environment, different children will learn at different speeds. This suggests that other factors are needed to explain intellectual development. For example, genetic or biological differences in intelligence may influence cognitive development in addition to social factors, but Vygotsky's theory does not mention these.

BAILLARGEON'S EXPLANATION OF EARLY INFANT ABILITIES

Baillargeon argues that babies are born with **innate physical reasoning** abilities

Just as horses have an innate ability to walk immediately after being born, for example, Baillargeon argues that babies are born with an ability to *understand the physical world.* This **physical reasoning system** is **innate** (i.e. present from birth).

Violation of expectation studies support Baillargeon's claim

One example of this is Baillargeon and Graber (1987). In this study, infants aged **5 – 6 months** were shown a rabbit travelling along a track and disappearing behind a wall with a hole in it:

- Scenario 1 (**possible event**): The rabbit is shorter than the lower edge of the window and so can't be seen in the hole in the wall.
- Scenario 2 (**impossible event**): The rabbit is taller than the lower edge of the window **but doesn't appear in the hole in the wall**.

Baillargeon and Graber observed that, on average, *infants looked at the impossible event for much longer than they looked at the possible event* (**33.07 seconds** vs. **25.11 seconds**).

This suggests that the infants (all less than 6 months old) *expected* the tall rabbit to appear in the gap in the wall and were *surprised* when it didn't – **it violated their expectations**.

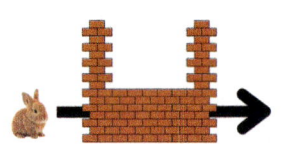

Possible

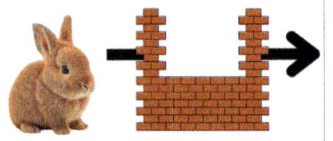

Impossible

This further suggests they had an understanding of **object permanence**, which contradicts Piaget's claim that infants don't understand object permanence before 8 months (see page 94).

Strengths:	• **Reliable:** Several violation of expectation studies have replicated Baillargeon and Graber's (1987) findings. For example, in Baillargeon and DeVos (1991), 3.5 month-old babies were shown a short carrot and a tall carrot travelling behind a wall with a hole in the top. Again, the babies paid more attention to the tall carrot scenario (the explanation being that they *expected* the top of the carrot to appear over the top of the wall and were *surprised* when it didn't).
Weaknesses:	• **Conflicting evidence:** Several researchers have replicated Baillargeon's experiments but found different results. For example, Rivera et al (1999) replicated Baillargeon's drawbridge experiment (another violation of expectation scenario) but found no difference between the amount of time infants looked at the impossible event vs. the possible event. • **Alternative explanations:** Bogartz et al (2000) and Cashon and Cohen (2000) conducted variations of Baillargeon's drawbridge experiment but concluded that it was *novelty* (i.e. new or more interesting events), not *impossibility*, that determined which event the infants paid more attention to. This suggests that Baillargeon's conclusion that infants have innate physical reasoning abilities may not be valid because the results may be explained another way.

Cognition and Development

DEVELOPMENT OF SOCIAL COGNITION – PERSPECTIVE TAKING

Perspective-taking is the ability to put yourself in another person's shoes

Selman (1980) described various scenarios to children of different ages and studied their responses. One such scenario was as follows:
- Holly injures herself falling out of a tree and promises her Dad she won't climb trees anymore.
- But one day, a friend's kitten is stuck up a tree and Holly is the only one who is able to climb the tree and save the kitten.
- Selman asked the children: *Should Holly climb the tree to save the kitten?*

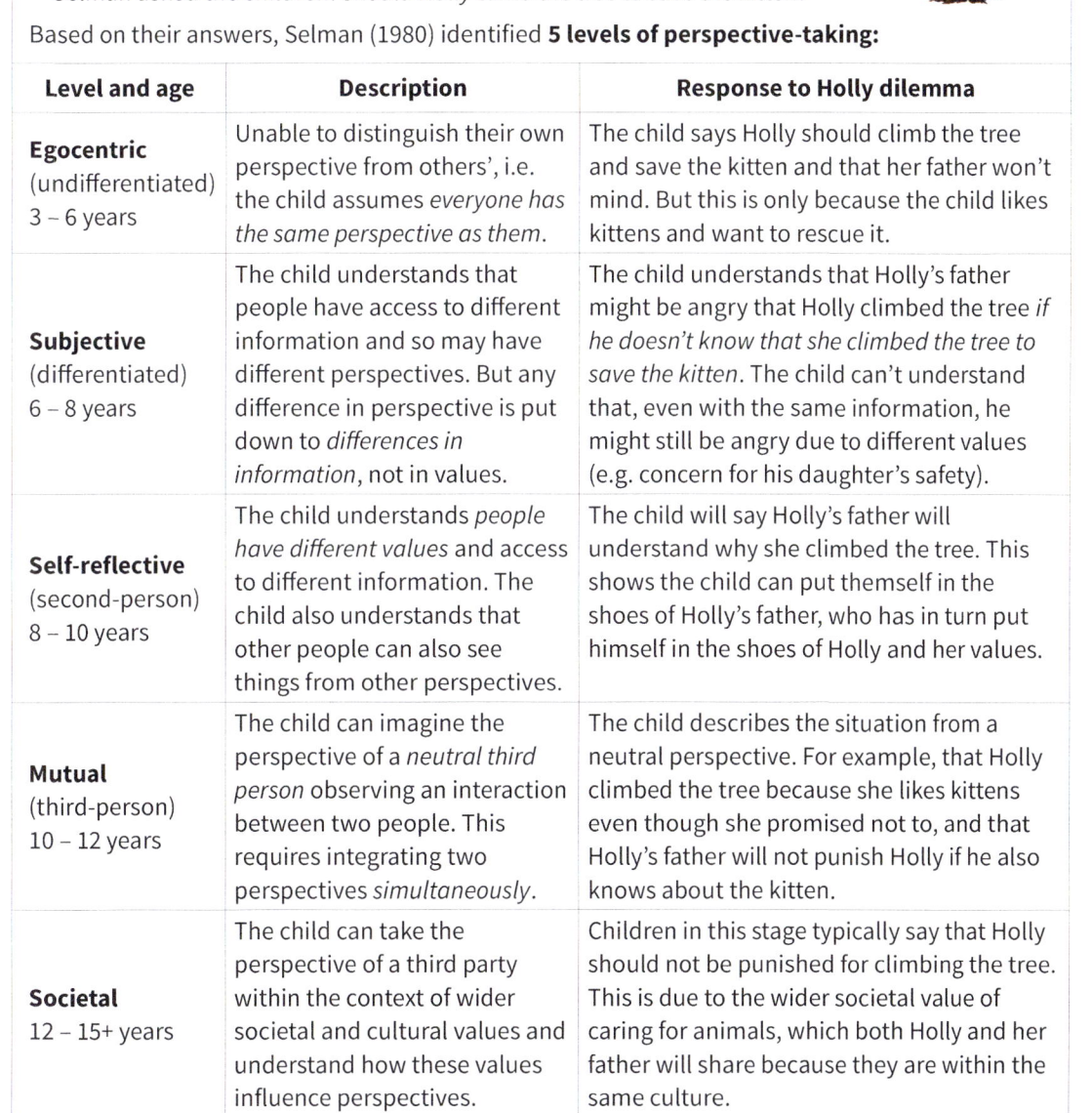

Based on their answers, Selman (1980) identified **5 levels of perspective-taking:**

Level and age	Description	Response to Holly dilemma
Egocentric (undifferentiated) 3 – 6 years	Unable to distinguish their own perspective from others', i.e. the child assumes *everyone has the same perspective as them*.	The child says Holly should climb the tree and save the kitten and that her father won't mind. But this is only because the child likes kittens and want to rescue it.
Subjective (differentiated) 6 – 8 years	The child understands that people have access to different information and so may have different perspectives. But any difference in perspective is put down to *differences in information*, not in values.	The child understands that Holly's father might be angry that Holly climbed the tree *if he doesn't know that she climbed the tree to save the kitten*. The child can't understand that, even with the same information, he might still be angry due to different values (e.g. concern for his daughter's safety).
Self-reflective (second-person) 8 – 10 years	The child understands *people have different values* and access to different information. The child also understands that other people can also see things from other perspectives.	The child will say Holly's father will understand why she climbed the tree. This shows the child can put themselves in the shoes of Holly's father, who has in turn put himself in the shoes of Holly and her values.
Mutual (third-person) 10 – 12 years	The child can imagine the perspective of a *neutral third person* observing an interaction between two people. This requires integrating two perspectives *simultaneously*.	The child describes the situation from a neutral perspective. For example, that Holly climbed the tree because she likes kittens even though she promised not to, and that Holly's father will not punish Holly if he also knows about the kitten.
Societal 12 – 15+ years	The child can take the perspective of a third party within the context of wider societal and cultural values and understand how these values influence perspectives.	Children in this stage typically say that Holly should not be punished for climbing the tree. This is due to the wider societal value of caring for animals, which both Holly and her father will share because they are within the same culture.

COGNITION AND DEVELOPMENT – SOCIAL COGNITION

AO3: **Strengths** of Selman's levels of perspective-taking

- **Supporting evidence:** Gurucharri and Selman (1982) followed 48 infant boys over several years. At different ages, their perspective-taking ability was measured using dilemmas such as the Holly example. They found the infants were able to take more perspectives the older they got, in line with the sequence of Selman's levels of perspective-taking described above.
- **Practical applications:** Boca et al (2018) found that encouraging perspective-taking in conflict resolution reduced hostility between the conflicting groups.

AO3: **Weaknesses** of Selman's levels of perspective-taking

- **Other factors:** Selman's perspective-taking focuses only on *cognitive* abilities. But this is too reductionist to be a complete account of social cognition. For example, social experiences (e.g. interactions with other people) and biological factors (e.g. genetics) are likely to play a part in both the development of perspective-taking and of social cognition more broadly.

Mirror neurons may be the *biological* basis of social cognition

Mirror neurons activate both when you perform an action and *when you observe someone else* perform that action. Rizzolatti et al (1996) first observed, in monkeys, the same areas of the brain activated when the monkeys reached for food as when they *watched someone else* reach for food.

Since then, studies have demonstrated the existence of mirror neurons in humans. It's proposed that mirror neurons enable us to **empathise** with others, enabling social cognition.

Given that mirror neurons are associated with social cognition, and **autism** (see page 101) is associated with *difficulties* in social cognition, Ramachandran and Oberman (2006) propose the '**broken mirror**' theory of autism – that it's caused in part by deficiencies of mirror neurons.

Strengths:	• **Supporting evidence:** Haker et al (2013) conducted fMRI brain scans while participants watched videos of people yawning. They observed that areas of the mirror neuron system (the Brodmann's area) activated while the participants watched the video. Based on this, they speculate that empathy via the mirror neuron system is why yawning is contagious.
Weaknesses:	• **Conflicting evidence:** Several studies cast doubt on the broken mirror theory of autism. For example, fMRI scans of people with autism by Dinstein et al (2010) found they had normal mirror neuron activity when observing people perform motor actions (e.g. moving their hands). • **Methodological concerns:** Hickok (2009) argues that observations in monkeys are overly generalised to human beings. For example, monkey studies such as Rizzolatti et al (1996) observe mirror neuron activity in monkeys watching people perform *motor actions* (e.g. reaching for food). But the mirror neuron explanation is then extended to higher cognitive processes in humans – such as *language* and *theory of mind* (see page 101) – which monkeys don't have.

Cognition and Development

DEVELOPMENT OF SOCIAL COGNITION – THEORY OF MIND

Theory of mind is the ability to imagine and model *other people's mental states*

For example, if you hear that your friend lost their job, you can *imagine* that your friend might be feeling upset or sad or angry. Even though you can't literally see into their mind, your **theory of mind** enables you to **imagine** and **understand** their mental state. This theory of mind also enables you to explain and predict their behaviour.

The **Sally-Anne test** is a way to test a person's theory of mind

Sally puts the marble in her basket

Sally leaves and Anne moves the marble to her box

When Sally comes back, where will she look to find the marble?

<<< The correct answer is that Sally will look in *her* basket for the marble. This is because Sally won't have seen Anne move the marble into her box and so will have the **false belief** that the marble is still in her basket. It requires theory of mind to put yourself in Anne's position and understand she has this false belief. Baron-Cohen et al (1985) devised the Sally-Anne test and asked 3 groups of participants *"where will Sally look to find the marble?"*:

- 85% of children with normal development answered correctly.
- 86% of children with Down's Syndrome answered correctly.
- But only **20%** of the children with **autism** answered correctly.

Autism is a developmental disorder characterised by difficulties with social cognition, such as difficulties interacting and communicating with people. The findings of this study suggest these difficulties are caused – at least in part – by problems with theory of mind. People with autism may be unable to understand the minds of others, such as what Sally will be thinking in the Sally-Anne test. This is sometimes referred to as **mind-blindness.**

Strengths:	• **Supporting evidence:** Baron Cohen et al's (1985) findings have been replicated several times, which suggests the Sally-Anne test is a *reliable* measure of autism. Further, brain scans by Happé et al (1996) compared brain activity in autistic children to non-autistic controls during a theory of mind test. The researchers observed that the controls had significant activity in the left medial prefrontal cortex of the brain but the children with autism had no activity in this area.
Weaknesses:	• **Conflicting evidence:** Tager-Flusberg (2007) points out that there are many examples of autistic children who *pass* theory of mind tests, such as the Sally-Anne test. This suggests theory of mind is not a complete explanation of autism. • **Overlap with other explanations:** There is a lot of overlap between theory of mind and perspective-taking (see page 99), so much so that they might actually be the same concept. For example, Rehfeldt et al (2007) found that perspective-taking tasks *also* provide an accurate measure of autism.

Cognition and Development

SCHIZOPHRENIA – CLASSIFICATION AND DIAGNOSIS

Schizophrenia has **positive** and **negative** symptoms

Schizophrenia is a psychological condition characterised by a **loss of contact with reality**. It affects around 0.7% of the population. There is no single symptom, but several:

Positive symptoms of schizophrenia	*Negative* symptoms of schizophrenia
These are experiences *in addition to* ordinary experience, such as: • **Hallucinations:** *Perceptions* that aren't based in reality, or distorted perceptions of reality. For example, hearing voices that aren't there. • **Delusions:** *Beliefs* that aren't based in reality. For example, believing that you're the victim of a grand conspiracy.	These are *a lack of* abilities associated with normal experience, such as: • **Speech poverty:** A reduction in the quality and amount of speech. For example, giving one word answers to questions. • **Avolition:** A lack of desire and motivation for anything. For example, not engaging in work, social activity, or maintaining hygiene.

There are 2 main systems for diagnosing schizophrenia: The American Psychiatric Association's *Diagnostic and Statistical Manual of Mental Disorders* (**DSM-5**) and the World Health Organisation's *International Statistical Classification of Diseases and Related Health Problems* (**ICD-10**). DSM-5 requires **at least one positive symptom**, but ICD-10 can diagnose on **negative symptoms alone**.

How **reliable** is schizophrenia diagnosis?

Remember reliability (page 61)? If multiple different doctors diagnose the same person as schizophrenic based on the same symptoms, then their diagnosis is **reliable**.

Study	Diagnostic system	Finding
Beck et al (1962)	Psychiatrist's own assessment	54% concordance rate
Söderberg et al (2005)	DSM	81% concordance rate
Jakobsen et al (2005)	ICD	98% concordance rate

Strengths:
- **Improvements in inter-observer reliability:** Although research is conflicting, more recent studies of schizophrenia diagnosis generally find higher concordance rates among psychiatrists compared to older studies. This suggests that diagnosis of schizophrenia has become more reliable over time.

Weaknesses:
- **Low reliability between diagnostic methods:** Cheniaux et al (2009) found the *same observer* would often diagnose schizophrenia differently depending on which manual they used (DSM vs. ICD). In general, the DSM classification is considered more reliable as the descriptions of symptoms are more specific.
- **Co-morbidity:** People with schizophrenia often suffer from psychological disorders in addition to schizophrenia, which confuses diagnosis. For example, people with schizophrenia often suffer from depression as well.

Schizophrenia – Chapter 12

SCHIZOPHRENIA – CLASSIFICATION AND DIAGNOSIS

Is schizophrenia diagnosis **valid**?

Validity (see page 61) refers to how **accurately** schizophrenia is diagnosed. For example, if doctors often diagnose patients with *autism* as having schizophrenia, then their diagnosis is **not valid**.

Key study: **Rosenhan (1973)** Healthy Volunteers Pretend to be Schizophrenic

Method	8 healthy volunteers (i.e. subjects who did not have schizophrenia) presented themselves to various psychiatric hospitals claiming to hear voices.
Results	All 8 volunteers were successfully admitted to the hospitals and diagnosed with schizophrenia. Doctors took between 7-52 days to release each 'patient'.
	In a later experiment, doctors were falsely told that healthy patients would attempt to admit themselves, which led the doctors to turn *genuine* schizophrenic patients away because they thought they were actors.
	Conclusion: *The doctors did not have valid methods for diagnosing schizophrenia.*

AO3: **Strengths** of the validity of schizophrenia diagnosis

- **Improvements in validity:** Although Rosenhan (1973) casts doubt on the validity of schizophrenia diagnosis, more recent studies suggest schizophrenia diagnosis has become more accurate. For example, Mason et al (1997) found that improvements to diagnostic manuals (DSM and ICD) over time led to more accurate diagnosis of schizophrenia.

AO3: **Weaknesses** of the validity of schizophrenia diagnosis

- **Symptom overlap:** Schizophrenia shares symptoms with disorders such as depression and autism. For example, people with schizophrenia and people with autism often suffer with speech poverty. This overlap of symptoms may reduce the validity of schizophrenia diagnosis because an evaluator may incorrectly attribute these symptoms to a different disorder.
- **Gender differences:** A meta-analysis from Aleman et al (2003) found men were 42% more likely to suffer from schizophrenia than women. However, Cotton et al (2009) suggest that the better interpersonal functioning of women may cause doctors to miss schizophrenia diagnosis in women, suggesting possible gender bias in schizophrenia diagnosis.
- **Cultural differences:** Several studies (e.g. Cochrane (1977)) have found ethnic minorities living in Britain (particularly those of Afro-Caribbean descent) are diagnosed with schizophrenia at higher rates than white people. However, rates of schizophrenia diagnosis among Afro-Caribbean people *living in the Caribbean* are roughly the same as white people in Britain. This suggests either that environmental stressors in Britain (e.g. racism, increased risk of flu) are causing increased rates of schizophrenia among people of Afro-Caribbean descent, or that Afro-Caribbean people are being *invalidly* diagnosed with schizophrenia.

SCHIZOPHRENIA – BIOLOGICAL EXPLANATIONS

Genetics are one biological explanation of schizophrenia

As always, **twin studies** (see page 38) are a useful way to determine whether or not a condition is hereditary – i.e. inherited through genetics. Gottesman (1991) found that the closer a person's genetic relationship is to someone with schizophrenia, the greater their own risk of developing it:

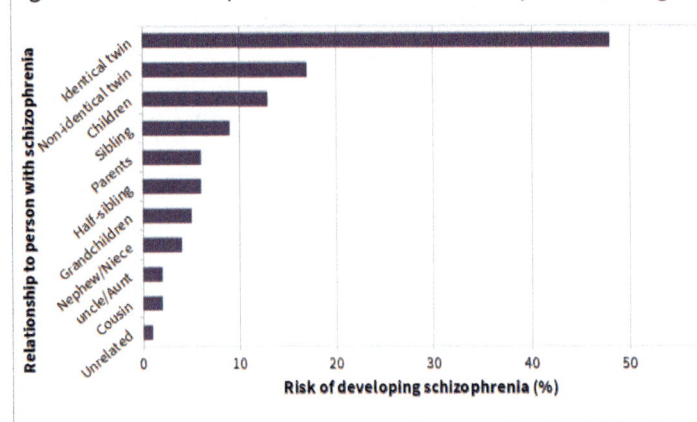

The **concordance rate** for schizophrenia among *identical* twins was 48%, whereas for non-identical twins it was 17%. And this is supported by Cardno et al (1999), who found similar concordance rates for schizophrenia. Such studies support the idea that genetics play a role in schizophrenia.

AO3: It's not like there's a *single* gene responsible for schizophrenia. Instead, multiple genes likely combine to increase a person's risk of developing schizophrenia. For example, in a study of more than 36,000 schizophrenic patients, Ripke et al (2014) found **108 different genetic variations** that were correlated with schizophrenia, supporting the genetic explanation. Further, many of these genetic variations were related to *dopamine transmission,* so genetic explanations can be combined with the dopamine hypothesis (page 105) for a holistic explanation of schizophrenia.

There are also various **neural correlates** of schizophrenia

- **Enlarged ventricles:** For example, Johnstone et al (1976) and Suddath et al (1990) found people with schizophrenia had enlarged ventricles compared to controls. This is particularly linked with the *negative symptoms* of schizophrenia, as shown in studies such as Andreasen et al (1982).
- **Reduced grey matter and cortical thinning:** MRI scans by Boos et al (2012) found schizophrenic patients had reduced grey matter and cortical thinning compared to their non-schizophrenic family members and the non-schizophrenic controls.
- Facial emotion processing: A common symptom of schizophrenia is difficulty perceiving emotions. A meta-analysis by Li et al (2010) compared fMRI scans of schizophrenic patients with non-schizophrenic controls during facial expression processing and found **reduced activity** in the **bilateral amygdala** and **right fusiform gyri** among the schizophrenic patients.

AO3: As always, correlations do not prove causation. For example, reduced activity in the bilateral amygdala of schizophrenic patients may *cause* difficulties in emotional processing, but it could also be that reduced blood flow and activity in the bilateral amygdala is an *effect* of reduced emotional processing (which may be caused by some other factor).

Schizophrenia

SCHIZOPHRENIA – BIOLOGICAL EXPLANATIONS

The **dopamine hypothesis** of schizophrenia...

...explains schizophrenia (at least partly) as a result of abnormal activity of the **neurotransmitter** dopamine.

The dopamine hypothesis became popular in the 1970s when studies (e.g. Seeman et al (1976), Creese et al (1976), and Snyder (1976)) reported that several drugs that reduce schizophrenia symptoms are **dopamine receptor antagonists**: They *reduce* dopamine activity. The implication is that schizophrenia is *caused* by increased dopamine activity and that these drugs work by *reducing* dopamine activity. Further evidence supporting the dopamine hypothesis includes:

- **Dopamine *agonists*:** These are the opposite of *ant*agonists – they *increase* dopamine activity. And several such drugs, like amphetamines, make schizophrenia symptoms worse.
- **Brain scans:** Some studies using brain-scanning techniques have found increased dopamine activity in schizophrenic patients. For example, Lindström et al (1999) compared PET scans of 12 schizophrenic patients with 10 controls and found the schizophrenic patients had increased dopamine activity in the striatum and parts of medial prefrontal cortex.

Strengths:	- **Supporting evidence:** See studies above. - **Revised dopamine hypothesis:** Over the years, the dopamine hypothesis has been refined. It's not as simple as *high dopamine = schizophrenia*. Instead, research suggests that schizophrenia is linked with high dopamine activity in *some* areas of the brain (e.g. the subcortex) but low dopamine activity in other areas (e.g. the prefrontal cortex).
Weaknesses:	- **Conflicting evidence:** The dopamine hypothesis is controversial. Farde et al (1990) compared brain scans of 18 schizophrenia patients with 20 non-schizophrenic controls. They found no difference in dopamine activity between the two groups. Similarly, a review of post-mortem studies by Haracz (1982) found little evidence to support the dopamine hypothesis. - **Other neurotransmitters:** Evidence suggests that other neurotransmitters besides dopamine are involved in the development of schizophrenia, such as *glutamate*. For example, a meta-analysis of brain scans by Marsman et al (2013) found decreased glutamate activity in schizophrenic patients compared to controls. And, like with the dopamine hypothesis, there is some evidence that drugs that alter glutamate activity can successfully treat schizophrenia. But the glutamate hypothesis does not necessarily contradict the dopamine hypothesis – both neurotransmitters may be involved in schizophrenia. - **Allegations of bias:** Psychiatrist David Healy (2004) argues that pharmaceutical companies *exaggerated* the dopamine hypothesis of schizophrenia to sell more drugs. The overly-simplified hypothesis that schizophrenia is caused by high dopamine makes it easy to market antipsychotic drugs as 'cures' for schizophrenia.

SCHIZOPHRENIA – BIOLOGICAL TREATMENT

Drugs for schizophrenia are either **typical** or **atypical antipsychotics**

	Typical antipsychotics	**Atypical antipsychotics**
Other names	First-generation	Second-generation
Used since	1950s	1970s
Aim	Reduce symptoms of schizophrenia	Reduce symptoms more effectively with less side effects
Neurotransmitters	Dopamine only	Dopamine and others
Examples	Chlorpromazine and haloperidol	Clozapine and risperidone

Typical antipsychotic drugs for schizophrenia work by blocking dopamine receptors – they are dopamine **antagonists** – and are thus strongly associated with the dopamine hypothesis of schizophrenia (page 105). Typical antipsychotic drugs, such as chlorpromazine and haloperidol, can cause several **side effects**. Among the most serious of these side effects are **extrapyramidal symptoms**, which are problems with movement similar to Parkinson's disease.

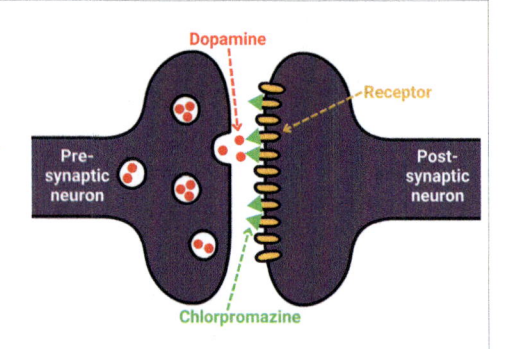

The aim of **atypical antipsychotic drugs** is to improve upon the efficacy of typical antipsychotics while reducing side effects. Atypical antipsychotics target **several neurotransmitters**, not just dopamine. For example, clozapine is an atypical antipsychotic that acts on the neurotransmitters dopamine, serotonin, and glutamate. Risperidone, another atypical antipsychotic, targets dopamine and serotonin. Some evidence suggests atypical antipsychotics are superior to typical antipsychotics. However, atypical antipsychotics also carry a risk of **side effects** including weight gain, increased risk of heart attack, increased risk of diabetes, and extrapyramidal symptoms.

Strengths:	• **Supporting evidence:** Several studies (e.g. Bagnall et al (2003)) have found both typical and atypical antipsychotics to be more effective than placebo for reducing schizophrenia symptoms.
Weaknesses:	• **Side effects:** All antipsychotics carry a risk of side effects to varying degrees. These side effects can range from mild (e.g. weight gain, dizziness) to potentially fatal (e.g. heart attack, stroke, neuroleptic malignant syndrome). Lieberman et al (2005) found that 74% of 1,342 schizophrenic patients discontinued antipsychotic drug treatment within 18 months due to side effects. • **Meaningless distinction:** A meta-analysis by Leucht et al (2013) found both efficacy and side effects of antipsychotic drugs varied greatly, and that this was equally true of typical and atypical varieties. As such, the authors question whether this distinction between typical and atypical is a medically useful one.

SCHIZOPHRENIA – PSYCHOLOGICAL EXPLANATIONS

Some psychologists have said **family dysfunction** can cause schizophrenia

For example, Bateson et al (1956) proposed the **double bind explanation of schizophrenia**. According to this explanation, children who get **conflicting messages** from their parents are more likely to develop schizophrenia. For example, a mother who loves her child but has trouble expressing it may exhibit **contradictory** behaviours (e.g. hugging the child but being critical with her words). Constant exposure to these mixed messages means the child is unable to form a coherent picture of reality. This leads to disorganised thinking which in extreme cases can manifest as symptoms of schizophrenia such as delusions and hallucinations.

Another familial explanation is that an environment with a high degree of **expressed emotion** – particularly *negative*, e.g. **criticism** and **hostility** – causes stress, increasing risk of schizophrenia.

Strengths:	• **Supporting evidence:** For example, Tienari et al (2004) found that adoptees raised in families rated as dysfunctional had much higher rates of schizophrenia (36.8%) compared to adoptees raised in families rated as healthy (5.8%).
Weaknesses:	• **Other factors:** Not everyone with schizophrenia was raised in a dysfunctional family and not everyone raised in a dysfunctional family goes on to develop schizophrenia. This suggests that other factors (e.g. genetics) are needed. • **Selection bias:** Bateson et al's double bind explanation is based on a handful of case studies and interviews. But some critics argue the researchers focused on examples that *support* the explanation while ignoring ones that contradict it.

Cognitive explanations look at differences in how schizophrenic people *think*

- **Dysfunctional thought processing**: *Metacognition* is the ability to think about and reflect on one's own thoughts, emotions, and behaviours. Metacognitive *dysfunction* may explain some symptoms of schizophrenia, such as hallucinations. For example, an inability of schizophrenic patients to recognise their thoughts *as their own* may explain hearing voices: They attribute their own thoughts to some external source outside their mind.
- **Cognitive biases:** Positive symptoms of schizophrenia, such as delusions, can be explained as a result of cognitive biases. For example, bias may mean a schizophrenic person interprets the ordinary actions of other people as sinister, supporting their delusion that they are a victim of a conspiracy or that people are trying to harm them.

Strengths:	• **Practical applications:** Cognitive explanations have been used to develop effective therapies for treating schizophrenia, such as CBT (see page 109).
Weaknesses:	• **Other factors:** Many people have the cognitive biases and distortions associated with schizophrenia and yet don't develop schizophrenia. This suggests that cognitive explanations *alone* are too reductionist. • **Describes, but doesn't explain:** Cognitive theories simply *describe* the thought processes of schizophrenia but don't explain *why* they occur in the first place.

SCHIZOPHRENIA – PSYCHOLOGICAL TREATMENTS

CBT is the main psychological treatment for schizophrenia

Example: A schizophrenic patient may have **delusional thoughts** that there is a conspiracy to kill them. These thoughts cause negative *emotions* (e.g. fear, anxiety) and irrational *behaviours* (e.g. hiding from or attacking people). **Cognitive behavioural therapy** involves talking through these irrational thoughts. The patient is encouraged to **describe** their thoughts and the therapist then helps the patient to **challenge** the reality of these thoughts. For example, the therapist may ask the patient to consider *how likely* these thoughts are to be true and to consider alternative explanations. The therapist may also help the patient tackle their symptoms from the *behavioural* angle (e.g. by teaching coping skills) and the *emotional* angle (e.g. teaching relaxation methods). CBT is commonly used in combination with antipsychotic drug therapy (see page 106).

Strengths:	• **Supporting evidence:** For example, a meta-analysis of 14 studies involving 1,484 schizophrenia patients by Zimmermann et al (2005) found CBT significantly reduced positive symptoms of the disorder. • **Low risk of side effects:** By comparison, antipsychotic drugs carry a risk of serious and potentially fatal side effects such as pyramidal symptoms.
Weaknesses:	• **Conflicting evidence:** However, a meta-analysis by Jauhar et al (2014) found CBT only had minor effects on schizophrenia symptoms. • **Not suitable for all:** Some patients may be too paranoid or anxious to develop a trusting alliance with a therapist and so are not suitable candidates for CBT.

Family therapy is based on the family dysfunction explanation

This involves getting the patient's family together with an aim to:
- **Improve communication patterns:** Increase positive communication and decrease negative communication among the family (i.e. reduce levels of *expressed emotion* – see page 107)
- **Increase tolerance and understanding:** Educate family members about schizophrenia and how to deal with it (e.g. how to support each other).
- **Reduce feelings of guilt and anger:** Family members may feel guilty (e.g. that they are responsible for causing schizophrenia) or angry towards the schizophrenic patient

A typical course of family therapy may consist of weekly sessions for a year, after which the family members will have developed skills that they can use after therapy has ended.

Strengths:	• **Supporting evidence:** Pilling et al (2002) analysed 18 studies of family therapy for schizophrenia and found it had a clear effect on reducing relapse rates. • **Low risk of side effects:** Again, compared to e.g. antipsychotic drugs. • **Cost effective:** The Schizophrenia Commission (2012) estimate that family therapy results in cost savings of around £1000 per patient over a 3 year period.
Weaknesses:	• **Not suitable for all:** Some schizophrenic patients do not have dysfunctional families and so family therapy is unlikely to be an effective treatment for them.

SCHIZOPHRENIA – TOKEN ECONOMIES AND DIATHESIS-STRESS

Token economies are a *behaviourist* treatment for schizophrenia

Remember **operant conditioning** (page 33)? In a token economy, schizophrenic patients receive **tokens** (that can be exchanged for rewards) in return for desirable behaviour.

Token economies are primarily used for schizophrenic patients who are in **institutions** for long time periods and are mainly used to treat **negative symptoms** of schizophrenia. For example, *avolition* (a negative symptom of schizophrenia) may mean the patient has little motivation to undertake tasks such as getting out of bed, washing, and socialising. Token economies provide an incentive for the patient to undertake these tasks, **positively reinforcing** this behaviour.

Strengths:	• **Supporting evidence:** A review by McMonagle and Sultana (2000) found token economies reduced the negative symptoms of schizophrenia. However, the researchers question the reliability of these studies and likelihood of relapse.
Weaknesses:	• **Ethical concerns:** Firstly, some argue that token economies are *dehumanising*. Secondly, some argue that token economies are *discriminatory:* Severely ill patients will have greater difficulty complying with behavioural demands and thus get fewer privileges than patients who are less severely ill. • **Relapse:** If improvements in behaviour are dependent on receiving tokens, the schizophrenic patient may relapse once token economy therapy is withdrawn.

Interactionist approaches to *explaining* and *treating* schizophrenia

Meehl's (1962) **diathesis-stress model** is an interactionist explanation. According to this model, genetics determines a person's *vulnerability* to schizophrenia (**biological diathesis**), but schizophrenia is only triggered in response to *environmental* stressors (**stress**). So, a person with a high genetic predisposition towards schizophrenia may never develop the disorder (e.g. if they live in a supportive low-stress environment) but a person with a lower genetic disposition may develop schizophrenia if exposed to enough environmental stress (e.g. dysfunctional family, drug abuse).

Strengths:	• **Holistic:** Rather than reducing schizophrenia to one single cause, the diathesis-stress model accounts for the multitude of factors that contribute to the disorder. This can be seen as a more complete picture of schizophrenia. • **Supporting evidence:** There is evidence supporting the role of both a biological diathesis (see e.g. Gottesman (1991) on page 104) and environmental triggers. For example, a meta-analysis by Varese et al (2012) found that stressful events in childhood increase the risk of schizophrenia. • **Practical applications:** Interactionist approaches may result in more effective treatment. For example, antipsychotic drugs can be *combined* with CBT or family therapy. In general, research suggests this is more effective than monotherapy.
Weaknesses:	• **Increased costs:** Multiple treatments will be more expensive than monotherapy. But if this results in lower relapse rates, this could save money in the long-term.

EATING BEHAVIOUR – EXPLANATIONS OF FOOD PREFERENCES

Evolutionary explanations say genes for healthy food preferences are *adaptive*

For example, if you had **genes** that resulted in a preference for **nutritious** and **commonly-found** foods, you'd be **less likely to starve** and more likely to reproduce and **pass on your genes**. But if your genes meant you really liked the taste of *deadly mushrooms*, say, then you probably wouldn't live long enough to reproduce and pass on those genes.

AO3: Preferences for sweet and calorie-dense foods would have evolved in a time when food was scarce, but this may be maladaptive in the modern era where food is plentiful, resulting in obesity.

Neophobia is an innate dislike of foods we haven't tried before. This makes sense from an evolutionary perspective as unfamiliar foods could potentially be poisonous or unhealthy. However, we overcome neophobia via *learning*. In a study of young children, Birch et al (1987) found that preference for new foods increased over time with repeated exposure to those foods.

AO3: Several studies (e.g. Steiner (1979) and Rosenstein and Oster (1988)) have analysed facial expressions and behaviours of babies after feeding them bitter- and sweet-tasting foods, finding that babies like sweet tastes and dislike bitter ones. The fact that babies have these preferences from such a young age suggests they are *innate*, supporting evolutionary explanations.

Taste aversion is when a person develops a dislike for a certain food **after becoming ill** from it.
Example: You eat yoghurt, get food poisoning, and from then on even the thought of eating yoghurt again makes you feel sick.

Seligman (1971) says this **biological preparedness** to develop taste aversion is evolutionarily adaptive: If certain foods are dangerous, it would be advantageous to learn this **as quickly as possible** because the next time you eat that food you might get ill again or die.

As well as genetics, food preferences may be *learned* from **social influences**

Social influences can affect food preferences in several ways:
- **During development:** In the womb, foods (and flavours) the mother eats are fed to the baby via amniotic fluid. After birth, flavours are transmitted from the mother to the baby via breast milk.
- **Social learning:** Children observe what parents and other role models eat, which they then imitate. This helps reduce neophobia, encouraging the child to eat a wider range of foods.
- **Operant conditioning:** If you enjoy eating a certain food, then that enjoyment serves as positive reinforcement, which increases the chances of you eating it again. However, research suggests that operant conditioning doesn't really work to *create* food preferences. For example, if parents try to teach their children to like certain foods (e.g. vegetables) through rewards (e.g. praise for eating vegetables), it may actually *decrease* preference for those foods.

AO3: Mennella et al (2005) found that genetics primarily determine food preferences in children (e.g. liking sweet tastes and disliking bitter ones) but by adulthood environmental factors are far more important, supporting learning explanations of food preferences.

Eating Behaviour – Chapter 13

EATING BEHAVIOUR – BIOLOGICAL MECHANISMS

Finally, another way food preferences may be *learned* is via **culture**

Different **cultures** have different eating behaviours and this too affects food preferences. For example, some **religious** cultures (e.g. Islam and Judaism) forbid eating pork. **Local** cultures also have different cuisines (e.g. eating snails in France (escargots)), which affect food preferences.

AO3: Advances in transportation (e.g. shipping) and technology (e.g. refrigeration) have reduced the influence of local culture and made food preferences more global. For example, avocados can't be grown in the UK, which in the past would mean people living in the UK wouldn't have developed a taste for avocados.

The **hypothalamus** is the **neural mechanism** that controls eating behaviour

The hypothalamus is the main section of the **brain** responsible for maintaining **homeostasis** (i.e. stability and normal functioning) within the body. It controls things like body temperature, sleep, and **hunger**.

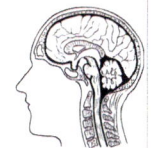

In the case of hunger, there are 2 sections that have opposite effects:

- *Lateral* **hypothalamus:** Responsible for making you feel *hungry* and *start eating*.
- *Ventromedial* **hypothalamus:** Responsible for making you feel full (*satiety*) and *stop eating*.

The process is as follows: When blood sugar (glucose) is low, the liver sends signals to the lateral hypothalamus. This causes neurons to fire that make you feel hungry and start eating. Then, when you eat, glucose is released into the blood, which is detected by the ventromedial hypothalamus. This causes neurons to fire that make you feel satiated (full).

AO3: The role of the hypothalamus in eating behaviour is supported by animal studies. For example, Baylis et al (1996) created lesions (cuts) in the ventromedial hypothalamus of 13 rats. The rats with damage to this area became obese compared to 13 age- and sex-matched controls.

Ghrelin is the **hormone** that makes you feel *hungry*

The **ghrelin** hormone is secreted by the **stomach** into the bloodstream, which is detected by the *hypothalamus* (see above), creating the sensation of **hunger**.

When you eat food, the stomach stops releasing ghrelin, which stops you feeling hungry. After the meal is eaten, ghrelin levels (and hunger) progressively increase until the next time you eat.

Leptin is the **hormone** that makes you feel *full*

Leptin is a hormone that makes you feel **full**. It is secreted by **fat cells** into the bloodstream, which signals to the *hypothalamus* that energy storage (fat deposits) is high and so you don't need to eat.

If you don't eat for a while, the body uses these fat deposits for energy, and so those fat cells no longer exist to produce leptin. This reduction in leptin makes you feel hungry.

EATING BEHAVIOUR – BIOLOGICAL EXPLANATIONS OF ANOREXIA

Anorexia nervosa: An eating disorder characterised by an obsession with losing weight, body image distortion, restriction of food, and low bodyweight.

Genetic explanations of anorexia are supported by twin studies

Holland et al (1988) found a **concordance rate** for anorexia of **56%** for **identical** twins and **5%** for **non-identical** twins. Similarly, Bulik et al (2006) estimate the heritability of anorexia to be **56%** based on analysis of 31,406 pairs of Swedish twins.

The role of genetics is further supported by **gene association studies** (e.g. Wang et al (2011) and Scott-Van Zeeland et al (2014)), which compare DNA profiles of anorexia sufferers with non-anorexic controls. These studies have found various genes to be correlated with anorexia, such as OPRD1, HTR1D, and EPHX2.

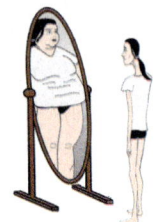

Strengths:	• **Supporting evidence:** See studies above.
Weaknesses:	• **Conflicting evidence:** Kortegaard et al (2001) found a concordance rate for anorexia of just 18% for identical twins and 7% for non-identical twins. This still supports a genetic explanation, but suggests other factors are more important. • **Genetics haven't changed significantly:** Anorexia was practically unheard of before 1950 but since then rates of anorexia have increased significantly. This change is far too quick to be explained by genetics, which suggests other factors (e.g. social learning theory) have caused the rise in anorexia diagnoses.

Neural explanations look at brain structures and neurochemistry

Some research has found *correlations* between reduced blood flow in the **lateral hypothalamus** of the brain (the area associated with *hunger* – see page 111) and anorexia.

Neurotransmitters may also play a role in anorexia. For example, several studies have found correlations between **serotonin** activity and anorexia, although the exact relationship is unclear. One hypothesis proposed by Kaye et al (2009) is that people with anorexia naturally have elevated serotonin activity, which causes them anxiety. Starvation reduces serotonin levels (because food is needed to produce serotonin), which reduces this anxiety and reinforces anorexic behaviour.

Strengths:	• **Practical applications:** Neural explanations of anorexia could lead to effective treatments. E.g. some studies suggest SSRIs can improve anorexia outcomes by altering neurotransmitter activity (although other studies disagree).
Weaknesses:	• **Conflicting evidence:** Much of the research linking neurotransmitter activity and anorexia is contradictory. For example, a review by Kontis and Theochari (2012) reports how different studies have suggested anorexia is linked with normal, increased, *and* decreased dopamine activity. • **Correlation is not causation:** For example, reduced blood flow in the lateral hypothalamus could be an *effect of starvation* rather than a *cause* of anorexia.

Eating Behaviour

PSYCHOLOGICAL EXPLANATIONS OF ANOREXIA

Minuchin et al (1978) proposed the **family systems theory of anorexia**

The researchers found that the families of anorexic patients often share **4 key features:**

- **Enmeshment:** The family members have no individual identity or independence but instead blur into one single unit. For example, they are very involved in each other's business, spend all their time together, and nobody has any unique role within the family.
- **Overprotective:** The family is very controlling and overprotective, which makes it more difficult for members to break free from the enmeshment and develop their own identity.
- **Conflict avoidance:** The family ignores or suppresses conflict.
- **Rigidity:** The family does not like change and tries to keep things as they are.

There are several **psychodynamic** explanations of how this dysfunctional family style can contribute to anorexia. For example, a child who fears their parents will split up due to arguing may become anorexic in order to distract from those arguments and *reduce conflict*.

A related explanation described in Bruch (1978) is that anorexia is a way for people to assert **autonomy** and **control**. For example, refusing to eat might be a way for a family member to assert their individuality and free will against their *overprotective* and *enmeshed* family.

Strengths:	• **Supporting evidence:** Minuchin et al (1978), observed 11 families of anorexic patients and 34 control families as they completed a group task. The researchers observed greater levels of enmeshment, overprotectiveness, conflict avoidance, and rigidity among the families of anorexic patients. • **Practical applications:** For example, Robin et al (1999) randomly assigned 37 anorexic patients to receive either family therapy or individual therapy. Although both treatments were found to be effective, the family therapy group saw greater weight gains and a faster return to health.
Weaknesses:	• **Conflicting evidence:** A review of 17 studies by Viesel and Allan (2014) found that anorexia and family dysfunction were correlated. However, the researchers did not find evidence for a *specific pattern* of family dysfunction (e.g. enmeshment), weakening support for Minuchin et al's family systems model. • **Correlation is not causation:** E.g. a child developing anorexia could cause a previously normal family to become enmeshed, not the other way round.

Cognitive explanations of anorexia look at *thoughts* and *beliefs*, such as:

- **Distortions:** People with anorexia have inaccurate perceptions of body image.
    - *Example:* The person sees their body as fat and overweight when actually it is skinny and underweight.
- **Irrational beliefs:** People with anorexia have incorrect, maladaptive, and exaggerated thoughts about eating food and gaining weight.
    - *Examples:* "If I eat one crisp, I'll get fat" or "If I can't control my weight, I'm worthless".

PSYCHOLOGICAL EXPLANATIONS OF ANOREXIA

AO3: **Strengths** of cognitive explanations of anorexia nervosa

- **Supporting evidence:** For example, Williamson et al (1993) used silhouette pictures to evaluate 37 anorexic patients' current and ideal body images. Compared to the control group, the anorexic patients' estimation of their current body size was larger and their ideal body image was thinner, supporting the role of cognitive distortions in anorexia.
- **Practical applications:** For example, Grave et al (2014) used cognitive behavioural therapy with 26 anorexia patients, which resulted in improvements in weight and anorexia symptoms that were still maintained at a 12-month follow up.

AO3: **Weaknesses** of cognitive explanations of anorexia nervosa

- **Conflicting evidence:** Cornelissen et al (2013) compared 30 anorexic women with 137 controls but found no significant difference in body image estimates, which contradicts Williamson et al (1993) and weakens support for the role of cognitive distortions in anorexia.

Social learning theory is all about observation and imitation of role models

See the approaches section (page 34) for more details. Applying the concepts of SLT to anorexia:

- **Modelling:** A *role model* who the anorexic patient either likes or wants to be like. For example, an older sister or a celebrity who is thin.
- **Vicarious reinforcement:** The anorexic person *observes* the role model being rewarded and praised for being thin. For example, the slim sister is complimented on her weight loss, or the slim celebrity has lots of followers on social media. These rewards create a *motivation* to imitate their behaviour and restrict eating.

Operant conditioning may then come in as well. For example, when the anorexic person starts imitating the behaviour themself, they may receive compliments for being slim *(positive reinforcement)* or people may stop criticising them for being overweight *(negative reinforcement)*.

Strengths:	• **Supporting evidence:** Dittmar et al (2006) showed 162 girls (aged 5-8) either Barbie dolls, Emme dolls (a US size 16), or no dolls and then got them to complete a body image assessment. The girls shown the Barbie dolls had lower body esteem and a *greater desire to be thin* than the other two groups, which suggests role models in the media and culture may contribute to anorexia. • **Explanatory power:** Anorexia has increased significantly in Western cultures since 1950 – far quicker than can be explained via changes in genetics. But social learning theory can explain this by pointing to things like growing emphasis on thinness in the media and culture during this time.
Weaknesses:	• **Other factors:** Even if social learning contributes to anorexia, it's unlikely this is the sole cause. For example, all people in Western countries are exposed to the same amount of media influence (more or less), and yet only some of them develop anorexia. This suggests other factors (e.g. biology) play a role too.

Eating Behaviour

EATING BEHAVIOUR – BIOLOGICAL EXPLANATIONS OF OBESITY

Obesity: A physical condition characterised by excess body fat, which may cause other health problems such as heart disease and diabetes.

There is evidence that **genetics** can make someone more likely to be obese

As always, twin studies (page 38) are your friend when seeing if something is genetically inherited:
- Stunkard et al (1990) compared **concordance rates** of obesity among identical twins *raised together* and identical twins *raised apart*. Male and female identical twins raised together had concordance rates of 74% and 69% respectively, whereas male and female twins raised apart had concordance rates of 70% and 66% respectively. The similarity between these two sets of figures suggests the different environments had little impact on obesity rates compared to genetics.

Strengths:	• **Supporting evidence:** In addition to Stunkard et al (1990) above, gene association studies have identified genes that may contribute to obesity. For example, Fall and Ingelsson (2012) and Frayling et al (2007) have found the FTO gene to be *correlated* with obesity.
Weaknesses:	• **Genetics haven't changed significantly:** In 1975, only around 10% of the UK population was obese (defined as having a BMI > 30) but by 2020 this figure was closer to 30%. This change has happened far too quickly to be explained by genetics as only a few generations have passed during this time. This suggests other factors (e.g. changing dietary habits) are needed to explain obesity.

Neural factors – i.e. brain structures and neurotransmitters – play a role too

As described on page 111, the **ventromedial hypothalamus** is the area of the brain responsible for making you feel full. Some neural explanations say damage to this area may cause obesity. Other neural explanations look at the role of **leptin** – the hormone that makes you feel full – saying that obesity can be caused by neurons that don't respond properly to this hormone.

Neurotransmitters are also implicated in obesity. For example, brain scans by Wang et al (2001) and Volkow et al (2008) found that obese individuals have reduced **dopamine** receptor activity compared to controls. Dopamine is associated with pleasure and reward and so the hypothesis is that obese people overeat to get the same pleasure and reward response as a non-obese person would get from eating less food. This is a similar mechanism to other addictions, such as smoking.

Strengths:	• **Supporting evidence:** See studies above. • **Practical applications:** For example, Heymsfield et al (1999) suggest leptin injections may be a successful treatment for obesity in some people.
Weaknesses:	• **Conflicting evidence:** For each neural explanation of obesity, there are often several studies that contradict it. For example, a meta-analysis of 33 studies by Benton and Young (2016) found lower dopamine receptor activity is *not* correlated with obesity, contradicting Wang et al (2001) and Volkow et al (2008).

EATING BEHAVIOUR – PSYCHOLOGICAL EXPLANATIONS OF OBESITY

Herman and Polivy (1984) proposed the **boundary model** of eating

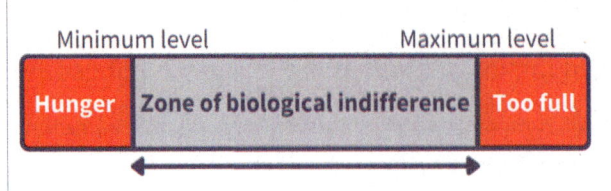

If food falls *below* a certain **minimum level**, the person feels the aversive (unpleasant) feeling of **hunger** that motivates them to eat. At the other end, eating too much food *exceeds* the **maximum level**, which causes the aversive feeling of being **too full**.

According to the boundary model, these levels are primarily determined by *biology*. The range in the middle is the **zone of biological indifference**, where a person's biology is satisfied. Within this zone, it is *psychological* – not *biological* – factors that determine whether a person eats.

Restraint theory says trying to eat less food paradoxically makes you eat *more*

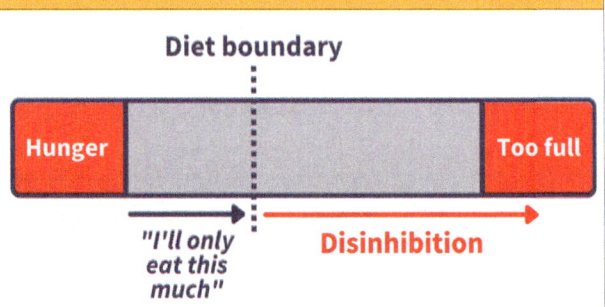

According to this explanation, a **restrained eater** sets a **diet boundary** (i.e. a self-imposed cognitive limit after which they won't eat any more). Setting this boundary causes the restrained eater to spend more time thinking about food than if they *hadn't* set a diet boundary. Also, the diet boundary may be **unrealistically low**, causing constant hunger and low mood. But when the person *crosses* their diet boundary (as often happens), their eating may become **disinhibited:** The person *gives up* trying to control their eating and will keep eating until they're full (or beyond). This **disinhibited eating** causes obesity.

Strengths:	• **Supporting evidence:** Herman and Mack (1975) took 45 women (either dieting or not dieting) and randomly allocated them into groups given either 1 glass of milkshake, 2 glasses of milkshake, or nothing. After the milkshakes, they were then given unlimited ice cream to eat. The researchers found that the women who *weren't* on diets ate less ice cream the more milkshakes they'd had (which is to be expected as presumably they were already full). However, the *dieting* women actually ate *more* ice cream the more milkshakes they'd had previously, which supports the idea that they had become disinhibited. • **Practical applications:** If dieting is actually counterproductive, this knowledge could lead to more effective obesity treatments. For example, Bergh et al (2009) suggests training people to eat *more slowly* could be more effective than dieting.
Weaknesses:	• **Conflicting evidence:** Many people lose weight via dieting. For example, in a longitudinal study of 163 women, Savage et al (2009) found that restrained eating and dieting were correlated with *weight loss*, not weight gain.

Eating Behaviour

EATING BEHAVIOUR – PSYCHOLOGICAL EXPLANATIONS OF OBESITY

Explanations of the success or failure of dieting

A diet is successful if the dieter loses the desired amount of weight and **keeps it off for the long-term.** There are many **factors** that contribute to the **success** or **failure** of dieting:

Factors that **increase the chance of diet success** include:
- **Realistic expectations:** Dieters are more likely to succeed if they follow a sustainable diet and steadily lose weight over **months** and **years**, setting *realistic* short- and long-term goals.
- **Incentives and motivation:** Dieters may *reward* themselves for achieving weight loss goals. For example, a dieter may buy new clothes to fit their slimmer physique. This works as a form of **operant conditioning**, reinforcing and motivating weight loss.
- **Social support:** Having support from **family** and **friends** makes a diet more likely to succeed. For example, Wing and Jeffery (1999) randomly assigned 166 participants to receive either a standard 4-month weight loss program or a standard 4-month weight loss program + social support. At follow up 6 months later, 66% of participants in the social support group had maintained their weight loss compared to just 24% in the group without social support.
- **Relapse prevention strategies:** Many dieters see dieting as a temporary measure after which they can return to their old eating habits. This results in a demotivating cycle of regaining lost weight and then dieting again (yo-yo dieting). Dieters who have strategies to avoid going back to their previous eating behaviours and **maintain a stable food intake** are more likely to succeed.

AO3: Understanding the factors that increase the likelihood of diet success could lead to more effective ways to treat obesity. For example, providing social support in addition to a realistic diet plan is likely to increase the chance of successful and sustainable weight loss.

Factors that **increase the chance of diet failure** include:
- **Overly-restrictive diets:** Dieters often try to follow diets that are **too strict**, such as limiting calories to under 1000 per day. This is unsustainable and when the dieter exceeds this limit they may lose motivation and indulge in **disinhibited eating** (in line with the predictions of restraint theory – see page 116).
- **Unrealistic expectations:** Dieters often expect to lose a lot of weight in a matter of **weeks** or months. However, obese people typically gained weight progressively over many years and so it is unrealistic to expect to reverse this in a short time period. If the dieter does not have realistic expectations, they may **lose motivation** and abandon the diet.

AO3: Individual differences mean the best approach is likely to vary from person to person. For example, *restrained* eaters are unlikely to successfully lose weight via calorie restriction because this will probably result in disinhibited eating. However, unrestrained eaters are likely to have more success with calorie restriction.

A general criticism of research on dieting is **gender bias:** Most research into dieting is done on females, and so the conclusions drawn from this research may not be valid in males.

STRESS – PHYSIOLOGICAL PROCESSES

We've all experienced and know what stress is. But the precise psychological understanding of **stress** is: When an individual *feels* (rightly or wrongly) that they are not able to cope with the demands of a situation.

Example: You *feel* you don't know enough to pass your psychology exam = stress.

Selye (1936) first described stress as **general adaptation syndrome**

Selye (1936) exposed rats to various **stressors** (i.e. causes of stress) such as extreme cold, forced exercise, and sub-lethal doses of drugs. He observed a common **3-stage physiological response:**

1. **Alarm reaction**>>>>>>>>>>	2. **Resistance**>>>>>>>>>>>>>>>	3. **Exhaustion**
Fight or flight – adrenaline and noradrenaline release.	*Coping* – adrenaline declines, cortisol increases.	*Weakening* – bodily resources are depleted, causing illness.

The fact that this **same general sequence** was observed *irrespective of the specific stressor* led Selye to characterise this 3-part stress response as **general adaptation syndrome**.

Strengths:	• **Supporting evidence:** Selye's (1936) experiments demonstrated the *same physiological sequence* in response to completely different stressors (e.g. extreme cold or forced exercise), suggesting a single explanation of stress.
Weaknesses:	• **Conflicting evidence:** In experiments on *monkeys*, Mason (1971) found that rather than exhibiting the *same* physiological response to the different stressors, the monkeys' physiological responses *differed* depending on the stressor. For example, exposure to extreme cold appeared to increase levels of cortisol whereas exposure to extreme heat decreased cortisol levels. • **Methodological concerns:** As Selye's (1936) physiological explanation of stress was derived from experiments on rats, general adaptation syndrome may not be valid when explaining the physiological process of stress in human beings.

The **sympathomedullary pathway** is associated with *acute* (short-term) stress

More recent explanations would break down Selye's alarm reaction stage into the following sequence *(Note: This is basically the fight or flight response described on page 46)*:

- The **hypothalamus** sends a signal to the **sympathetic** part of the **autonomic nervous system**
- This signal triggers the **adrenal medulla** of the adrenal glands to release the hormones **adrenaline** and **noradrenaline**
- These hormones increase bodily activities to prepare to deal with the stressor. For example, **heart rate** and **breathing** are increased to improve **blood flow** and oxygenation, and bodily systems that are not essential for dealing with the stressor (e.g. digestion) are decreased.

Once the stressor has passed, the parasympathetic part of the autonomic nervous system switches back to rest and digest, reducing bodily activity.

Stress – Chapter 14

PHYSIOLOGICAL PROCESSES AND STRESS-RELATED ILLNESS

The **hypothalamic-pituitary-adrenal system**...

...is associated with **chronic** (long-term) stress. The short-term sympathomedullary response can't be maintained forever because it consumes too many bodily resources. And so, if a stressor *remains* for an extended time period, the hypothalamic-pituitary-adrenal system takes over:
- The hypothalamus starts releasing **corticotropin-releasing hormone** (CRH)
- CRH tells the **pituitary gland** to start releasing **adrenocorticotropic hormone** (ACTH)
- ACTH tells the **adrenal cortex** of the adrenal glands to release **cortisol**, which provides energy.

Cortisol is the stress *hormone*

Cortisol is a glucocorticoid hormone that **increases blood sugar** by converting protein to glucose. This increased blood sugar provides **energy** to replace energy lost during the sympathomedullary response (see above) and help overcome the stressor. However, cortisol has negative effects on the body – especially over the long term – increasing the risk of **stress-related illness** (see below).

Stress can cause **cardiovascular disorders** and **immunosuppression**

Immunosuppression means a reduction in the ability of the immune system to fight off disease. The immune system identifies foreign things like bacteria and viruses within the body and destroys them. However, **cortisol reduces the production of immune cells** (e.g. natural killer cells and T helper cells), which reduces the effectiveness of the immune system.

AO3: A study illustrating this is Kiecolt-Glaser et al (1984). In this natural experiment, researchers took blood samples from 75 medical students a month before their exams and again on the day of their exams. They found the number of natural killer cells was much lower on the day of their exams (high stress), demonstrating a *correlation* between stress and immunosuppression.

However, the relationship between stress and immunosuppression is not simple. For example, Schedlowski (1993) measured natural killer cell activity in 45 first-time parachute jumpers 2 hours before their jump, immediately after their jump, and 1 hour after their jump, finding that natural killer cell activity *increased* immediately after the parachute jumps and then fell below baseline 1 hour post-jump. This suggests acute stress (initially) increases immunity.

Cardiovascular disorders are problems of the heart. There are several ways stress can cause cardiovascular disorders. For example, stress causes **blood pressure** to increase and causes **fat to accumulate on arterial walls**. There are also more indirect mechanisms – for example, stress may increase the likelihood that a person takes up **smoking**, which in turn increases the risk of cardiovascular issues.

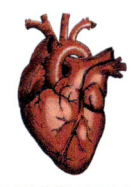

AO3: Yusuf et al (2004) compared lifestyle factors of 15,152 people who'd had a heart attack with a control group of 14,820 who had not had a heart attack. The researchers found strong *correlations* between stress (e.g. workplace stress, stressful life events, daily hassles) and heart attack.

STRESS – SOURCES OF STRESS

Workplace stress comes in many forms, such as...

- **Workload:** *How much work* a person has. If a person is given too many tasks to do within a time period, this causes stress. The higher the workload, the more stress.
- **Control:** The extent to which a person *has influence* over what work they do and how much. The less control a person has over their work, the greater the stress.

The key theory that brings these 2 factors together is Karasek's (1979) **demand-control model**. According to this model, high workload increases the likelihood of stress-related illness, but this risk is *reduced* when the employee has more control over their work.

Strengths:	• **Evidence supporting *workload*:** Kivimäki et al (2006) conducted a meta-analysis of 14 studies that included at a total of 83,104 employees and found that workload was correlated with coronary heart disease (CHD). They estimate that workplace stress makes employees 50% more likely to suffer from CHD. • **Evidence supporting *control*:** The 'Whitehall Studies' conducted by Marmot et al (1997) followed 10,308 employees in the UK civil service over a period of 5 years. The researchers found that employees with low levels of control over their work were significantly more likely to suffer from heart attacks compared to employees with high levels of control over their work.
Weaknesses:	• **Conflicting evidence on *workload*:** Although the Whitehall Studies found a correlation between low levels of *job control* and heart disease, they found no such correlation between level of *workload* and heart disease. • **Conflicting evidence on *control*:** Meier et al (2008) found that, for employees with an *external locus of control*, greater level of job control was actually correlated with *increased* levels of stress-related illness. • **Confounding variables:** Researchers in the Whitehall Studies only looked at workload and control, but there are other factors that may explain higher levels of stress-related illness. For example, jobs with lower levels of control may also be paid less, and this may be what increased the risk of stress-related illness.

Life changes can also be a major source of stress

Holmes and Rahe (1967) created the **social readjustment ratings scale** (SRRS) to quantify stress associated with **life changes**. It includes 43 examples of life changes, which are ranked from 1-43.

To get these rankings, Holmes and Rahe asked subjects to rate how stressful each event was. Based on their responses, each life event was given a **life change unit** (LCU) score. The more LCUs a person scores, the greater their risk of stress-related illness. If a person scores **more than 300 LCUs**, the SSRS predicts they are at **high risk** of illness.

Event	Rank	LCUs
Death of spouse	1	100
Marriage	7	50
Retirement	10	45
Vacation	41	13

Stress

STRESS – SOURCES OF STRESS AND SELF-REPORT MEASURES

AO3: **Strengths** of stress caused by life changes and the SSRS

- **Supporting evidence:** Rahe et al (1970) got 2664 navy sailors to complete the SRRS prior to a 6-8 month tour of duty during which their medical records were recorded. The researchers observed a *positive correlation* (+0.118) between LCUs on the SRRS and illness during the tour of duty. This suggests the SRRS is a valid measure of stress.
- **Practical applications:** The SSRS could potentially be used to prevent stress-related illness. For example, a doctor could get patients to complete the SSRS and if the patient scores more than 300 LCUs, the doctor could prescribe or advise treatments to manage stress.

AO3: **Weaknesses** of stress caused by life changes and the SSRS

- **Doesn't distinguish between positive and negative:** The SSRS assumes all life changes are stressful, when many may actually be the exact opposite. For example, the SSRS includes 'vacation' (13 LCUs), but many people find vacations *relaxing* rather than stressful.
- **Correlation is not causation:** Even if scores on the SSRS are *correlated* with illness, this does not prove *causation*. For example, illness could be what causes life changes (e.g. time off work from being ill leads to the life change of losing a job) rather than the other way round.
- **Less scientific:** As a self-report method, the SSRS relies on the participant's subjective interpretation of events (e.g. "trouble with in-laws" is open to interpretation). As such, the SSRS can be said to be less scientific than physiological measures such as skin conductance response (page 122), which produce objective and quantifiable data.

Daily hassles are an obvious source of stress

Kanner et al's (1981) **hassles and uplifts scale** includes 117 examples of such **daily hassles**, defined as *"irritating, frustrating, distressing demands that to some degree characterise everyday transactions with the environment"*. However, stress caused by these hassles may be counteracted by **uplifts** – positive experiences.

Examples of daily hassles	Examples of uplifts
Concerns about weight	Relating well with your spouse or lover
Poor health of a family member	Relating well with friends
Rising prices of common goods	Completing a task
Home maintenance	Feeling healthy
Too many things to do	Getting enough sleep

The researchers (Kanner et al) got 100 participants to complete the hassles and uplifts scale by ticking which hassles and uplifts they had encountered over the previous month each month for 9 months. They found **high scores for hassles** were *positively correlated* with **stress** and **health problems.** They also found that high scores for uplifts were *negatively correlated* with stress and health problems – but only among women.

STRESS – WAYS OF MEASURING STRESS

AO3: **Strengths** of the hassles and uplifts scale

- **Supporting evidence:** Kanner et al (1981) compared the correlation between stress-related illness and scores on their hassles and uplifts scale with the correlation between scores on the SRRS and stress-related illness. They found a stronger correlation with stress-related illness from scores on the hassles and uplifts scale compared to the SRRS.

AO3: **Weaknesses** of the hassles and uplifts scale

- **Evidence against the role of uplifts:** DeLongis et al (1982) gave 100 adults aged 45-64 the hassles and uplifts scale and found uplifts made little difference to stress-related illness.
- **Methodological concerns:** In addition to the 'correlation is not causation' argument, the hassles and uplifts scale is *retrospective*, meaning respondents must remember hassles and uplifts over a time period. But if a person has a bad memory, their responses may not be valid.
- **Less scientific:** Like the SSRS, the hassles and uplifts scale is a self-report method that relies on subjective interpretation. For example, what counts as "relating well with friends" may differ from person to person and can't be objectively measured.

Skin conductance response is a *physiological* method of measuring stress

Water conducts electricity. And when a person is stressed, they **sweat** more. So, when a person is stressed, their skin conducts electricity more easily. This is how **skin conductance response** measures stress. You might have heard it referred to as a *polygraph* test (AKA lie detector test):

- **Electrodes** are attached to the subject's fingers and apply a tiny electrical current.
- The subject is asked to sit still for 30 mins to establish **baseline** (non-stressed) skin conductance.
- The subject is asked questions. If the subject lies when answering, this causes stress, triggering the sympathetic nervous system to increase **sweat**
- This increase in stress is detected as an **increase in skin conductance** relative to their baseline (non-stressed) level of skin conductance.

Strengths:	• **Supporting evidence:** Several studies demonstrate correlations between levels of stress and skin conductance. For example, Kurniawan et al (2013) found that trained polygraph operators were able to accurately determine whether a person was experiencing high stress or low stress 70% of the time. • **More scientific:** Skin conductance response uses objective and quantifiable data to measure stress. As such, it can be said to be more scientific than self-report measures of stress, which rely on subjective interpretations. • **Practical applications:** For example, police detectives can use polygraph testing to help determine whether a suspect is telling the truth.
Weaknesses:	• **Conflicting evidence:** Skin conductance is not a perfect measure of stress (or lying). For example, even though Kurniawan et al (2013) above found a 70% success rate, this still leaves 30% of the time when they got it wrong.

STRESS – INDIVIDUAL DIFFERENCES

Certain **personality types** appear to be more prone to **cardiovascular disorders**

Friedman and Rosenman (1959) identified certain patterns of behaviour, which they characterised into two personality types: **Type A** and **Type B**.

Type A personality (stressed)	**Type B personality** (less stressed)
Time-urgent, impatient, rushed	More patient
Competitive, perfectionistic	Less competitive
Hostile, aggressive, irritable	More calm
More prone to developing heart disease	*Less prone to developing heart disease*

Strengths:	• **Supporting evidence:** Rosenman et al's (1976) Western Collaborative Group Study determined the personality type (A or B) of 3,154 employed men who were not suffering from heart disease. At the follow-up 8.5 years later, *257* had developed heart disease. Type A personalities were approximately twice as likely to be among these 257 men than type B personalities, which supports a link between type A personality and heart disease.
Weaknesses:	• **Conflicting evidence:** Ragland and Brand (1988) followed up again with the 257 subjects who had suffered heart disease in Rosenman et al (1976) above. They found that of the 231 subjects who *survived* a heart attack, type B personalities were more likely to have died at this follow up than type A personalities.
	• **Classification issues:** Matthews and Haynes (1986) and Dembroski et al (1989) found that *hostility alone* predicts heart disease just as accurately as type A personality does. This suggests that some components of the type A personality (e.g. being competitive) are not relevant to differences in stress-related illness.

Greer and Watson (1985) identified a **Type C** personality, at greater risk of **cancer**

People with a **Type C personality** are **introverted**, **neurotic**, **avoid conflict**, **repress their emotions**, and are **people-pleasers**. These personality types are said to be more prone to stress than people who express their emotions freely and assert themselves.

Greer and Watson (1985) found type C personalities are at higher risk of developing **cancer**.

Strengths:	• **Supporting evidence:** Several studies support a link between type C personality and cancer. For example, Temoshok (1987) looked at cancer rates and type C personality traits, such as a tendency to repress emotions (particularly anger). She found these personality traits *were* correlated with increased risk of cancer.

AO3: A general point with these links between personality types and stress-related illness is that the risks are relative: Even if it is true that type C personalities are *more likely* to get cancer, this does not mean it is *likely* (in absolute terms) that type C personalities will get cancer. Further, all these studies are simply *correlational* – they do not necessarily prove causation.

STRESS – INDIVIDUAL DIFFERENCES

According to, Kobasa (1979) **hardy personalities** have 3 key features:

- **Commitment:** Hardy people are **highly committed** to what they do. They feel a strong sense of purpose and meaning in their life and activities – their work, their relationships, their hobbies, and so on.
- **Challenge:** Hardy people interpret stressors as **challenges to be overcome** and an opportunity to grow and improve. For example, they may seek out activities and tasks that other people find stressful, such as endurance races.
- **Control:** Hardy people have an *internal* **locus of control** (page 9). This means they see their own choices as shaping their life instead of factors outside their control.

Non-hardy personalities are the opposite: They give up easily (low commitment), feel unable to cope with stressors (rather than seeing them as challenges), and have an external locus of control.

Strengths:	• **Supporting evidence:** Kobasa (1979) used the SRRS (see page 120) to identify 161 subjects who had undergone high levels of stress over the last 3 years. Of these 161 stressed individuals, 75 had suffered stress-related illness, whereas 86 had not. She then compared the personality traits of these two groups and found the 86 subjects who did not get ill scored much higher for hardiness than the 75 subjects who did get ill. This suggests hardy personality types are more resistant to stress-related illnesses *even when actual levels of stress are similar*.
Weaknesses:	• **Vague:** Funk (1992) points out that several different scales are used to measure hardiness and that there is little research comparing these different scales. Further, it may be that some of these scales actually measure *neuroticism* – and that it is *low neuroticism*, not hardiness, that prevents stress-related illness. • **Correlation is not causation:** For example, it may be that hardy people are more likely to seek the *challenge* of physical exercise, in which case it may be this that causes lower levels of stress-related illness, not hardiness itself.

There may also be **gender differences** in coping with and responding to stress

For example, page 71 describes how Taylor et al (2000) found the female stress response is better characterised as '**tend and befriend**' rather than '**fight or flight**'. A potential mechanism for these differences in stress behaviours is differences in **oxytocin** levels (see page 87).

Similarly, a meta-analysis by Tamres et al (2002) found women were more likely than men to use **social support** (see page 126) to cope with stress, supporting the 'tend and befriend' response.

AO3: Although Tamres et al (2002) supports a *dispositional* **explanation** of gender differences in coping with stress, the researchers also found support for *role-constraint theory:* The idea that men and women face *different* stressors. For example, women tend to be more involved in looking after other people than men – and the stresses involved with this require a different response. These (social) differences in roles may partly explain gender differences in coping with stress.

Stress

STRESS – WAYS OF MANAGING STRESS

Drug therapy is a *biological* method of managing stress

Benzodiazepines, such as **Valium**, increase the effects of a neurotransmitter called gamma-aminobutyric acid (**GABA**). GABA is an *inhibitory* **neurotransmitter** which means it *decreases* the likelihood that the neuron will fire (see page 45 for more). By increasing the effects of GABA, benzodiazepines **reduce activity in the nervous system** and counteract the effects of excitatory neurotransmitters such as serotonin. This reduced activity causes feelings of calm and reduced stress and anxiety.

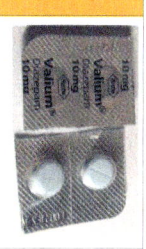

Another type of drug for stress are **beta blockers**, which work by blocking **beta-adrenergic receptors**. As mentioned on page 118, stressors cause the release of the hormones **adrenaline** and **noradrenaline**. When these hormones stimulate beta-adrenergic receptors in the heart and brain, it causes an increase in heart rate and blood flow. Beta blockers work by occupying these beta-adrenergic receptors – *blocking them* – so that **adrenaline and noradrenaline can't produce their usual effects**. This reduces the physical symptoms of stress, such as increased heart rate.

Strengths:	• **Supporting evidence:** Randomised controlled trials have found both drugs to be much more effective than placebo at reducing stress.
Weaknesses:	• **Side effects:** Both drugs produce side effects that must be weighed against the benefits of stress reduction. For example, beta blockers may cause fatigue. • **Addictive:** Benzodiazepines are highly addictive. So, while they reduce stress in the short-term, they can potentially create greater problems over the long-term.

Stress inoculation therapy is a form of *cognitive behavioural therapy*

Meichenbaum (1985) describes the **3 components of stress inoculation therapy** (SIT):
- **Conceptualisation:** The therapist helps the patient identify and understand stressors in their life. Negative strategies for dealing with stressful situations are identified. For example, some people make their stress worse with exaggerated or unrealistically negative thinking (e.g. "I can't cope with this work, I'm going to get fired").
- **Skill acquisition and rehearsal:** The therapist teaches the patient ways to deal with stressors more effectively. This may include *relaxation* strategies (e.g. breathing techniques or meditation) or *cognitive* strategies, such as replacing exaggerated thoughts with realistic alternatives.
- **Application:** The therapist and patient practice using these newly-learned skills and techniques. This may just involve visualisation or role-play at first, before using them in real-life.

Strengths:	• **Supporting evidence:** A meta-analysis by Saunders et al (1996) concluded that SIT was effective at reducing anxiety and improving performance under stress. • **Long-term:** Whereas drug therapy only lasts as long as a person takes the drugs, the techniques learned from SIT can be applied to future stressful situations.
Weaknesses:	• **Difficult:** Stress inoculation therapy is time-consuming and takes a lot of effort on behalf of the patient. As such, many patients may quit without seeing results.

STRESS – WAYS OF MANAGING STRESS

Biofeedback teaches people to *recognise* and *control* physiological processes

- **Awareness:** Machines such as heart rate and blood pressure monitors provide feedback (e.g. via a visual display on a screen) to make the patient *aware* when they're experiencing stress.
- **Control:** Next, the patient is taught ways to *control* these physiological symptoms when they occur (e.g. meditation or breathing techniques). The patient practices these techniques while paying attention to feedback from the machine (e.g. looking at heart rate on a heart rate monitor) to try and **reduce this physiological response** (e.g. trying to make heart rate go down).
- **Positive reinforcement:** Feedback from the machine can act like a sort of game, providing *positive reinforcement* (see page 33) of effective stress-reduction techniques. The increased feelings of **relaxation** also positively reinforce the stress-reduction techniques.
- **Application:** When the patient is able to control their physiological stress response, they *apply* the techniques they've learned in biofeedback to **real-life** stressful situations.

Strengths:	• **Supporting evidence:** A randomised controlled trial by Lemaire et al (2011) found biofeedback resulted in significant and lasting stress reductions (as measured by a questionnaire) that were not observed in the control group.
Weaknesses:	• **Methodological concerns and conflicting evidence:** Stress in Lemaire et al (2011) was assessed using a self-report questionnaire. But when Greenhalgh et al (2010) reviewed randomised controlled trials of biofeedback for reducing high blood pressure (an objective measure), they found no difference in results between biofeedback and placebo. This could suggest biofeedback only reduces *feelings* of stress without actually reducing the risk of stress-related illness.

Social support – e.g. from friends and family – takes different forms:

- **Instrumental support:** *Practical help.* For example, if a friend is stressed out because they can't pay their bills, instrumental support might involve giving them some money.
- **Emotional support:** Helping improve someone's mood by providing *care and comfort.* For example, if a friend is stressed out by relationship problems, emotional support may involve listening to them and empathising with their situation.
- **Esteem support:** Helping improve someone's *confidence* in their ability to deal with a stressor. For example, if a colleague is stressed out by a difficult work assignment, esteem support may involve telling them how skilled they are and reminding them of past successes.

AO3: Orth-Gomér et al (1993) conducted a 6-year longitudinal study of 736 Swedish men aged 50. The researchers found smoking and *lack of social support* were the 2 factors most strongly correlated with heart disease, which suggests social support is effective at managing stress. Further, Stachour (1998) found *quality* of social support (as measured by questionnaires) was protective against stress-related illness, but *quantity* (i.e. how many friends a person has) wasn't. Despite this research, it's not clear *how* social support reduces the risk of stress-related illness.

AGGRESSION – BIOLOGICAL MECHANISMS

The **limbic system** is the main area of the *brain* associated with aggression

Several studies point to the **amygdala** of the limbic system as playing a key role:
- Gospic et al (2011) used **fMRI scans** to measure brain activity during a game designed to provoke aggression. **Aggressive** responses were **correlated** with increased activity in the **amygdala**. Further, participants who were given drugs that reduced amygdala activity were less aggressive.
- Brain scans of **convicted murderers** by Raine et al (1997) found abnormalities in the amygdala (and other areas of the limbic system) compared to controls.

Strengths:	• **Supporting evidence:** See studies above.
Weaknesses:	• **Conflicting evidence:** There are people with limbic system abnormalities who are not overly aggressive, and aggressive people with normal limbic systems. • **Deterministic:** If aggressive behaviour is explained solely in terms of brain structures, it leaves no room for the free will of the individual (see page 73) and means people are not in control of their behaviour. This implies people cannot be held morally responsible for aggressive behaviour (as it is not freely chosen).

Low levels of the *neurotransmitter* **serotonin** may cause aggressive behaviour

Some studies suggest **low serotonin** levels increase aggression. For example:
- Virkkunen et al (1994) found that **impulsive violent offenders** in Finnish prisons had **lower serotonin** levels (as measured by 5-HIAA levels, a serotonin metabolite) compared to controls.
- Berman et al (2009) randomly assigned 80 subjects (40 with a history of aggression, 40 without) to receive either paroxetine (a drug that **increases serotonin**) or placebo. Among participants with a history of aggression, those who had been given paroxetine behaved **less aggressively** than those given placebo when playing a game that involved delivering electric shocks.

Strengths:	• **Supporting evidence:** See studies above.
Weaknesses:	• **Methodological concerns:** For example, Berman et al (2009) based their conclusions on games played in *laboratory conditions*, which may not reflect behaviours in real life. Similarly, Virkkunen et al (1994) used criminal convictions as a measure of aggression, but this may not be an accurate measure of real-life aggression. As such, these studies may lack *ecological validity*.

The *hormone* **testosterone** is heavily linked to aggressive behaviour

Testosterone is the primary sex hormone in **males** (see page 86). Studies link it to aggression, e.g.:
- When Albert et al (1989) **injected female rats** with testosterone, they behaved more aggressively.
- Van Goozen et al (1995) found that administering testosterone to **female-to-male transgender** people resulted in **more aggressive behaviour**. Conversely, male-to-female transgender people given drugs to lower their testosterone levels behaved less aggressively.

AGGRESSION – BIOLOGICAL MECHANISMS

AO3: **Strengths** of testosterone as an explanation of aggression
- **Supporting evidence:** The studies above suggest *causation*, not simply correlation because the behaviours of both rats and humans changed directly after testosterone administration.

AO3: **Weaknesses** of testosterone as an explanation of aggression
- **Conflicting evidence:** Although there is a lot of evidence supporting a link between testosterone and aggression, not all studies agree. For example, Tricker et al (1996) randomly assigned 43 men to receive either 600mg of testosterone per week or placebo but observed no differences in aggression between the two groups.

Genetics are an important biological mechanism of aggression

Whenever genetic explanations are mentioned, you know a **twin study** is never far away:
- Coccaro et al (1997) found the **concordance rate** for physical violence was **50% among identical twins** and **19% among non-identical twins**.
- Christiansen (1977) analysed the concordance rates for **criminal convictions** (a proxy for aggression) among 3,586 pairs of twins. Among males, concordance rates were **35% for identical twins** and **12% for non-identical twins**. Among females, the concordance rates were **21% for identical twins** and **8% for non-identical twins**.

The **MAOA gene** is *especially* associated with aggression. It's responsible for producing **monoamine oxidase A** (MAOA), which is an **enzyme** that processes neurotransmitters such as *serotonin*. The **low-activity** form of the gene (*MAOA-L*, sometimes called the "**warrior gene**") results in lower levels of MAOA and is associated with aggression.

The link between the MAOA gene and aggression was discovered by **Brunner et al (1993)** in a study of a family in the Netherlands. 5 members of this family had a history of impulsive aggression and crime. Genetic analysis revealed that **all 5 had dysfunctional MAOA genes**, which resulted in an MAOA deficiency. The correlation between the MAOA gene and aggression further supports genetic explanations of aggression.

Strengths:	• **Supporting evidence:** See studies above. • **Supports other explanations:** Genetic explanations may tie in with the other biological mechanisms described above. For example, a person may have genetics that predispose them to low serotonin activity, or genetics that encode for limbic system abnormalities, which in turn causes aggression.
Weaknesses:	• **Other factors:** If aggression was 100% genetic, concordance rates among identical twins would be 100%. However, the twin studies outlined above found concordance rates to be lower than 50% among identical twins. Similarly, many people have the MAOA-L gene and are not aggressive. This all suggests other factors besides genetics are needed for a complete explanation of aggression.

Aggression

AGGRESSION – ETHOLOGICAL EXPLANATIONS

Ethological explanations of aggression are based on *animal* behaviour

Lorenz (1966) argued aggression is an **innate** response that **evolved** to help animals survive and pass on their genes – e.g. to help win competitions for mates or territory. He argued that, just like hunger builds up until an animal eats food, **aggression builds up** until it gets released. Something in the environment (e.g. a rival animal) triggers an **innate releasing mechanism**, which triggers a **fixed action pattern** of behaviour that releases the built-up aggression. The cycle then **repeats**.

Innate releasing mechanisms are biologically hard-wired pathways...

...such as brain structures/neural pathways responsible for building up **aggression** and releasing it in response to **environmental cues** (e.g. the red belly of a rival stickleback – see below). When the innate releasing mechanism is *triggered*, it releases a **fixed action pattern of behaviour**.

Fixed action patterns are pre-set *routines* of aggressive behaviour...

...that are **universal** (i.e. the same) across the entire species. Once a fixed action pattern is initiated, the animal will **keep going** until the behaviour pattern is complete. For example:

- During the mating season, male **stickleback fish** build nests where females lay eggs.
- (Male sticklebacks also develop **red bellies** during this time).
- If another male enters their territory, the stickleback will **attack** it.

Tinbergen (1952) demonstrates how fixed action patterns in sticklebacks are universal. When he presented male sticklebacks with **models** of fish with red bellies (even when the model was not realistic looking – see above), they all responded with the **same fixed action pattern of fighting behaviour**. The universal nature of this behaviour suggests the fixed action pattern is **innate**.

AO3: **Strengths** of ethological explanations of aggression

- **Supporting evidence:** There are many examples of fixed action patterns in animals beyond Tinbergen (1952). For example, if an egg (or similar looking object) is placed near a Grelag goose, it will instinctively try to roll the egg into its nest in a fixed action pattern.

AO3: **Weaknesses** of ethological explanations of aggression

- **Conflicting evidence:** Schleidt (1974) argues that 'fixed' action patterns are often quite varied. For this reason, some ethologists prefer the term *modal action pattern*.
- **Methodological concerns:** Sticklebacks (or even higher primates like chimpanzees) are very different to humans, so ethological explanations of aggression may not be valid in humans.
- **Pre-meditated aggression:** Ethological explanations can't explain pre-meditated aggression. For example, a pre-meditated murder is the result of cognitive processes and consideration rather than a fixed action pattern as an immediate response to an environmental cue.

AGGRESSION – EVOLUTIONARY EXPLANATIONS

Evolutionary explanations say aggression has *survival* advantages

And if you're more likely to survive, you're **more likely to pass on your genes**.

One way aggression could help an animal survive is by helping it **gain access to resources**. For example, aggression (physical or otherwise) may be an effective way to gain resources such as food or territory. Having resources like food, for example, mean you are less likely to starve to death.

Aggression also **protects against injury and death**. For example, if you don't fight back when someone is aggressive with you, then they might keep going until they kill you.

Evolutionary explanations say aggression may have *reproductive* advantages

Genes for aggressive behaviour may also increase the likelihood that a human **reproduces** and passes on their genes. This is more true for **men** rather than women, for the following reasons:

- Aggression helps **win competitions for mates:** Anisogamy (see page 77) means women must be selective over who they have children with. As such, **men compete with other men for status** and resources so that women will choose them as a mate. Pinker (1997) argues that competing for women is the **main reason** aggression evolved in men.
- Aggression may **deter infidelity**: Anisogamy also means women can be certain of paternity (i.e. that their children are theirs) but men can't. Raising another man's child is evolutionarily disadvantageous so men may have evolved aggression to prevent women from cheating on them.

AO3: **Strengths** of evolutionary explanations of aggression

- **Explanatory power:** Men are generally more aggressive than women (see page 86). The evolutionary explanation can explain this as aggression means males are more likely to win competitions for female mates, which makes them more likely to pass on their genes.
- **Supporting evidence:** Wilson and Daly (1985) looked at data from 690 murders in Detroit in 1972 and found the vast majority were committed by and perpetrated against young men – the most common reason being "status competition". This fits with the evolutionary explanation that men evolved aggression in order to gain status and compete for females.

AO3: **Weaknesses** of evolutionary explanations of aggression

- **Other factors:** If aggression was 100% explained by evolution, aggressive behaviour would be uniform across the human species. However, there are significant differences in aggression between different cultures. For example, aggression among the !Kung people of the Kalahari desert results in *loss* of status, whereas aggression among the Yanomami people of South America is correlated with *high* status. These differences suggest that other factors – such as cultural influences – are needed for a complete explanation of human aggression.
- **Methodological concerns:** Evolutionary hypotheses are difficult to test because evolution takes so long to occur. We can't run a controlled experiment over *millions of years*, say, that compares genes for aggression vs. less aggressive genes to see which become more common.

Aggression

AGGRESSION – PSYCHOLOGICAL EXPLANATIONS

Bandura's Bobo studies support a **social learning explanation of aggression**

See page 34 for full details of Bandura et al (1961), but the key take-away was that children were more likely to behave **aggressively** towards the Bobo doll if they'd seen a **role model** do so beforehand. This supports the social learning theory explanation of aggression, that aggressive behaviour is the result of **observation** and **imitation** of **role models**.

A complete social learning explanation of aggression will also reference **mediating processes**: The *cognitive* factors in between observation and imitation that determine whether someone decides to imitate a behaviour or not. For example, if someone observes the role model being rewarded for aggressive behaviour, this provides **motivation** to imitate that behaviour and makes aggression more likely. There is also **vicarious reinforcement:** If a person sees the role model rewarded for behaving aggressively, they are more likely to imitate the aggressive behaviour.

Strengths:	• **Supporting evidence:** See Bandura et al (1961 and 1963) on page 34. • **Practical applications:** If aggression is learned through observation and imitation of role models, then aggressive behaviour can be reduced by altering the role models and their behaviour. For example, aggressive role models in the media could be replaced with non-aggressive role models.
Weaknesses:	• **Doesn't explain all forms of aggression:** For example, a person who is threatened may act aggressively towards the threat in order to *protect themselves*, not because they are imitating the behaviours of a role model. • **Other factors:** Boys showed more aggression than girls in Bandura's studies. This suggests other factors (e.g. testosterone levels – see page 127) are needed for a complete explanation of aggressive behaviour.

De-individuation increases the likelihood of aggressive behaviour

De-individuation is when a person **loses a sense of personal identity** and **personal responsibility**. According to the de-individuation explanation, **anonymity** (e.g. by being part of a large crowd or wearing a disguise) makes a person more likely to behave aggressively.

Festinger et al (1952) coined the phrase **de-individuation** to describe a phenomenon where people in crowds **lose their sense of personal identity and responsibility** and instead identify with the morals and beliefs of a group. This feeling of anonymity in the crowd means people who might ordinarily be polite and civil may act aggressively and violently. A classic example of this would be a football fan who gets swept up in the crowd and behaves violently.

In addition to anonymity in a crowd, anonymity in other ways may cause de-individuation. For example, Dodd (1985) got 203 students to anonymously describe what they would do **if nobody could identify them** or hold them responsible for their actions. 36% of the responses involved some form of **antisocial behaviour**, with the most common answer being to **rob a bank**.

AGGRESSION – PSYCHOLOGICAL EXPLANATIONS

AO3: **Strengths** of the de-individuation explanation of aggression

- **Supporting evidence:** In Zimbardo (1969), participants were randomly allocated to either an *individuated* group (where they wore name badges met the other participants) or a *de-individuated* group (where they wore hoods and weren't referred to by name) and completed a task where they could deliver electric shocks to a confederate. Participants in the de-individuated group delivered shocks for twice as long as participants in the other group.
- **Explanatory power:** De-individuation might explain why online abuse is so common; people feel more *anonymous* and de-individuated when they're behind a screen.

AO3: **Weaknesses** of the de-individuation explanation of aggression

- **Conflicting evidence:** In Gergen et al (1973), participants were put together in a dark room so they couldn't see each other (i.e. they were de-individuated) and told to do whatever they wanted. Rather than behaving *aggressively*, the participants would *kiss and touch* each other.
- **Doesn't explain all forms of aggression:** People often behave aggressively in situations where they are *not* de-individuated, so other factors are needed to fully explain aggression.

Dollard et al (1939) proposed the **frustration-aggression hypothesis**

According to this hypothesis, **aggression** is a response to **frustration**. Frustration is defined as **being prevented from achieving a goal**. For example, if you're trying to beat someone at tennis (your goal) but they keep beating you, this causes feelings of frustration.

The likelihood of aggressive behaviour is *proportional* to the level of frustration. The **more frustrated** someone is, the **more likely they are to act aggressively**. For example, if a goal is really important and something prevents them from achieving it, that person is more likely to get frustrated and behave aggressively than if it was a goal they didn't care about.

Further, the **consequences** of aggressive behaviour may *increase* or *decrease* the likelihood of aggression in response to frustration. For example, if aggressive behaviour is likely to help achieve your goal, then aggressive behaviour becomes more likely. But if aggressive behaviour is likely to result in punishment, or won't help achieve a goal, then aggressive behaviour is less likely.

Strengths:	• **Supporting evidence:** Geen (1968) conducted an experiment where male subjects were frustrated while trying to complete a jigsaw puzzle. After the jigsaw, subjects were able to deliver an electric shock to a confederate. Participants in groups that had been frustrated delivered more intense electric shocks than those in the control (non-frustrated) group.
Weaknesses:	• **Conflicting evidence:** However, Buss (1966) found no correlation between level of frustration and aggression, weakening support for the hypothesis. • **Methodological concerns:** Much of the evidence supporting the frustration-aggression hypothesis comes from games conducted in laboratory conditions. As such, the frustration-aggression hypothesis may lack ecological validity.

AGGRESSION – INSTITUTIONAL AGGRESSION IN PRISONS

Aggression in **prisons** is much higher than in ordinary contexts – *why?*

There are 2 types of answer: **Dispositional explanations** and **situational explanations**.
- **Dispositional:** People sent to prison have a *natural disposition* towards aggressive behaviour.
- **Situational:** The *prison environment* makes ordinary people behave more aggressively.

The **importation model** is a **dispositional explanation** proposed by Irwin and Cressey (1962). According to this explanation, aggressive norms and behaviours are *imported* **into the prison from the outside.**

For example, people may be part of a **thief or convict subculture** that follows a criminal code that is more aggressive than the social norms of ordinary, **legitimate**, subcultures. For whatever reason (biological factors, social factors, etc.), people from these subcultures have a **disposition** towards these behaviours – *they act this way even when they aren't in prison*. And because these behaviours are more aggressive, these people are more likely to commit crimes and get arrested. This explains why aggressive behaviour is more common in prison – aggressive people *get sent there.*

Supporting evidence: DeLisi et al (2005) supports the dispositional explanation. They looked at the prison records of 831 US male inmates and found a strong correlation between gang membership and prison violence. This correlation supports the dispositional explanation that the increased aggression of gang members is *imported* into prisons.

The **deprivation model** is a **situational explanation** described by Sykes (1958). According to this model, the **prison environment** deprives inmates of the following **5 things:**
- **Liberty:** Prisoners are deprived of the freedom to go where they want.
- **Goods and services:** Prisoners can't access the goods and services they want.
- **Relationships:** Heterosexual prisoners do not have access to opposite-sex partners and so are deprived of sex and the emotional intimacy of romantic relationships.
- **Autonomy:** The lives of prisoners are controlled – e.g. when they go outside, what they eat, etc.
- **Security:** Prisons are violent environments and so prisoners do not feel safe. As such, prisoners are constantly on edge, which makes aggression and violence more likely.

According to Sykes, these 5 '**pains of imprisonment**' *make people* behave more aggressively.

Supporting evidence: Megargee (1977) found that disruptive behaviour was highly *correlated* with crowding within prisons, supporting the situational explanation.

Conflicting evidence: Camp and Gaes (2005) analysed data from 561 US male prisoners, who were randomly allocated to either a low-security California prison or a high-security California prison. Despite the differing prison environments, there was no significant difference in aggression between the two groups, which weakens support for situational explanations.

AO3: Both situational and dispositional explanations likely play a role. For example, Jiang and Fisher-Giorlando (2002) found aggression towards *prison staff* was best explained by *situational* factors whereas aggression towards *other inmates* was best explained by the *importation model*. Rather than arguing just one explanation is right, you can always take an interactionist approach.

AGGRESSION – MEDIA INFLUENCE ON AGGRESION

The media and video games may **desensitise** people to violence and aggression

Example: The first time you watched someone get murdered in a horror film, you were probably pretty shocked. But as an adult, these sorts of films don't produce the same response.

The natural reaction to aggression and violence is anxiety. But **repeated exposure** to such stimuli may **reduce** this emotional response – a person becomes *desensitised* to violence and aggression. In theory, this desensitisation increases aggression because natural emotional reactions that would *prevent* aggressive behaviour (e.g. anxiety, stress, revulsion, etc.) are not as strong.

Supporting evidence: Krahé et al (2011) measured participants' skin conductance (see page 122) as they watched a violent video clip. Participants who regularly watched violent films or played violent video games (as determined by questionnaire) demonstrated lower levels of stress when watching the violent video clip compared to those who didn't, suggesting they were desensitised.

Behaviour in video games is **disinhibited**, which may transfer to real life

Inhibitions restrain us from behaving inappropriately or aggressively in real life. But these **inhibitions aren't present** in video games. In theory, inhibitions that normally prevent someone from behaving aggressively are **worn down** when playing violent video games, making a person more likely to behave aggressively in real life.

Example: When playing a video game, there are no *real* consequences for attacking a random person on the street – the character can't actually fight back, you can't actually get arrested, and there is no social penalty. Things that inhibit aggressive behaviour aren't there in video games.

Aggressive behaviour in the media may **prime** people to copy it

Cognitive priming is the idea that aggressive behaviours **seen** in the media are **remembered** and thus '*prime*' a person to behave similarly when in similar situations. We **absorb** certain **scripts** for behaviour from media influences, and then **play out these scripts** in similar situations.

Example: A man who watches a drama where a husband and wife argue over a comment made during dinner may remember and on some level *learn* this behaviour. If the man's wife makes a negative comment during dinner, he is primed to argue with her like he saw in the drama.

AO3: A meta-analysis of 136 studies across multiple cultures by Anderson et al (2010) found that exposure to violent video games was *correlated* with increases in aggressive behaviour and aggressive thoughts. In general, a good meta-analysis is a high standard of evidence (see page 63) because it includes data from multiple studies, so this is strong support for the hypothesis that exposure to aggression in the media – in particular video games – increases aggressive behaviour. However, as always, correlation does not necessarily prove causation. It could be, for example, that when people are feeling aggressive they seek out video games as a source of catharsis.

FORENSIC PSYCHOLOGY – OFFENDER PROFILING

The **top-down approach** *starts with the general profile* then fills in the details

Police in **America** tend to use the **top-down approach**. Douglas et al (1986) describes the sequence of the FBI's top-down approach to offender profiling: First, data is *assimilated* (i.e. evidence from the scene is gathered), then the culprit is classified into 1 of 2 **offender profiles**:

Organised **offender profile**	*Disorganised* **offender profile**
Above-average or high intelligence	Below-average or low intelligence
Crime is planned and thought out	Crime is impulsive with little or no planning
Clears evidence from the scene	Evidence left behind
Skilled (e.g. has an advanced job)	Unskilled (e.g. low-skill job or unemployed)
Socially and sexually competent (e.g. married)	Socially/sexually incompetent (e.g. lives alone)

After *reconstructing* the crime (timeline of events, etc.), the profiler then generates a profile. This involves filling in more **specific details** about the criminal – e.g. physical and psychological characteristics – beyond those described in the general organised or disorganised profiles.

AO3: **Strengths** of the top-down approach to offender profiling

- **Supporting evidence:** Gregg McCrary and Ed Grant used the top-down approach to develop a profile of the man responsible for the murders of several prostitutes in the late 1980s. This profile turned out to match for the offender, Arthur Shawcross, who was found guilty.
- **Evidence-based:** The organised and disorganised offender profiles were developed by the FBI from interview and data from 36 US murderers, including Ted Bundy and Charles Manson.

AO3: **Weaknesses** of the top-down approach to offender profiling

- **Conflicting evidence:** Pinizzotto and Finkel (1990) compared the accuracy of profiles created by 6 US-trained profilers (using a top-down approach) against profiles created by control groups. When participants had to create a profile for a sexual assault case, the profiles created by the trained profilers were no more accurate than profiles created by the control groups.
- **Overly simplistic:** For example, it's possible that a high IQ person could commit a spontaneous and unplanned murder in a fit of rage. However, high IQ is a characteristic of the organised profile, but a spontaneous crime is characteristic of the disorganised profile and so sticking too rigidly to these offender profiles could lead to inaccurate profiling.

The **bottom-up approach** *starts with specific details* and builds up from there

Police in **Britain** tend to use a **bottom-up approach**. This approach starts with the criminal's characteristics and develops the profile based on that. In other words, it's the opposite way round to top-down: Specific details of the crime come first and the general profile comes second.

FORENSIC PSYCHOLOGY - OFFENDER PROFILING

Investigative psychology is a key part of the bottom-up approach

A key concept within investigative psychology, described in Canter (1994), is **interpersonal coherence**. This means that the way a criminal behaves **when they are committing a crime** will be consistent with how they behave **in everyday life**. For example, a killer who commits aggressive murders is likely to be an aggressive person in general. So, if there is evidence of an aggressive murder, the profile of the suspect will include an aggressive personality.

Statistical analysis is used to identify common themes and patterns of behaviour across several crime scenes (e.g. type of victim, what acts are committed, how evidence is disposed of, etc.). This can be used to identify crimes committed by the same person. Because of *interpersonal coherence*, this data may also provide details about the criminal and narrow down the range of suspects.

Geographical profiling uses statistics to work out the offender's rough *location*

The **circle hypothesis** says that serial offenders carry out their crimes within a *geographical circle*. The circle hypothesis also predicts that the offender's home will be within this circle.

Canter and Larkin (1993) tested the circle hypothesis by studying the locations of sexual assaults committed by 45 British serial offenders. They found that 39 of the 45 offenders (87%) lived within the circle predicted by the circle hypothesis, suggesting it is valid. However, they also describe a *commuter model*, where the offender travels from home to a familiar area and then commits crimes within a range of that area.

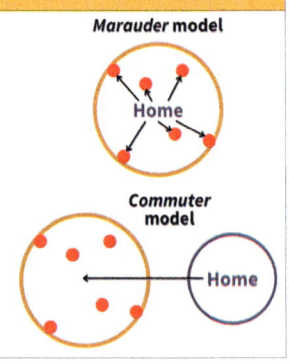

Marauder model

Commuter model

AO3: **Strengths** of the bottom-up approach to offender profiling

- **Supporting evidence:** Canter used bottom-up profiling to develop a profile of the 'Railway Rapist' – responsible for several rapes and murders of women near railway stations in the 1980s. Canter's profile was of a man in his mid-late 20s, with a criminal record, working a semi-skilled job, poor relationships with women, knowledge of the railways, and living near the crime scenes. This profile turned out to closely match the offender, John Duffy.
- **Wider range of applications:** Whereas the top-down approach only really works for crimes with a particular *modus operandi*, such as rape and murder, the bottom-up approach has much wider applications. For example, geographical profiling only requires the locations of the crimes, so this bottom-up approach can be applied to basically any type of crime.

AO3: **Weaknesses** of the bottom-up approach to offender profiling

- **Conflicting evidence:** Copson (1995) surveyed 184 UK police officers on the use of offender profiles created by trained profilers. Although 83% of the police surveyed said the profiles were 'useful', just 3% of profiles created by trained profilers resulted in identification of the offender. This suggests bottom-up profiles are not particularly useful in practice.

BIOLOGICAL EXPLANATIONS OF CRIMINAL BEHAVIOUR

Atavistic form says criminals are savage evolutionary throwbacks

If that sounds a bit wild, it's described as *'an historic approach'* on the syllabus because most scientists don't take it seriously today.

An **atavism** is when an ancestral genetic trait that has disappeared reappears – like a human that grows a vestigial tail (it happens). According to 19th century criminologist Cesare Lombroso, criminals have more in common with our evolutionary ancestors than normal humans do. Hence, Lombroso's theory is called **atavistic form**: The idea is that criminality represents the behaviours of earlier, more savage, pre-human species – like Neanderthals or homo habilis.

Lombroso argued that atavism also results in criminals having **distinctive facial features**, such as a **heavy brow**, strong jaw, and **extra fingers, toes, or nipples**. Further, Lombroso argued, *different types* of criminal have typical facial features. For example, he argued that murderers typically have curly hair and bloodshot eyes, whereas sex offenders have swollen and fleshy lips.

Strengths:	• **Supporting evidence:** Lombroso collected measurements of the facial features of thousands of Italian criminals, which he used to support his theory. • **Historical influence:** Although not a popular explanation nowadays, Lombroso played an important role in advancing criminology and scientific explanations of criminal behaviour. Prior to Lombroso, explanations of criminal behaviour tended to be religious (e.g. bad spirits, Satan, etc.) or moralistic (e.g. weak-mindedness). In providing an evolutionary explanation, Lombroso paved the way for more scientific explanations of criminal behaviour, such as genetics.
Weaknesses:	• **Methodological concerns:** Lombroso did not use a non-criminal control group to compare his measurements of criminals' facial features against. Without comparing the features of criminals against the features of non-criminals, it's impossible to say whether criminals do actually have distinctive features that differentiate them from non-criminals, as Lombroso claimed.

There is evidence for genetic explanations of criminal behaviour though

For example, Christiansen's (1977) twin study found **concordance rates** for criminal convictions among were **35% for identical male twins** and **12% for non-identical male twins**.

Adoption studies also support a link between genetics and criminal behaviour. For example, Mednick et al (1984) looked at 14,427 adopted children and compared the likelihood that a child would grow up to engage in criminal activity if their *biological* parent or *adoptive* parents were convicted criminals. The results are in the table opposite:

	Criminal *adoptive* parent	Non-criminal *adoptive* parent
Criminal *biological* parent	24.5%	20%
Non-criminal *biological* parent	14.7%	13.5%

These results suggest *biological* factors (genetics) are more important than environmental factors.

Forensic Psychology

BIOLOGICAL EXPLANATIONS OF CRIMINAL BEHAVIOUR

AO3: **Strengths** of genetic explanations of criminal behaviour

- **Supporting evidence:** In addition to the studies above, Brunner et al (1993) – see page 128 – suggests the MAOA-L gene may explain criminal behaviour.

AO3: **Weaknesses** of genetic explanations of criminal behaviour

- **Other factors:** If criminal behaviour was entirely determined by genetics, the concordance rate would be 100% among identical twins. However, Christiansen (1977) found the concordance rates for criminal behaviour among identical twins to be less than 100%, which suggests other factors are needed for a complete explanation of criminal behaviour.
- **Methodological concerns:** Adoptees are often raised by their biological parents for a long time before being adopted, so the correlation between having a biological parent who is a criminal and becoming a criminal seen in Mednick et al (1984) could be due – at least in part – to environmental factors rather than genetics.

Neural explanations include *brain structures* and *neurotransmitters*

Raine et al (1997) compared **brain scans** conducted on 41 convicted murderers and with **brain scans** conducted on 41 control participants. The researchers observed that the murderers had reduced activity in the **prefrontal cortex**, the superior parietal gyrus, and left angular gyrus, and the corpus callosum compared to the control group. This suggests that criminals may have certain **brain structures** that cause criminal behaviour.

Neurotransmitters may also explain criminal behaviour. For example, Brunner et al (1993) – see page 128 – demonstrates a link between the MAOA-L gene and criminal behaviour. This gene results in abnormal processing of neurotransmitters, such as **serotonin**, which may be the mechanism through which these genes increase violent behaviour.

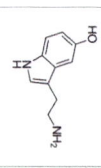

Strengths:	- **Supporting evidence:** See studies above.
Weaknesses:	- **Small sample sizes:** The population of serious criminals (e.g. murderers) are hard to gain scientific access to. Further, brain-scanning tools (such as fMRI) are highly expensive. These considerations mean studies of neural explanations of criminal behaviour often use small sample sizes. These small sample sizes mean such studies may not be valid when applied to the wider population. - **Ethical issues:** An implication of Raine's research is that brain scans in childhood could be used to identify potentially violent criminals of the future. This policy, if enacted, could potentially reduce crime but is socially sensitive because it could lead to discrimination against people with these brain structures. - **Conflicting evidence:** Evidence linking neurotransmitters and aggressive or criminal behaviour is often contradictory. For example, the MAOA-L gene results in *high* serotonin and is associated with criminal behaviour, but some studies suggest *low* serotonin causes aggressive behaviour (see page 127 for more).

Forensic Psychology

PSYCHOLOGICAL EXPLANATIONS OF CRIMINAL BEHAVIOUR

Cognitive distortions may explain criminal behaviour

One such example of a cognitive distortion is **hostile attribution bias**, which is where a person has a bias that causes them to **misinterpret** people's actions as in some way **hostile** or **negative**.
Example: Someone with hostile attribution bias may interpret an innocent look from someone as aggressive, which may cause them to respond aggressively or violently.

Supporting evidence: Schönenberg and Jusyte (2013) showed pictures of 'emotionally ambiguous' faces to 55 violent offenders and 55 matched control subjects. The violent offenders were more likely to interpret these ambiguous stimuli as aggressive than the controls were, which supports the explanation that hostile attribution bias may explain (violent) criminal behaviour.

Another cognitive distortion associated with criminal behaviour is **minimalisation**. This is where a person **downplays** how bad their criminal behaviour really is (e.g. by using rationalisations).
Example: A thief may tell himself that his victim was rich and he's poor so it's fair to steal from them. Or a violent offender may tell herself that an assault wasn't that bad.

Supporting evidence: Pollock and Hashmall (1991) conducted a *content analysis* (see page 58) of the clinical records of 86 child molesters. They found the records often contained attempts to *minimise* the seriousness of their crimes. Excuses including denying their actions were sexual (35%) and arguing that the actions were consensual (36%).

AO3: **Weaknesses** of cognitive distortions as an explanation of criminal behaviour

- **Limited applications:** There are many types of crime that cognitive distortions don't explain well. For example, it's easy to see how hostile attribution bias could lead to *impulsive* violence (e.g. the offender misinterprets an innocent look from someone and assaults them) but it's hard to see how this bias could explain *planned* violence (e.g. a pre-meditated murder).

Kohlberg (1984) says there are **3 stages of moral development and reasoning:**

Pre-conventional morality	*Bad* = an action that gets *punished*. *Good* = an action that gets *rewarded*.	Actions are chosen according to **self-interest** (e.g. if I don't get caught it's OK to steal).
Conventional morality	*Bad* = an action that others *disapprove* of. *Good* = an action that others *approve* of.	Actions are chosen according to wider **societal interests** (e.g. I shouldn't steal because it's against the law and people would judge me).
Post-conventional morality	Bad = an action that violates abstract *moral laws*. Good = an action in line with moral laws.	Actions are chosen according to **abstract moral principles** (e.g. Even though it's against the law, it's OK to steal in situations where stealing results in a greater good).

Another explanation of criminal behaviour is that criminals don't **cognitively** progress past the *pre-conventional* morality stage. According to Kohlberg, this makes them **more likely to commit crime**.

PSYCHOLOGICAL EXPLANATIONS OF CRIMINAL BEHAVIOUR

AO3: **Strengths** of moral reasoning as an explanation of criminal behaviour

- **Supporting evidence:** Palmer and Hollin (1998) used questionnaires to compare the moral reasoning abilities of 126 male convicted offenders with 122 male non-offenders. The researchers found that male offenders had significantly poorer moral reasoning compared to the male non-offenders, supporting moral reasoning as an explanation of criminal behaviour.

AO3: **Weaknesses** of genetic explanations of criminal behaviour

- **Limited applications:** Thornton and Reid (1982) found criminals convicted of *robbery* were more likely to be at the pre-conventional morality stage than criminals convicted of *assault*. This suggests moral reasoning is a better explanation of some criminal behaviours than others.
- **Other factors:** There are examples of criminals of all stages of moral reasoning, which suggests that other factors besides pre-conventional moral reasoning (e.g. biological factors or learning approaches) are needed for a complete explanation of criminal behaviour.

Eysenck's (1947) **theory of personality** may explain criminal behaviour

According to Eysenck, our biology (genetics) *predisposes* us to certain personality traits. There are **3 main personality trait spectrums** that are measured by the *Eysenck Personality Questionnaire*: Extroversion vs. introversion, neurotic vs. stable, and psychotic vs. non-psychotic. Applied to **criminal behaviour**, the following traits make someone more likely to commit crime:

- **High extroversion:** A highly *extroverted* person is more likely to take risks and act impulsively, increasing the likelihood of criminal behaviour. Extroverts are also thrill-seekers, so the excitement of criminal behaviour is likely to be more appealing.
- **High neuroticism:** A highly *neurotic* person feels negative emotions more strongly, which increases the likelihood of them committing a criminal act in the heat of the moment.
- **High psychoticism:** A *psychotic* person lacks empathy, doesn't feel guilt, is aggressive and unconventional. A highly psychotic person is more likely to commit a crime because they are not put off by feelings of guilt or empathy for a potential victim. High psychoticism is also associated with increased aggression, increasing the likelihood of violent criminal behaviour.

Strengths:	• **Supporting evidence:** Furnham (1984) tested 210 subjects using Eysenck's personality theory, a social skills test, and a test of anomie (which basically means moral values). Of these 3 tests, the results of Eysenck's personality theory were the most accurate predictors of criminal behaviour.
Weaknesses:	• **Some factors more important than others:** For example, the correlation between being highly *psychotic* and criminal behaviour is much stronger than the correlation between being highly *neurotic* and criminal behaviour. • **Methodological concerns:** Self-report techniques, such as the *Eysenck Personality Questionnaire*, are often unreliable as the answer the participant gives varies depending on their mood.

Forensic Psychology

PSYCHOLOGICAL EXPLANATIONS OF CRIMINAL BEHAVIOUR

Sutherland's (1939) **differential association theory** is a *learning* explanation

According to differential association theory, criminal behaviour is learned by **associating with people who commit crimes**. Through associations with criminals, a person learns both specific *methods* of crime (e.g. how to source and supply drugs) as well as certain *attitudes* towards crime (e.g. that being a successful thief drug dealer is worthy of respect and that police are the bad guys).

A person becomes more likely to engage in criminal activity *the more* of these criminal differential associations they have, *the closer the relationships* to these criminals are (e.g. parents and siblings), and the *longer the duration of time spent interacting with them is*. Sutherland (1939) argues these factors can be used to *mathematically predict* how likely a person is to be a criminal.

Strengths:	• **Supporting evidence:** Alarid et al (2000) applied differential association theory to 1,153 newly-imprisoned criminals and found that it could accurately explain their criminal behaviour (e.g. which crimes they committed) in many cases. • **Explanatory power:** Differential association theory is able to explain why rates of recidivism (see page 142) are so high: People who are sent to prison will be surrounded by other criminals who teach and encourage criminal behaviour.
Weaknesses:	• **Exceptions:** There are many examples of people raised around criminals who don't go on to commit crimes and vice versa, weakening support for the theory.

Psychodynamic explanations of criminal behaviour focus on the superego

According to Freud, the **superego** is the '**moral**' part of personality (see page 40). Blackburn (1993) describes 3 ways the superego may fail to develop properly, resulting in criminal behaviour:

- **Under-developed:** If the same-sex parent is absent during the *phallic stage* (3-5 years), the child is unable to *identify* with them and *internalise* their values into their superego (see page 90 for more). This under-developed (weak) superego means the ego is less likely to feel guilt and thus more likely to give in to the (potentially criminal) impulses of the id.
- **Over-developed:** If the superego is over-developed (too strong), the person may feel excessive guilt. However, rather than making them *less likely* to commit crime, an over-developed superego makes a person *more likely* to commit crime because of an *unconscious desire to be caught* and punished in order to alleviate the intense feelings of guilt created by the superego.
- **Deviant :** The child successfully *identifies* with their same-sex parent and *internalises* their values into their own superego. However, the same-sex parent's values are *deviant* (e.g. the boy's father is a criminal), which the child internalises, making them more likely to commit crimes.

AO3: In addition to the usual criticisms of Freud (e.g. the theory is unscientific, unfalsifiable, etc. - see page 41), there is also conflicting evidence. According to Freud, women have weaker superegos than men. But if this were true, women should commit *more* crimes than men because women would be more likely to have an underdeveloped superego. However, the *opposite* is true, which suggests that psychodynamic explanations of criminal behaviour are inaccurate.

Forensic Psychology

DEALING WITH CRIMINAL BEHAVIOUR – CUSTODIAL SENTENCING

Custodial sentencing (i.e. sending criminals to prison) has several aims:

- **Retribution:** This is about justice – criminals suffer in exchange for the suffering *they* caused.
- **Rehabilitation:** Helping offenders so that they are less likely to commit crimes in the future.
- **Deterrence:** Prison is an negative consequence of criminal behaviour and so this makes the offender (and the general public) less likely to commit crimes.
- **Protection:** Imprisoning an offender also protects the public from them committing further crimes. For example, a serial killer will be unable to kill any more people while locked up in prison.

The psychological effects of custodial sentencing can include:

- **Institutionalisation:** If someone spends too long in prison, they may come to **see prison life as normal** and find life outside of prison difficult. For example, a homeless person may come to *prefer* life in prison (e.g. the routine, regular meals, and shelter) to life on the street.
- **Mental health problems:** The mental breakdowns of 'prisoners' in the Stanford prison study (page 6) demonstrates potential mental health issues resulting from imprisonment (though, as an *experiment*, this study may lack ecological validity). However, Fazel et al (2011) found rates of **suicide** in prison were roughly **3 times higher** than in the general population.

Recidivism – i.e. *reoffending* – rates after being released from prison are high

According to the UK Ministry of Justice proven reoffending statistics, **around 25% of adult offenders reoffend within 1 year** of being convicted of a crime.

However, recidivism is *negatively correlated* with length of sentence. For example, offenders given custodial sentences longer than 10 years are significantly less likely to reoffend (~10% recidivism rate) than offenders given custodial sentences of 6 months or less (~60% recidivism rate).

AO3: **Strengths** of custodial sentencing

- **Positive outcomes:** Rehabilitation schemes in prison may result in the offender changing their life for the better. For example, an offender who used crime to support themselves financially may learn skills that enable them to make an honest living upon release. This results in a positive contribution to society and gives the offender a second chance.

AO3: **Weaknesses** of custodial sentencing

- **Negative outcomes on criminal behaviour:** For example, institutionalised prisoners may be more likely to commit crimes when released, which is the opposite of deterrence. Similarly, prison may reinforce criminal behaviour (e.g. differential associations may reinforce criminal values and teach better methods of crime), which is the opposite of rehabilitation. These criticisms are supported by the high rates of recidivism described above.
- **Negative psychological outcomes:** E.g. Fazel et al (2011) described above.

Forensic Psychology

OTHER WAYS OF DEALING WITH CRIMINAL BEHAVIOUR

Behaviour modification uses *operant conditioning* to discourage criminality

An example of a behaviour modification techniques is the use of **token economies** (like are used to treat schizophrenia – see page 109). In a *prison* token economy, **offenders earn tokens** for **good behaviour** (e.g. following the rules, participating in rehabilitation programs, etc.) and these tokens can be used to buy things (e.g. food and cigarettes), which **positively reinforces** good behaviour.

Strengths:	• **Supporting evidence:** Milan and McKee (1976) found token economies were more effective at improving prisoner behaviour (e.g. keeping a clean cell and completing tasks) compared to direct orders or praise for good behaviour.
Weaknesses:	• **Not effective long term:** Once a prisoner leaves prison and is no longer incentivised by tokens, they may lapse back into criminal behaviour.

Anger management CBT for criminal offenders has 3 stages:

- **Cognitive preparation:** The therapist will help the offender reflect back on times when they have been angry in the past and identify potential triggers that make them angry.
- **Skill acquisition:** The therapist teaches skills to help manage anger in anger-inducing situations.
- **Application practice:** The therapist and the offender practice using the newly-learned skills in situations that may require them (e.g. role-playing anger-inducing scenarios).

Strengths:	• **Supporting evidence:** Ireland (2004) compared anger levels of 50 prisoners who underwent anger management therapy with a control group of 37 prisoners who didn't. In the anger management group, mean anger ratings (as measured by questionnaire) fell from 42.7 *before* therapy to 27.3 *after* therapy. In the control group, mean anger ratings did not change significantly (39.7 vs. 36.6).
Weaknesses:	• **Only useful for offenders whose crimes were the result of anger.**

Restorative justice is about making amends with victims and undoing damage

In the case of *vandalism*, for example, restorative justice might require the vandal to **fix** what they damaged. With something like *assault*, restorative justice may involve **communication** between offender and victim – e.g., via in-person meeting or letter-writing – where the victim can express how they were affected and the offender can express their **remorse** and **apologise**.

AO3: Restorative justice only works if both offender and victim *consent* to the program, which limits its potential applications. It's also highly important that restorative justice programs do not cause the victim any further trauma. Despite these limitations, there is good supporting evidence: A meta-analysis by Latimer et al (2005) found restorative justice programs resulted in greater victim satisfaction, greater offender satisfaction, and lower rates of recidivism compared to custodial sentencing and probation. However, this effect could be the result of selection bias: Restorative justice programs are *voluntary*, so offenders involved in them will *already* be motivated to change.

Forensic Psychology

ADDICTION – SYMPTOMS AND RISK FACTORS

The 3 symptoms that **describe addiction:** *Dependence*, *tolerance*, and *withdrawal*

- *Physical* **dependence:** When someone experiences *withdrawal symptoms* (e.g. pain, shaking, seizures – see below) when they stop using a substance.
- *Psychological* **dependence:** When someone has a strong *desire* to use the substance or engage in the addictive behaviour.

Tolerance is when a person needs *higher doses* of a drug to achieve the *same effect* as before. It occurs because the body adjusts to use of the drug in order to maintain **homeostasis** (feeling and functioning normally). This creates a new 'normal' so the person has to consume more next time in order to get the same buzz as before.

Cross-tolerance is when tolerance to one drug often creates increased tolerance to other drugs. For example, nicotine (cigarettes) increase tolerance to caffeine because they have similar effects.

Withdrawal syndrome is when a person develops **unpleasant symptoms** upon *stopping* or *reducing* drug use. These may include pain, anxiety, depression, insomnia, and shaking. Withdrawal symptoms are often the **opposite** of the ones created by the drug. For example, a person addicted to painkillers may experience severe pain when they stop using the painkillers.

A person's **genetics** may make them more susceptible to addiction

As always, **twin studies** are useful when it comes to genetic explanations. And **concordance rates** for alcohol and heroin addiction are much higher among identical twins than non-identical twins. For example, a meta-analysis of twin and adoption studies by Verhulst et al (2015) estimated that **alcohol addiction** is approximately **50% heritable**.

AO3: It's impossible for addiction to be *100%* genetic. A person with a genetic predisposition towards heroin addiction, for example, can't become addicted to heroin if they never encounter the drug in the first place! So, as is often the case, an interactionist explanation (see page 74) makes most sense: Genetic vulnerability must *interact* with environment to cause addiction.

Stress is a risk factor for addiction – both in the short term and *historically*

In the *short term*, people may turn to addictive substances as a way of **coping** with stress. E.g. someone may turn to alcohol after a stressful day at work, increasing likelihood of addiction.

Further, *historical* stress is also a risk factor for addiction. For example, Epstein et al (1998) found women who were sexually abused in childhood were twice as likely to develop alcohol addiction.

Strengths:	• **Supporting evidence (short-term stress):** Tavolacci et al (2013) assessed stress levels of French students using a questionnaire and found that stressed students were more likely to smoke, abuse alcohol, or develop cyberaddiction.
Weaknesses:	• **Correlation vs causation:** Being addicted is *itself* stressful and so the direction of causation could go the other way: Addiction may cause stress.

ADDICTION – RISK FACTORS

Certain **personality types** may also be at greater risk of addiction

Cloninger's (1987) **tri-dimensional theory** looks at **3 key personality traits**. According to Cloninger, people with the following combination of personality traits are most at risk of addiction:
- *High* **novelty seeking:** People who seek new experiences and sensations are more likely to seek out and become addicted to drugs.
- *High* **reward dependence:** People who learn quickly from rewarding stimuli (i.e. the pleasant sensations of drugs) will become addicted to rewards from drugs more quickly.
- *Low* **response to danger:** People who are less worried about the dangers of drugs are more likely to try them and become addicted.

AO3: *Some* evidence supports personality traits as a risk factor for addiction. For example, a meta-analysis by Howard et al (1997) found *high novelty seeking* was correlated with increased risk of alcohol abuse in teenagers and young adults – just as Cloninger's tri-dimensional theory predicts. However, the same meta-analysis did not support a link with addiction and the other 2 traits.

Influence from **family** and **friends** increases the likelihood of addiction

According to **social learning theory** (page 34), people **imitate** behaviours of **role models** they identify with. For example, a child may *identify* with their cigarette-smoking father (role model) and observe the reward (pleasure/stress relief) he gets from smoking. This provides **vicarious reinforcement** of cigarette-smoking behaviour, making the child more likely to smoke cigarettes.

Strengths:	• **Supporting evidence:** Akers and Lee (1996) looked at smoking behaviours of 454 adolescents over a 5 year period. They found that family influence made the children more likely to start and continue smoking cigarettes.

Like family, **peer influence** may also increase the likelihood that a person develops an addiction. For example, if a person's friendship group all starts smoking cigarettes, it makes that person more likely to try smoking – their friends may offer them cigarettes, or the person may feel left out if they don't smoke when everyone else is. Again, social learning theory comes in here: People *identify* with their friends, and if people think the friend is cool for smoking, this creates *vicarious reinforcement*.

Weaknesses:	• **Methodological concerns:** A review by Bauman and Ennett (1996) found many studies cite peer influence as a reason for substance abuse without actually testing this claim against evidence. • **Correlation vs. causation:** For example, an alcoholic may *seek out* friends who like going to pubs and drinking as this enables them to indulge their addiction. In this case, the addiction causes the friendships, not the other way round.

AO3: The relationship between peer and family influence and addiction is likely to vary according to many factors. For example, if a child's father smokes but the child identifies more with its mother, this would likely reduce the strength of family influence. Similarly, a 40 year old would probably be less influenced by friends who smoke cigarettes than they would as a teenager.

NEUROCHEMICAL EXPLANATIONS OF NICOTINE ADDICTION

Neurochemical explanations of nicotine addiction: *Dopamine* and *nAChRs*

In short, the **dopamine desensitisation hypothesis** says nicotine binds to **nAChRs** receptors, which causes **dopamine** release and feelings of **pleasure**. The full sequence of this is as follows:

- Neurons in the brain have *nicotinic acetylcholine receptors* (**nAChRs**).
- **Nicotine binds** to these nAChRs receptors, which **causes dopamine release** (in particular from the *ventral tegmental* area of the brain).
- Dopamine activity (particularly in the *nucleus accumbens* and *frontal cortex*) creates a pleasurable feeling of mild **euphoria**, **stress relief**, and increased **alertness.**
- This pleasurable feeling becomes *associated* with nicotine intake.
- Repeated exposure to nicotine causes nAChRs receptors to shut down and **no longer respond as easily** (i.e. the receptors are *downregulated*: They become *desensitised* to nicotine).
- This increases **tolerance** (page 144): *More nicotine* is needed to achieve the *same effect*.

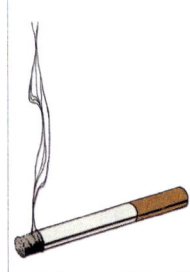

Further neurochemical explanation of nicotine addiction comes in the form of the **nicotine regulation model**.

According to this model, when a smoker goes without nicotine for a while, nAChRs receptors become **resensitised** to nicotine (i.e. they are *upregulated*). This state of having loads of nAChRs receptors available but not stimulated causes **withdrawal symptoms** such as anxiety. Cigarettes alleviate these withdrawal symptoms (see page 144), which *reinforces* smoking behaviour.

Strengths:	• **Supporting evidence:** Several studies – in both animals and humans – support the role of dopamine in nicotine addiction. For example, Brody et al (2004) conducted brain scans of a group of 20 nicotine-dependent smokers after which they had a 10 minute break. During this break, 10 of the participants smoked a cigarette and the other 10 did not smoke a cigarette (the control group). After the break, the researchers repeated the brain scans and found that the group who had smoked a cigarette had more dopamine activity than the control group. • **Explanatory power:** The nicotine regulation model explains why smokers find the first cigarette of the day to be the most satisfying: During sleep, nAChRs receptors are *upregulated* and become more sensitive, which results in a greater dopamine release than usual when smoking resumes in the morning.
Weaknesses:	• **Other factors:** Although dopamine almost certainly plays a role in nicotine addiction, it's likely that other neurochemical factors are at play. For example, nicotine also triggers the release of endogenous *opioids*, which also have pleasurable effects in the body. This suggests that the dopamine desensitisation hypothesis is an incomplete explanation of nicotine addiction.

Addiction

THE LEARNING THEORY EXPLANATION OF NICOTINE ADDICTION

Learning theory explains nicotine addiction through *operant conditioning*

Remember **operant conditioning** (page 33)? According to learning theory, smoking behaviour is both *positively* and *negatively* reinforced:

- **Positive reinforcement:** *Smoking causes pleasant feelings* of mild euphoria and stress relief. This reward makes the person more likely to smoke again.
- **Negative reinforcement:** Stopping smoking causes unpleasant withdrawal symptoms (see page 144) such as anxiety, low mood, and difficulty sleeping. The person is thus more likely to smoke again in order to *avoid these unpleasant feelings*.

Learning theory explanations of nicotine addiction may also include **social learning**, such as peer influence (see page 145).

The pleasant sensations of smoking can also become *associated* with **cues** in the **environment** via **classical conditioning**. For example, if a person regularly smokes cigarettes *when they're in a pub*, then they may condition themselves to associate pubs with smoking. Once this association is learned, going to the pub may trigger an urge to smoke. This is known as **cue reactivity**:

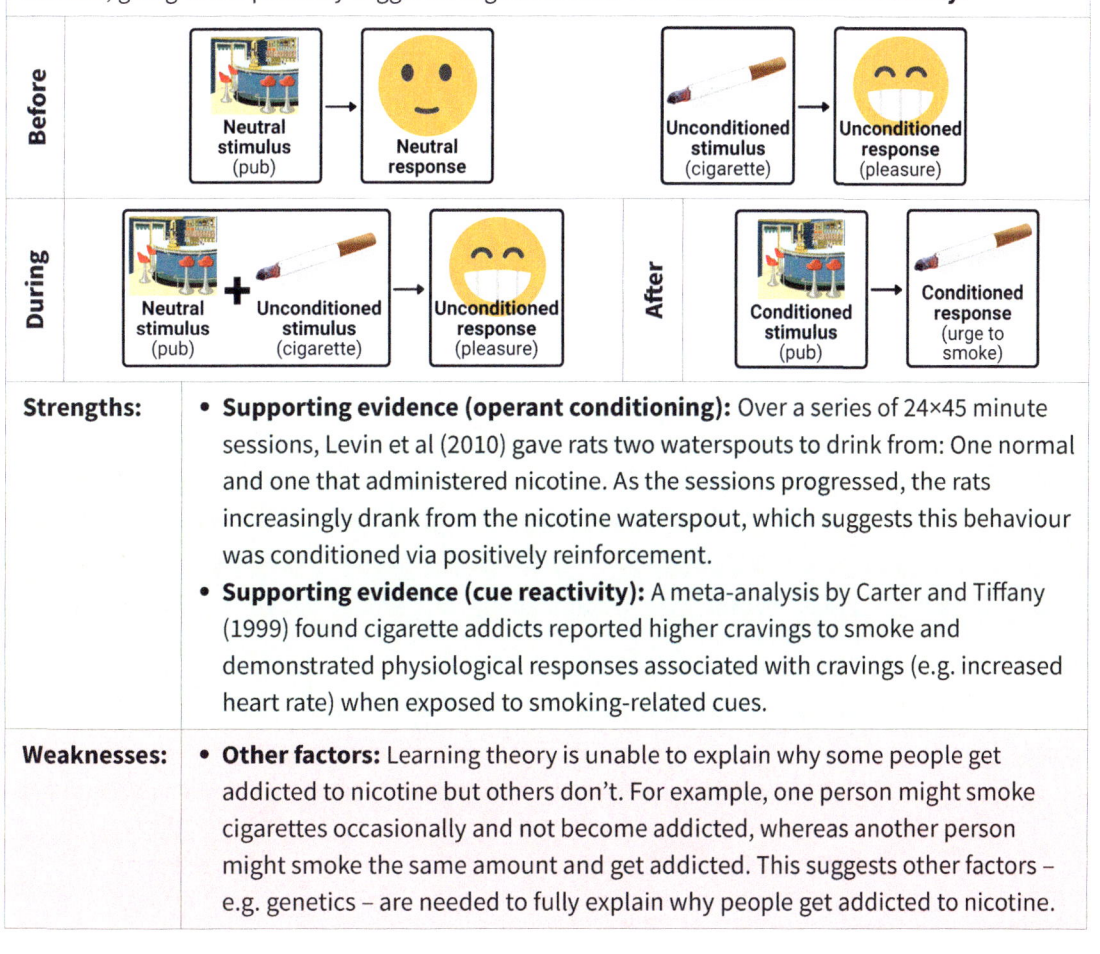

Before	Neutral stimulus (pub) → Neutral response	Unconditioned stimulus (cigarette) → Unconditioned response (pleasure)
During	Neutral stimulus (pub) + Unconditioned stimulus (cigarette) → Unconditioned response (pleasure)	**After**: Conditioned stimulus (pub) → Conditioned response (urge to smoke)

Strengths:	• **Supporting evidence (operant conditioning):** Over a series of 24×45 minute sessions, Levin et al (2010) gave rats two waterspouts to drink from: One normal and one that administered nicotine. As the sessions progressed, the rats increasingly drank from the nicotine waterspout, which suggests this behaviour was conditioned via positively reinforcement. • **Supporting evidence (cue reactivity):** A meta-analysis by Carter and Tiffany (1999) found cigarette addicts reported higher cravings to smoke and demonstrated physiological responses associated with cravings (e.g. increased heart rate) when exposed to smoking-related cues.
Weaknesses:	• **Other factors:** Learning theory is unable to explain why some people get addicted to nicotine but others don't. For example, one person might smoke cigarettes occasionally and not become addicted, whereas another person might smoke the same amount and get addicted. This suggests other factors – e.g. genetics – are needed to fully explain why people get addicted to nicotine.

THE LEARNING THEORY EXPLANATION OF GAMBLING ADDICTION

Learning theory explains gambling addiction through *operant conditioning*

The **positive reinforcement** of gambling is obvious: **Winning money**. Other factors, such as the lights and sounds of the machines, provide further positive reinforcement. But gamblers typically *lose* more money than they win. These **losses** *should* serve as **negative reinforcement** that makes the person less likely to repeat the behaviour. *So why do people get addicted to gambling?*

The answer is to do with **schedule of reinforcement**. Skinner's research on rats and pigeons (see page 33) found that schedule was important for creating *lasting* behavioural change:

- **Continuous reinforcement:** When a behaviour is rewarded *every time* it is performed.
- **Partial reinforcement:** When behaviour is rewarded *some*, but not all, times it is performed.

Skinner found that animals rewarded with *continuous* reinforcement schedules **quickly stopped** the target behaviour **when the rewards stopped**. But when the reward schedule was *partial* and *unpredictable*, animals continued the target behaviour for much longer **after rewards stopped**.

Gambling companies use the same principles. For example, a slot machine with a **fixed ratio** pays out every x spins (or every x minutes) – e.g. every 3rd coin:

But this is often too predictable, so slot machines typically pay out according to **variable ratios:**

Variable ratios are typically the most addictive (and most profitable). When the rewards are **unpredictable**, the gambler thinks *"maybe next time I'll win"* and their gambling behaviour is maintained **even after successive losses**. This is how gambling addiction forms.

Strengths:	• **Supporting evidence:** Parke and Griffiths (2004) describe ways gambling behaviour is reinforced, such as winning money, the thrill of gambling, and praise from peers. They also argue that some losses – *near misses* – positively reinforce gambling behaviour, because these raise hopes of future success.
Weaknesses:	• **Other factors:** Operant conditioning can't explain why some people get addicted and others don't. For example, one person may become addicted to gambling after a few wins whereas another person may never gamble again after the exact same experience. This suggests other factors – e.g. genetics, personality – are needed to fully explain why people get addicted to gambling. • **Can't explain why people *start* gambling:** Operant conditioning only explains why people continue to gamble, not why they start gambling in the first place. As such, other learning theory explanations, such as social learning theory, may be needed to provide a complete account of gambling addiction.

Addiction

THE COGNITIVE EXPLANATION OF GAMBLING ADDICTION

Cognitive explanations of gambling addiction focus on the *thought processes*

Gambling addicts are prone to several **cognitive biases**, such as:

- **Overestimating skill:** Gambling addicts often believe they have control over things that are just luck. For example, a gambler may believe they can tell where the ball is going to land on a roulette wheel.
- **Faulty perceptions:** For example, many gamblers believe that past outcomes influence future outcomes even though they are statistically independent, e.g. after a streak of losses, a gambler may think "well, I'm *owed* a win next time". This is known as the *gambler's fallacy*.
- **Rituals:** Gambling addicts often have superstitious beliefs and rituals. For example, a gambler may believe that wearing their lucky shirt makes them more likely to win.
- **Selective recall:** Gambling addicts focus on wins and ignore or forget about losses.

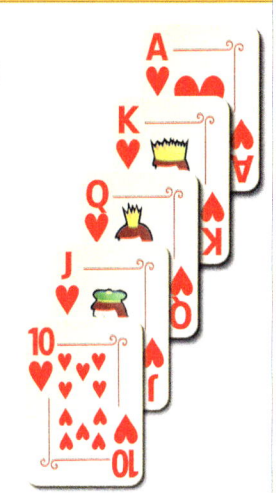

According to cognitive explanations of gambling addiction, these **irrational thought processes** and **cognitive biases** are what cause and sustain gambling addiction.

Strengths:	• **Supporting evidence:** A key study supporting cognitive explanations of gambling addiction is Griffiths (1994). In this study, 30 regular gamblers and 30 controls were each given £3 to gamble on slot machines. Griffiths recorded what the participants said as they gambled and interviewed them after. He found the regular gamblers were more than 5 times as likely to say irrational things (e.g. "the machine doesn't like me") as the controls, and that the regular gamblers were significantly more likely to believe winning was about skill rather than luck. This supports the idea that gambling addicts are prone to cognitive bias. • **Practical applications:** For example, some addicts may not be aware their thoughts are irrational (e.g. overestimating the role of skill and paying selective attention to wins while ignoring losses) and so cognitive behavioural therapy could help gambling addicts identify these thoughts, challenge them as irrational, and break their gambling addiction.
Weaknesses:	• **Methodological concerns:** Much of the evidence for cognitive explanations of gambling addiction come from self-report methods, which may not be valid. For example, Dickerson and O'Connor (2006) argue that much of what people say when gambling does not reflect what they actually believe in day-to-day life. • **Correlation vs. causation:** Even if cognitive bias and gambling addiction are *correlated*, it doesn't automatically prove that cognitive bias *causes* gambling addiction. For example, it could be the other way round: Over time, gambling addiction causes one's thinking to become more irrational and biased rather than irrational and biased thinking causing gambling addiction.

ADDICTION – WAYS TO REDUCE ADDICTION

Drug therapy for addiction takes several forms, such as:

- **Agonists:** Create a similar effect to the addictive drug (by activating the same neuron receptors). *Example:* Nicotine in patches and gum binds to nAChRs receptors (see page 146) and cause a similar dopamine release to smoking. This reduces withdrawal symptoms when quitting.
- **Antagonists:** Reduce the effects of the addictive drug (by binding to and blocking the neuron receptors the addictive drug acts on). *Example:* Naltrexone reduces the pleasant feelings caused by heroin and alcohol, reducing desire to take them.
- **Aversives:** Cause an unpleasant feeling when the drug is taken. This creates a negative association with the drug via classical conditioning, making the addict no longer want to take it. Example: *Disulfiram* (see below).

Strengths:	• **Supporting evidence:** This obviously varies depending on the drug and which addiction it is used to treat, but several drug therapies are supported by evidence. For example, a meta-analysis by Hughes et al (2003) found over-the-counter nicotine replacement therapy (e.g. gum, patches) was effective at helping people quit smoking.
Weaknesses:	• **Side effects:** Many drugs used to treat addiction have serious side effects that have to be weighed against the benefits. For example, methadone (the agonist used to treat heroin and opiate addiction) is itself highly addictive, although typically less so than the drugs it replaces. Drug therapies may also cause dangerous or unpleasant side effects (e.g. headaches, nausea), which increase the likelihood of the addict discontinuing the therapy.

Aversion therapy is a *behaviourist* treatment that uses classical conditioning...

...to **replace** the *positive* associations of an addictive substance with *negative* associations. The *emetic* (vomit-inducing) drug **disulfiram** works on this principle to treat alcohol addiction:

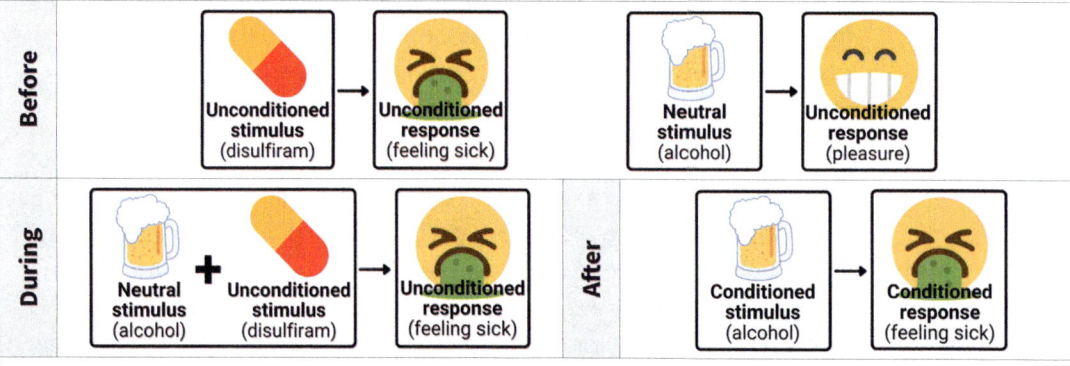

Before:
Unconditioned stimulus (disulfiram) → Unconditioned response (feeling sick)
Neutral stimulus (alcohol) → Unconditioned response (pleasure)

During:
Neutral stimulus (alcohol) + Unconditioned stimulus (disulfiram) → Unconditioned response (feeling sick)

After:
Conditioned stimulus (alcohol) → Conditioned response (feeling sick)

In addition to emetics, there are other ways to create **negative associations** with an addictive substance. For example, researchers have tried using electric shocks to treat gambling addiction and getting smokers to rapidly smoke cigarettes one after the other to induce sickness.

ADDICTION – WAYS TO REDUCE ADDICTION

The other behaviourist treatment for addiction is **covert sensitisation**

Covert sensitisation also operates on the behaviourist principle of **classical conditioning** but uses *imagination* rather than real-life unpleasant stimuli.

Example: To treat nicotine addiction, a therapist may get the patient to **imagine feeling sick** while **smoking cigarettes**. In theory, the stronger and more realistic the mental image is, the more successful the therapy is. So, the therapist may use **graphic** and **disgusting** imagery to treat the addiction (e.g. getting the patient to imagine smoking cigarettes covered in faeces). The therapist may then get the patient to imagine feelings of happiness at *not* having to smoke cigarettes, creating *positive* associations with *not smoking* cigarettes.

AO3: There is *some* evidence supporting both covert sensitisation and aversion therapy – though this of course differs depending on the type of addiction and treatment. For example, a review of 25 trials by Hajek and Stead (2001) did not support aversion therapy for *nicotine* addiction, but Elkins (1991) found 60% of *alcoholics* treated with emetic drugs were alcohol-free one year later.

A downside of aversion therapy is side effects. Disulfiram, for example, can result in heart attack and death in extreme cases. In contrast, covert sensitisation only uses *imagination*, so is the safer and arguably more ethical of the two behaviourist options. There is also evidence to suggest covert sensitisation is effective: In a study of alcohol addicts by Ashem and Donner (1968), 40% of patients treated with covert sensitisation were alcohol-free after 6 months compared to 0% of controls. However, covert sensitisation may only work on people with vivid imaginations.

CBT is particularly useful for addictions with a strong cognitive basis...

...such as gambling. For example, a gambling addict may tell themself *"I'll stop when I win back what I've lost"*. A therapist could get the patient to **reflect on** and **challenge** such thoughts and realise how they make their situation worse. This is the **functional analysis** part of CBT.

The behavioural component of CBT for addiction is **skills training**. This may include:

- **Drug refusal skills:** E.g. how to turn down alcohol at social events and not be peer-pressured.
- **Problem-solving:** Addicts often relapse when confronted with the problems and stresses of everyday life. The therapist may teach the patient more healthy ways to deal with challenges.
- **Relaxation skills:** E.g. Meditation techniques to deal with stress instead of smoking cigarettes.

Strengths:	• **Supporting evidence:** Petry et al (2006) randomly assigned 231 gambling addicts to receive 1 of 3 treatment plans: Gamblers Anonymous meetings, Gamblers anonymous meetings + cognitive behavioural workbook exercises, or Gamblers Anonymous meetings + 8 sessions of CBT. The groups that received cognitive behavioural treatments saw greater reductions in gambling activity.
Weaknesses:	• **May not work long-term:** Cowlishaw et al (2012) found CBT to be an effective treatment for gambling addiction in the short term (0-3 months post-treatment) but not long-term (9-12 months post-treatment).

ADDICTION – THEORIES OF BEHAVIOUR CHANGE

According to Ajzen's (1991) **theory of planned behaviour**...

...changing addictive behaviour is all about **intention.** The greater the level of intention, the more likely a person is to give up their addiction. Intention is determined by **3 factors:**

- **Personal attitudes:** The person's attitude to their addiction. If a person recognises their addiction is harmful, they will have *greater* intention to quit than e.g. someone in denial.
- **Subjective norms:** The attitudes and norms of the people in their life. If a drug addict socialises with other addicts who don't want to quit, this will *reduce* their intention to quit.
- **Perceived behavioural control:** Whether a person believes they're in control of their behaviour. E.g. if an addict thinks they're too weak willed to quit, this reduces their intention to quit.

Strengths:	**Supporting evidence:** Hagger et al (2011) found support for all three factors – personal attitudes, subjective norms, and perceived behavioural control – in predicting how many units of alcohol recovering alcoholics consumed.
Weaknesses:	**Conflicting evidence:** A meta-analysis of 47 studies by Webb and Sheeran (2006) found *some* correlation between level of intention and behavioural change but the effect was very small, weakening support for the theory.

Prochaska's (1983) **6-stage model** of the steps between addiction and recovery:

Stage	Description	Intervention
Pre-contemplation	*Not considering* changing addictive behaviour at all. E.g. denial ("I'm not an addict") or demotivated ("What's the point of trying to quit?").	Intervention focuses on *helping the person recognise that they are an addict* (if in denial) and getting them to consider the need to quit.
Contemplation	Considering quitting *within the next 6 months*. Weighing up the costs and benefits of quitting.	Intervention focuses on *helping the addict reach a decision* and realise the benefits outweigh the costs.
Preparation	*Deciding* to quit and *making plans* to do so within the next month.	Intervention focuses on *helping the addict make a plan* to quit.
Action	The person has *done something* to quit within the last 6 months.	Intervention focuses on *helping the person quit* (e.g. social support).
Maintenance	Behavioural change *maintained for over 6 months* without relapse.	Intervention focuses on *preventing relapse* (e.g. continued support).
Termination	*Abstinent* for a long time.	Behavioural change is now *habit*.

AO3: A meta-analysis of five studies by Velicer et al (2007) found that a smoker's stage within the 6-stage model was a more accurate predictor of quitting than demographic factors such as age, race, or gender. Although this supports the *predictive* power of the model, it's not clear if this results in more effective treatment methods. For example, Aveyard et al (2009) randomly assigned 2,471 smokers to receive either treatment tailored to their stage in the 6-stage model or general treatment that was not tailored to their stage of quitting but found no significant difference in effectiveness between the two treatments.

THE AQA PSYCHOLOGY EXAM FORMAT (7182)

Paper 1: **Introductory Topics in Psychology** (7182/1)

Section A: Social influence
(24 marks for this section)

Section B: Memory
(24 marks for this section)

Section C: Attachment
(24 marks for this section)

Section D: Psychopathology
(24 marks for this section)

- 2 hours long
- 96 available marks:
  - 24 marks for Social Influence.
  - 24 marks for Memory.
  - 24 marks for Attachment.
  - 24 marks for Psychopathology.

Paper 2: **Psychology in Context** (7182/2)

- 2 hours long
- 96 available marks:
  - 24 marks for Approaches in Psychology.
  - 24 marks for Biopsychology.
  - 48 marks for Research Methods.

Section A: Approaches in psychology
(24 marks for this section)

Section B: Biopsychology
(24 marks for this section)

Section C: Research methods
(48 marks for this section)

Paper 3: **Issues and Options in Psychology** (7182/3)

Section A: Issues and debates in psychology
(24 marks for this section)

Section B: Choose from:
- Relationships
- Gender
- Cognition and development

(24 marks for this section)

Section C: Choose from:
- Schizophrenia
- Eating behaviour
- Stress

(24 marks for this section)

Section D: Choose from:
- Aggression
- Forensic psychology
- Addiction

(24 marks for this section)

- 2 hours long
- 96 available marks:
  - 24 marks for Issues and Debates.
  - 24 marks for Section B
    - (Choose 1 topic of 3).
  - 24 marks for Section C
    - (Choose 1 topic of 3).
  - 24 marks for Section D
    - (Choose 1 topic of 3).

ASSESSMENT OBJECTIVE 1 (AO1)

Exam responses are graded according to **3 assessment objectives:**
- **AO1:** Knowledge and understanding.
- **AO2:** Application.
- **AO3:** Evaluation.

Longer questions often require a mixture of two or more of the following skills, whereas shorter questions may only test for one of these skills. The question won't tell you how many marks are available for each assessment objective, but the way it's worded will give you an idea.

AO1: Knowledge and Understanding

To pick up these marks, you just need to demonstrate that you know about the specific psychology concept, experiment, or technique you are asked to explain. This typically involves a short **description** or sometimes answering a multiple-choice question.

The following words in a question indicate marks available for AO1:
- *Outline...*
- *Describe...*
- *Identify...*

Model answer for an AO1 question:

Describe how Asch investigated conformity to group consensus. [4 marks]

Asch recruited 123 male student participants. He told them they were taking part in a study of visual perception. The experiment involved putting the participants in groups with 7-9 confederates and asking them to say which example line was closest in length to another line. In some trials, the confederates would all give the same wrong answer (the independent variable) in order to measure the extent to which the participants would conform to an incorrect group consensus (the dependent variable). The extent to which participants conformed to the incorrect group consensus was compared against the results of a control group, who completed the same task alone.

The question is asking you to *describe* (AO1) how Asch investigated conformity to group consensus – <u>not</u> to evaluate it. You wouldn't get any marks for saying, for example, that Asch's experiments may lack ecological validity because of the specific nature of the task, or that they may suffer from gender bias because all the participants were male – because that's evaluation.

You wouldn't even get any marks for describing the *results* (that 32% conformed), because the question is asking you to describe how Asch *investigated* conformity – not the results of that investigation. It's not the end of the world to include such details, but it does waste time.

Exam Format and Assessment Objectives

ASSESSMENT OBJECTIVE 2 (AO2)

AO2: Application

To pick up these marks, you need to **apply** your knowledge of psychology to a **particular issue** or **example**. You can tell which questions include AO2 marks, as they will usually have some sample material before the question, such as:

- A short extract
- A description of a person
- A table of results

Paper 2 (Psychology in Context) has more marks available for AO2 than the other papers. A lot of the research methods (section C) questions are AO2 questions because you'll typically get a description of a study – potentially including results in the form of quantitative or qualitative data – and be asked questions about that study.

Model answer for an AO2 question:

Daniel and Benjamin are identical twins. Benjamin recently failed his school exams and Daniel is worried this means he will fail his school exams too.

Using your knowledge of genotype and phenotype, explain why Daniel's twin brother failing the test does not necessarily mean Daniel will also fail the test. [4 marks]

A person's genotype is their actual genes (inherited from the mother and father), which cannot change. Because Daniel and Benjamin are identical twins, they will have an identical genotype. In contrast, a person's phenotype is how these genes present in response to the environment – this may differ between Daniel and Benjamin because they may have different environment and experiences. So, even though Daniel and Benjamin have an identical genetic predisposition for passing exams, these genes may present differently depending on environmental factors. For example, Benjamin may not have studied for his school exams at all but if Daniel has put in many hours of revision he may pass his school exams even though his twin brother did not.

This could be an AO1 question – *outline the difference between genotype and phenotype* – but the fact that the examiner has added in this little extract at the start about Daniel and Benjamin makes it AO2 – you're going to have to *apply* your knowledge of the difference between genotype and phenotype to their situation.

AO2 questions are usually pretty obvious. If you get a short extract like this before the question, it's AO2. So, be sure to *refer* to the sample material given. For example, here the answer refers to the specific names (Daniel and Benjamin) and their particular situation (passing or failing school exams).

Exam Format and Assessment Objectives

ASSESSMENT OBJECTIVE 3 (AO3)

AO3: Analysis, interpretation, and evaluation

For example, you may be asked to **evaluate** a psychological study or psychological theory from the syllabus. The following words in a question indicate marks available for AO3:
- *Discuss…*
- *Outline a limitation of…*
- *Briefly discuss a strength…*

General evaluation points – *validity, correlation vs. causation,* too *reductive,* etc.

Throughout this book, I've included a bunch of evaluation points below each topic – such as supporting or conflicting evidence. But this is a lot to remember, so having **generic evaluation points** enables you to evaluate explanations, studies, or theories on the fly in the exam:

Too reductive (see page 75)	Most psychological explanations, *in isolation,* can be accused of being too reductive – because there's always an exception that doesn't fit the explanation or some other factor that may explain a result. *Example:* Explaining OCD solely in terms of genetics (page 30) is too reductive because there are people who have genetics for OCD but don't develop OCD. So, a complete (holistic) explanation will need to include other factors.
Deterministic (see page 73)	Certain theories and explanations – particularly biological – are deterministic: They don't leave room for the free will of the individual. *Example:* If criminal behaviour is the result of genetics (page 137), this means it isn't a free choice. But this would make it unfair to punish criminals.
Ethical issues (see page 62)	Did a study inflict harm on participants? Did they give informed consent? What steps could be done to make the study more ethical? *Example:* Milgram's experiments caused distress to participants. But they were debriefed after, and the study's results were worth the distress caused.
Ecological validity (see page 61)	Many psychological theories and explanations are based on lab experiments. But lab experiments are *artificial,* so the results may not apply in real life. *Example:* Zimbardo's prison study may not reflect real-life prison behaviour.
Correlation vs. causation (see page 59)	The easiest example to illustrate this is *reversing* the direction of causation. *Example:* The cognitive explanation of depression (page 28) says negative thoughts *cause* negative emotions. And while it's true that negative thoughts and negative emotions are *correlated,* the direction of causation could go the other way: Negative emotions could cause negative thoughts.
Methodological issues	This depends. *Self-report method?* Participants' subjective interpretations may mean the results aren't reliable. *Animal study?* It may not be valid in humans. *Small sample size?* It may not apply to the wider population.

Exam Format and Assessment Objectives

ASSESSMENT OBJECTIVE 3 (AO3)

Model answer for an AO3 question:

Briefly explain one strength and one limitation of the behaviourist approach. [4 marks]

One strength of the behaviourist approach is that it has practical applications. For example, behaviourism has led to successful treatments for phobias, such as flooding and systematic desensitisation. These treatments are effective in many cases, reducing phobias and improving the lives of people who have received these treatments. This shows that the behaviourist approach can result in positive outcomes when applied to human beings, which is a strength of the approach.

However, a limitation of the behaviourist approach is its reliance on animal studies. A basic assumption of behaviourism is that the same processes that govern human behaviour also govern the behaviour of non-human animals. For example, Pavlov experimented on dogs and generalised the results to humans, and Skinner experiment on rats and pigeons and generalised the results to humans. However, humans are different from animals such as rats, pigeons, and dogs and so the behaviourist conclusions drawn from animal studies may not be valid when applied to human psychology.

A good format for structuring your evaluation points is **point**, **evidence**/example, **explanation**. Both paragraphs above use this structure:

Strength:
- **Point:** Behaviourism has practical applications.
- **Evidence:** Flooding and systematic desensitisation have been successfully used to treat phobias.
- **Explanation:** This is a strength of behaviourism because it shows the approach can be used to improve people's lives.

Weakness:
- **Point:** Behaviourism relies on animal studies.
- **Evidence:** Pavlov's studies of dogs and Skinner's experiments on dogs and pigeons.
- **Explanation:** This is a weakness of behaviourism because animals are different from humans and so the results may not be valid in humans.

As a general rule, one or two *detailed* evaluation points is better than just listing many evaluation points without going into any detail or explaining them. Throughout this book, the evaluation points I have given below each topic are generally too short – just one or two lines. In the exam, be sure to *expand* on them – breaking them down into point, evidence, explanation.

EXTENDED RESPONSE QUESTIONS

> **16 mark** extended response questions may include **all 3** assessment objectives

Michael and Jack are identical twins but were adopted by different families when they were six months old. Michael's adoptive parents were both doctors and when Michael left school he also became a doctor. Jack's adoptive parents were both plumbers but when Jack left school he became a music teacher. From a young age, both Michael and Jack loved music, and they both play guitar as adults.

Describe and evaluate genetics as a way of explaining people's behaviour. Refer to Michael's and Jack's experiences in your answer. **[16 marks]**

> You may use this space to plan your answer.
>
> AO1: Genetics, genetic explanations, genotype vs. phenotype.
>
> AO2: Identical twins means Michael and Jack share 100% of their genes. Genes: Music (both Michael and Jack). Environment: Jobs (e.g. Michael a doctor).
>
> AO3: Strengths: Supporting evidence (twin studies). Weaknesses: Overly reductive (e.g. Michael and Jack have the same genes but different lives, so other factors i.e. environment needed), deterministic.

Genetics are biological traits inherited from a person's parents. Just as physical characteristics (e.g. eye colour) are determined by genetics, genetic explanations of behaviour say that behaviours are also determined by genetics. Genetic explanations distinguish between genotype (i.e. a person's actual genes) and their phenotype (i.e. how those genes present in response to the environment). For example, a person may have genes that make them susceptible to schizophrenia but these genes may only be triggered if they are raised in a stressful environment. As identical twins, Michael and Jack share 100% of their genetics but these genes may present differently because they were raised in different environments.

A strength of genetic explanations of behaviour is that there is supporting evidence in the form of twin studies. The concordance rate in a twin study is the rate at which twins share the same trait. If the concordance rate for a behaviour is higher among monozygotic (identical) twins than dizygotic (non-identical) twins, this suggests the behaviour is genetically determined. Twin studies have found higher concordance rates among identical twins for many behaviours and psychological disorders (e.g. Gottesman (1991) for

EXTENDED RESPONSE QUESTIONS

schizophrenia, and Verhulst et al (2015) for alcoholism), which supports genetic explanations of these behaviours. The fact that both Michael and Jack love music and both play guitar – despite being raised in different environments – suggests this may be a genetic trait because Michael and Jack are identical twins and so share 100% of their genes.

However, a weakness of genetic explanations of behaviour is that they are overly reductive because they ignore other factors such as environment. Michael and Jack share 100% of their genetics and yet have very different lives and behaviours (for example, Michael is a doctor and Jack is a teacher). If behaviour was 100% genetic, Michael and Jack would behave in exactly the same way and so other factors besides genetics are needed to explain their different behaviours. For example, the fact that Michael was raised in an environment where both parents were doctors may explain why Michael became a doctor but Jack did not. This shows that genetic explanations of behaviour are often incomplete.

A further weakness of genetic explanations of behaviour is that they are deterministic. Our genetics are outside of our control and so genetic explanations of behaviour leave no room for free will. If free will doesn't exist and behaviour is 100% genetic then it means people are not in control of their lives. An implication of this is that people are not morally responsible for their actions and so genetic explanations could potentially excuse criminal behaviours.

In conclusion, although there is a lot of evidence supporting genetic explanations of behaviour, genetics do not provide a complete and holistic explanation. Environmental factors also affect peoples behaviour and so an interactionist approach – where genes interact with environment – is best for explaining Michael's and Jack's behaviours.

The available marks for this question would be broken down as follows:

- **AO1 = 6**
- **AO2 = 4**
- **AO3 = 6**

For more model answers to practice questions, check out the **practice papers with A* model answers** available from psychologyalevel.com.

PRACTICE QUESTIONS

Social Influence Practice Questions

Outline two variables that affect conformity. [4 marks]

Discuss locus of control as an explanation of resistance to social influence. [8 marks]

Outline two explanations of conformity. [4 marks]

Discuss what psychological research has told us about why people obey authority. [16 marks]

At university, Zach agreed to take part in a psychology student's research project which he was told was an investigation of human colour perception. For the experiment, Zach was placed in a room with 15 other students and shown various colours and asked to identify them. The third colour Zach was shown was mostly blue but had hints of green. Before Zach gave his answer, the 14 other students had all said "green". Zach was originally going to answer "blue" but when asked said "green".
Using your knowledge of conformity, outline two variables that affected why Zach gave the answer he did. [4 marks]

Describe how Milgram investigated obedience to authority. [4 marks]

Discuss ethical issues in social influence research. [8 marks]

Outline and evaluate research into conformity to social roles. [8 marks]

Outline how minority influence can lead to social change. [4 marks]

Briefly outline what is meant by compliance as a type of conformity. [2 marks]

Identify two variables that affect obedience. [2 marks]

Discuss what psychological research has told us about why people resist social influence. [16 marks]

Pippa works at a marketing agency with eight other colleagues. Pippa believes that their daily meetings are an inefficient use of time and that the time spent in meetings would be better spent catching up with work. She would like to reduce the number of meetings from five meetings per week to one meeting per week. Her colleagues do not agree but have told Pippa they are willing to have a meeting about it.
Using your knowledge of minority influence, explain how Pippa might be able to persuade her colleagues to accept her view. [6 marks]

Outline one variable that affects obedience. [2 marks]

Describe how Zimbardo investigated conformity to social roles. [4 marks]

Outline one explanation of why people may resist authority (disobedience). [4 marks]

Outline and evaluate the agentic state explanation of obedience. [8 marks]

PRACTICE QUESTIONS

Memory Practice Questions

Which one of the following best describes capacity in memory? Shade one box only. [1 mark]

A	How long the information is stored for.	☐
B	How accurate the memory is.	☐
C	The format the information is stored as.	☐
D	How much information can be stored.	☐

Outline and evaluate the cognitive interview as a way of improving eyewitness testimony. [8 marks]

Describe interference as an explanation of forgetting. [4 marks]

The different storage systems of the multi-store model of memory differ in terms of coding. Using an example, explain what is meant by coding in memory. [3 marks]

Outline and evaluate the working model of memory. [16 marks]

Explain how misleading information can affect the accuracy of eyewitness testimony. [4 marks]

Outline the phonological loop of the working memory model. [2 marks]

Strong passwords contain a mixture of letters, numbers, and symbols and are greater than 9 characters in length. In contrast, weak passwords consist of a single word that is less than 9 characters in length. However, most people would struggle to remember a long password consisting of random letters, numbers, and symbols.

Discuss the multi-store model of memory. Refer to the information above in your answer. [16 marks]

Using an example, explain what is meant by context-dependent failure. [3 marks]

Outline one strength of the multi-store model of memory. [2 marks]

Outline and evaluate research into capacity in memory. [8 marks]

Laura was out in town with a friend when she witnessed a crime. Two men had broken into a jewellery store. After hearing the sound of smashing glass, Laura saw the men running away from the scene with a bag. Laura's friend was on the other side of the road when this was happening. Laura and her friend called the police and remained there until the police arrived.

Explain how the police could use the cognitive interview to help Laura's recall of the event. [6 marks]

Ryan was able to hold a conversation with a friend whilst driving his car. However, when reading a newspaper later that day, Ryan has to stop what he was doing in order to have a conversation with his friend.

With reference to the working memory model, explain Ryan's different experiences. [4 marks]

PRACTICE QUESTIONS

Attachment Practice Questions

Describe how Harlow studied attachment using animals. [4 marks]

Rebecca is pregnant and her baby is due in a month's time. The baby's father, John, will help raise the baby but works long hours and so Rebecca will be the primary caregiver. Rebecca's parents – the baby's grandparents – live far away but have said they will come and visit Rebecca and the baby from time to time.
Using Schaffer's stages of attachment, explain how Rebecca can expect her baby to behave towards her and other people during the first two years of development. [6 marks]

Outline one difference in attachment shown by infants who have an insecure-avoidant attachment and infants who have a secure attachment. [2 marks]

Outline and evaluate the learning theory of attachment. [8 marks]

Discuss the influence of early attachment on relationships as an adult. [8 marks]

Outline Bowlby's monotropic theory of attachment. [4 marks]

Outline findings from research into the role of the father in attachment. [4 marks]

Jay and Gigi are a British couple who are adopting an 18-month old baby called Amy. The adoption agency has told Jay and Gigi that Amy was raised in an orphanage with many other children in poor conditions ever since she was two weeks old. John and Gigi are concerned how these early experiences may affect her development.
Discuss the effects of institutionalisation and Bowlby's maternal deprivation hypothesis. Refer to Jay and Gigi's situation above in your answer. [16 marks]

Jenny is discussing her childhood with her mother.
When Jenny asks what she was like as a toddler, Jenny's mother replies: "You were always happy when we were together but would sometimes throw tantrums when I dropped you off at nursery. When I came to pick you up, you always ran towards me for a hug."
Identify the type of attachment that Jenny's mother is describing. [1 mark]
Distinguish between two other types of attachment. [4 marks]

Identify three of Schaffer's stages of attachment. [3 marks]

Discuss caregiver-infant interactions in humans. [16 marks]

Discuss one limitation of Bowlby's monotropic theory of attachment. [4 marks]

Briefly outline what is meant by interactional synchrony in caregiver-infant interactions. [2 marks]

Ainsworth's 'Strange Situation' procedure uses controlled observations of infant attachments. Outline one advantage of controlled observations. [3 marks]

Outline and evaluate one or more animal study of attachment. [8 marks]

Practice Questions

PRACTICE QUESTIONS

Psychopathology Practice Questions

Which two of A, B, C, D, and E are examples of failure to function adequately? Shade two boxes only. [2 marks]

A	Causing discomfort to others.	☐
B	Statistical infrequency.	☐
C	Resistance to stress.	☐
D	Eccentricity.	☐
E	Personal distress.	☐

Which two of A, B, C, D, and E are behavioural characteristics of phobias? Shade two boxes only. [2 marks]

A	Irrational beliefs about the stimuli that causes fear.	☐
B	Avoiding the stimuli that causes fear.	☐
C	Extreme anxiety.	☐
D	Screaming.	☐
E	Difficulty concentrating.	☐

Describe the cognitive approach to treating depression. [4 marks]

Discuss one strength of the genetic explanation of obsessive-compulsive disorder. [4 marks]

Jimmy has a phobia of dogs. As a child, he was bitten on the hand by a dog when he went to stroke it. Now, as an adult, Jimmy avoids parks and areas where he might encounter dogs.
Discuss the behaviourist approach to treating phobias. Refer to Jimmy's phobia of dogs in your answer. [16 marks]

Outline two emotional characteristics of depression. [4 marks]

Outline and evaluate one or more biological treatment for obsessive-compulsive disorder. [8 marks]

Outline and evaluate the statistical infrequency definition of abnormality. [8 marks]

Outline two weaknesses of the deviation from social norms definition of abnormality. [4 marks]

Identify one cognitive characteristic of obsessive-compulsive disorder. [1 mark]

Outline Ellis' ABC model of depression. [4 marks]

Outline one neural explanation of obsessive-compulsive disorder (OCD). [4 marks]

Briefly evaluate the failure to function adequately definition of abnormality. [4 marks]

Discuss cognitive explanations of depression. [16 marks]

PRACTICE QUESTIONS

Approaches in Psychology Practice Questions

Which of the following statements about the behaviourist approach is FALSE? Shade one box only. [1 mark]

A	Inferences about internal mental processes are made on the basis of behaviour.	☐
B	Animal studies are a valid way to learn about human behaviour.	☐
C	Behaviour is learned from experience.	☐
D	Internal mental processes are subjective and so should not be studied scientifically.	☐

Describe the role of the ego according to the psychodynamic approach. [2 marks]

Briefly explain one strength and one limitation of the humanistic approach. [4 marks]

Johnnie is playing Goblin Quest, an online video game. When Johnnie completes quests with his character, he is awarded in-game gold and a bell rings. However, if Johnnie doesn't log in for a week, his character will start to lose gold and so Johnnie plays Goblin Quest regularly to avoid this. After staying up all night playing Goblin Quest, Johnnie was late for school and got told off by his parents and teachers for playing Goblin Quest too much.

Identify and outline three types of reinforcement. Refer to Johnnie's experience in your answer. [6 marks]

Researchers investigating the influence of genetics on intelligence used data on twin concordance rates for their study. They found that concordance rates for 'gifted' IQ scores were 50% among monozygotic twins and 25% among dizygotic twins.

Explain why this data supports a genetic influence on intelligence. [3 marks]

Outline and evaluate the humanistic approach. [16 marks]

Timmy is a 7 year-old boy. He sees a television advert for a new toy, called 'Zoomer Man', which shows a popular male influencer playing with the toy. In the advert, the influencer picks up Zoomer Man and is transformed into a superhero who can fly. Zoomer Man fights a villain and arrests him, and then a crowd of people cheer. After watching the advert, Timmy starts punching his toy bear and pretending to fly.

Outline and evaluate social learning theory. Refer to Timmy's behaviour in your answer. [16 marks]

Describe one practical application of cognitive neuroscience. [4 marks]

Outline and evaluate Wundt's role in the emergence of psychology as a science. [8 marks]

Outline the structure of personality according to the psychodynamic approach. [4 marks]

Outline the way in which Bandura studied social learning. [4 marks]

PRACTICE QUESTIONS

Biopsychology Practice Questions

Which type of neuron would be associated with transmitting information between the central nervous system and muscles? Shade one box only. [1 mark]

A	Sensory neruon.	☐
B	Motor neuron.	☐
C	Relay neuron.	☐
D	Terminal neuron.	☐

Briefly outline the components of the central nervous system and their functions. [4 marks]

Discuss ways of studying the brain. [16 marks]

Using an example, outline the function of the endocrine system. [4 marks]

Neurotransmitters can have excitatory or inhibitory effects. Briefly describe the difference between these two effects. [2 marks]

Using an example, explain what exogenous zeitgebers are. [2 marks]

Discuss research into localisation of function in the brain. [16 marks]

Emma is a 16 year old girl who was involved in a car accident that caused damage to her motor cortex.
Describe the symptoms Emma might experience following the car accident. [2 marks]
Using your knowledge of functional recovery after trauma, discuss what Emma can expect during her recovery. [8 marks]

Give one difference between the autonomic nervous system and the somatic nervous system. [1 mark]

Using an example, briefly outline the function of glands. [2 marks]

Outline and evaluate split-brain research. [8 marks]

Explain one strength and one weakness of fMRI as a way of studying the brain. [4 marks]

Outline the fight or flight response and explain why this could be helpful in a stressful situation. [4 marks]

Describe the structure and function of a neuron. [6 marks]

Outline and evaluate research into the effects of endogenous pacemakers and exogenous zeitgebers on circadian rhythms. [8 marks]

Information is passed from one neuron to another via neurotransmitters. Explain how neurotransmitters enable synaptic transmission. [3 marks]

Discuss research into neuroplasticity and functional recovery of the brain after trauma. [16 marks]

PRACTICE QUESTIONS

Research Methods Practice Questions

A recent study found that consuming caffeine before participating in a memorisation task improved memory. However, an earlier study found that consuming caffeine before participating in a memorisation task reduced memory. Alice wanted to find out which of these two studies was accurate.

Alice approached 10 participants in a local coffee shop and asked them to take part in her study. In the first trial, participants were given one minute to memorise a list of 20 words. In the second trial, participants were given a cup of coffee containing 450mg of caffeine 20 minutes prior to being given one minute to memorise a different list of 20 words. After each trial, Alice recorded how many words each participant could remember.

Write an appropriate hypothesis for this experiment. [3 marks]

Did Alice use independent groups or repeated measures? Explain your answer. [2 marks]

What is the independent variable in this experiment? Explain your answer. [2 marks]

Identify the sampling method Alice used in this experiment. Explain one strength and one limitation of using this method for this study. [5 marks]

Is Alice gathering quantitative or qualitative data? Explain your answer. [2 marks]

A study of infants found that girls are more sociable than boys. In order to test this, two psychology researchers observed the behaviours of 20 infants (10 girls and 10 boys) at a nursery school. The researchers compared sociable behaviours among the girls and the boys. The first researcher observed the infants between 9:00 and 10:00 and the second researcher observed the infants between 13:00 and 14:00. Every 15 minutes, the students would record whether or not each child was behaving sociably.

Identify the study design the researchers used. [1 mark]

Explain one strength of using this study design for this study. [2 marks]

Should the researchers' hypothesis be directional or non-directional for this study? Explain your answer. [2 marks]

Which behaviour sampling method did the researchers use? Explain your answer. [2 marks]

Describe how the researchers could assess inter-observer reliability for this study. [3 marks]

Outline two ethical issues the researchers should have considered before conducting this study. [4 marks]

During the observation, the researchers noticed that girls and boys tended to choose different toys to play with. On average, the girls preferred to play with toy dolls whereas the boys preferred to play with toy trucks. The researchers decided to investigate this further by conducting an experiment.

Design a matched pairs experiment the researchers could conduct. In your answer you will be awarded credit for providing appropriate details of: The aim of the experiment, identification and manipulation of variables including details of the task, participant sampling and selection, and controls to minimise the effects of extraneous variables. [12 marks]

PRACTICE QUESTIONS

More Research Methods Practice Questions

Which one of the following best describes temporal validity? Shade one box only. [1 mark]

A	The study's results are also accurate outside of the environment it was conducted in.	☐
B	The study's results are similar to the results of a relevantly similar study.	☐
C	The study appears to accurately measure what it is supposed to measure.	☐
D	The study's results remain accurate over time.	☐

A researcher placed an advert in a university psychology department asking for students to participate in an experiment. 10 students responded to the advert and took part in the study. Each student had an app installed on their phone for the one-month study. Each evening, the students would rate their mood for that day on a scale from 1-10 and record it in the app. The app also recorded how many hours they spent using social media each day.

Identify the dependent variable in this study. [1 mark]

Identify the sampling method used in this study. [1 mark]

Explain one strength and one limitation of using this sampling method in this study. [4 marks]

Explain one limitation of assessing mood using a rating scale of 1-10. [2 marks]

Rating mood on a scale of 1-10 is an example of quantitative data. Give one strength of collecting quantitative data in this study. [2 marks]

The researcher's results are presented in table 1 below:

	Daily social media use (hours)	Mood rating (1-10)
Participant A	3	6
Participant B	4	5
Participant C	2	7
Participant D	7	3
Participant E	1	6

Using the data in Table 1, calculate the mean daily social media use in hours for all the participants. Show your workings. [3 marks]

Using the data in Table 1, calculate the standard deviation of daily social media use for all the participants. Use your answer to the question above. Give your answer to two significant figures. Show your workings. [5 marks]

The researcher observed a negative correlation between social media use and mood rating.

Explain why it would not be appropriate for the researchers to conclude from this correlation that increased social media use causes low mood. [2 marks]

PRACTICE QUESTIONS

Issues and Debates Practice Questions

Which one of the following best describes a holistic approach in psychology? Shade one box only. [1 mark]

A	Explaining behaviour in a complicated way in terms of complex mechanisms.	☐
B	Explaining behaviour in one way and ignoring all other explanations.	☐
C	Explaining behaviour in multiple different ways at the same time.	☐
D	Explaining behaviour in a scientific way.	☐

Discuss socially sensitive research in psychology. [8 marks]

What is psychic determinism? [2 marks]

Explain why behaviourism could be seen as a psychologically reductionist approach. [4 marks]

Discuss the free will vs. determinism debate in psychology. [16 marks]

What is alpha bias? [2 marks]

Outline and evaluate how cultural bias can impact psychological research. [8 marks]

Discuss the nature-nurture debate in psychology. [16 marks]

Explain one strength and one limitation of using a idiographic approach in psychology. [4 marks]

Using an example of research from elsewhere in the course, discuss gender bias in psychological research. [8 marks]

Name the opposite of the idiographic approach. [1 mark]

Discuss the reductionism vs. holism debate in psychology. [16 marks]

Using an example, explain what is meant by biological determinism. [3 marks]

What is meant by soft determinism? [4 marks]

Explain why the humanistic approach to psychology could be seen as a psychologically holistic approach. [4 marks]

What is interactionism in the context of the nature-nurture debate? [2 marks]

Using an example from elsewhere in the course, explain what is meant by socially sensitive research. [4 marks]

In an experiment on the effects of workload on mental health, a researcher measured cortisol levels to determine how stressed participants were.

Explain why measuring cortisol levels in this situation could be an example of biological reductionism. [2 marks]

Explain why the psychodynamic approach has elements of an idiographic approach to psychology. [4 marks]

PRACTICE QUESTIONS

Relationships Practice Questions

Discuss what psychological research has told us about parasocial relationships. [16 marks]

Outline one difference in reproductive behaviours between men and women. [2 marks]

What is meant by absence of gating in virtual relationships? [2 marks]

Outline and evaluate evolutionary explanations of partner preferences. [8 marks]

Outline and evaluate the equity theory of romantic relationships. [8 marks]

Outline Duck's phase model of relationship breakdown. [4 marks]

Outline and evaluate physical attractiveness as a factor affecting attraction. [8 marks]

What is the matching hypothesis? [2 marks]

Gender Practice Questions

Outline the difference between sex and gender. [2 marks]

Discuss the role of hormones in gender development. [16 marks]

Outline the physical and psychological effects of Klinefelter's syndrome. [4 marks]

Outline and evaluate psychodynamic explanations of gender development. [16 marks]

Outline and evaluate biological explanations of gender dysphoria. [8 marks]

What is meant by androgyny? [2 marks]

Describe gender schema theory. [4 marks]

Outline and evaluate social learning explanations of gender development. [16 marks]

Cognition and Development Practice Questions

Discuss Piaget's theory of cognitive development. [16 marks]

Describe Selman's levels of perspective taking. [5 marks]

Outline theory of mind and explain how the Sally-Anne test may be used to test a person's theory of mind. [6 marks]

What is meant by 'object permanence' according to Piaget's theory? [2 marks]

Outline and evaluate Baillargeon's research into early infant abilities. [8 marks]

What is the zone of proximal development? [2 marks]

Discuss what psychological research has told us about the mirror neuron system. [8 marks]

Outline one strength of Vygotksy's theory of cognitive development. [4 marks]

PRACTICE QUESTIONS

Schizophrenia Practice Questions

Briefly discuss two limitations of cognitive explanations of schizophrenia. [6 marks]

What is the diathesis-stress model of schizophrenia? [4 marks]

Outline the differences between typical and atypical antipsychotic drugs for the treatment of schizophrenia. [4 marks]

Outline and evaluate the role of dopamine in schizophrenia. [8 marks]

Identify two negative symptoms of schizophrenia. [2 marks]

Discuss psychological explanations of schizophrenia. [16 marks]

Discuss biological explanations of schizophrenia. [16 marks]

Outline and evaluate research into the validity of schizophrenia diagnosis. [8 marks]

Eating Behaviour Practice Questions

Discuss biological explanations of obesity. [16 marks]

Outline and evaluate research into cognitive explanations of anorexia nervosa. [8 marks]

Outline and evaluate evolutionary explanations of food preferences. [8 marks]

Outline the restraint theory explanation of obesity. [4 marks]

Outline the roles of ghrelin and leptin in eating behaviour. [4 marks]

Briefly explain one strength and one weakness of biological explanations of anorexia nervosa. [4 marks]

Outline and evaluate neural explanations of obesity. [8 marks]

Outline one factor that increases the success of dieting. [2 marks]

Stress Practice Questions

Discuss one strength and one limitation of the hassles and uplifts scale. [6 marks]

Outline two forms of social support. [4 marks]

Discuss research into life changes as a source of stress. [16 marks]

Outline and evaluate skin conductance response as a measure of stress. [8 marks]

Explain the role of the sympathomedullary pathway in the physiology of stress. [4 marks]

Outline and briefly evaluate research into workplace stress. [8 marks]

Briefly outline one strength and one limitation of biofeedback for managing stress. [4 marks]

Discuss individual differences in stress. [16 marks]

PRACTICE QUESTIONS

Aggression Practice Questions

Briefly discuss research into the effects of genetics on aggressive behaviour. [8 marks]

Discuss one or more psychological explanation of aggression. [16 marks]

Briefly explain how desensitisation might influence aggressive behaviour. [2 marks]

Outline the social learning explanation of aggression. [4 marks]

Outline the role of innate releasing mechanisms and fixed action patterns in the context of the ethological explanation of aggression. [6 marks]

Outline the frustration-aggression hypothesis. [4 marks]

Discuss evolutionary explanations of aggressive behaviour. [16 marks]

Outline and evaluate the situational explanation of aggression in prisons. [8 marks]

Forensic Psychology Practice Questions

Outline and briefly evaluate the top-down approach to offender profiling. [8 marks]

Discuss one or more biological explanation of offending behaviour. [16 marks]

Outline one strength and one limitation of restorative justice. [6 marks]

What is geographical profiling? [4 marks]

Discuss cognitive explanations of criminal behaviour. [16 marks]

Briefly outline Eysenck's theory of personality as an explanation of criminal behaviour. [4 marks]

Outline and evaluate psychodynamic explanations of offending behaviour. [8 marks]

Briefly outline two aims of custodial sentencing. [4 marks]

Addiction Practice Questions

Outline the neurochemical explanation of nicotine addiction. [4 marks]

Outline two symptoms of addiction. [4 marks]

Briefly discuss behaviourist treatments for reducing addiction. [8 marks]

What is cue reactivity? [2 marks]

Outline one or more learning explanation(s) of gambling addiction. Compare this explanation(s) of gambling addiction with cognitive explanations of gambling addiction. [16 marks]

Discuss research into risk factors for addiction. [16 marks]

Outline one weakness of the learning theory explanation of nicotine addiction. [4 marks]

Briefly outline and evaluate Prochaska's 6-stage model. [8 marks]

BIBLIOGRAPHY AND REFERENCES

Adorno, T. W., Frenkel-Brunswik, E., Levinson, D. J., & Sanford, R. N. (1950). The authoritarian personality. Harpers.

Ainsworth, M. D. S., Blehar, M. C., Waters, E., & Wall, S. (1978). Patterns of attachment: A psychological study of the strange situation. Lawrence Erlbaum.

Ajzen, I. (1991). The theory of planned behavior. Organizational Behavior and Human Decision Processes, 50(2), 179–211. https://doi.org/10.1016/0749-5978(91)90020-T

Akers, R.L., & Lee, G. (1996). A Longitudinal Test of Social Learning Theory: Adolescent Smoking. Journal of Drug Issues, 26, 317-343.

Alarid, L. F., Burton, V. S., Jr., & Cullen, F. T. (2000). Gender and crime among felony offenders: Assessing the generality of social control and differential association theories. Journal of Research in Crime and Delinquency, 37(2), 171–199. https://doi.org/10.1177/0022427800037002002

Albert, D. J., Jonik, R. H., Walsh, M. L., & Petrovic, D. M. (1989). Testosterone supports hormone-dependent aggression in female rats. Physiology & behavior, 46(2), 185–189. https://doi.org/10.1016/0031-9384(89)90253-9

Aleman, A., Kahn, R. S., & Selten, J. P. (2003). Sex differences in the risk of schizophrenia: evidence from meta-analysis. Archives of general psychiatry, 60(6), 565–571. https://doi.org/10.1001/archpsyc.60.6.565

Alexander, G. M., Wilcox, T., & Woods, R. (2009). Sex differences in infants' visual interest in toys. Archives of sexual behavior, 38(3), 427–433. https://doi.org/10.1007/s10508-008-9430-1

Altman, I., & Taylor, D. A. (1973). Social penetration: The development of interpersonal relationships. Holt, Rinehart & Winston.

Anderson, C. A., Shibuya, A., Ihori, N., Swing, E. L., Bushman, B. J., Sakamoto, A., Rothstein, H. R., & Saleem, M. (2010). Violent video game effects on aggression, empathy, and prosocial behavior in eastern and western countries: a meta-analytic review. Psychological bulletin, 136(2), 151–173. https://doi.org/10.1037/a0018251

Andreasen, N. C., Olsen, S. A., Dennert, J. W., & Smith, M. R. (1982). Ventricular enlargement in schizophrenia: relationship to positive and negative symptoms. The American journal of psychiatry, 139(3), 297–302. https://doi.org/10.1176/ajp.139.3.297

Asch, S. E. (1955). Opinions and social pressure. Scientific American, 193(5), 31–35. https://doi.org/10.1038/scientificamerican1155-31

Aschoff, J., & Wever, R. (1976). Human circadian rhythms: a multioscillatory system. Federation proceedings, 35(12), .

Ashem, B., & Donner, L. (1968). Covert sensitization with alcoholics: a controlled replication. Behaviour research and therapy, 6(1), 7-12 .

Atkinson, R. C., & Shiffrin, R. M. (1968). Human memory: A proposed system and its control processes. In K. W. Spence & J. T. Spence, The psychology of learning and motivation: II. Academic Press. https://doi.org/10.1016/S0079-7421(08)60422-3

Aumer, K., Elaine, H., & Frey, R. (2007). Examining Equity Theory across Cultures. Interpersona : An International Journal on Personal Relationships. 1. 10.5964/ijpr.v1i1.5.

Aveyard, P., Massey, L., Parsons, A., Manaseki, S., & Griffin, C. (2009). The effect of transtheoretical model based interventions on smoking cessation. Social Science & Medicine, 68(3), 397–403. https://doi.org/10.1016/j.socscimed.2008.10.036

Avtgis, T. A. (1998). Locus of control and persuasion, social influence, and conformity: A meta-analytic review. Psychological Reports, 83(3, Pt 1), 899–903. https://doi.org/10.2466/PR0.83.7.899-903

Baddeley, A. D., & Hitch, G. (1974). Working memory. Psychology of Learning and Motivation, 47–89. https://doi.org/10.1016/s0079-7421(08)60452-1

Baddeley, A., & Della Sala, S. (1996). Working memory and executive control. Philosophical transactions of the Royal Society of London. Series B, Biological sciences, 351(1346), 1397–1404. https://doi.org/10.1098/rstb.1996.0123

Bagnall AM, Jones L, Ginnelly L, et al. A systematic review of atypical antipsychotic drugs in schizophrenia. 2003. In: NIHR Health Technology Assessment programme: Executive Summaries. Southampton (UK): NIHR Journals Library; 2003-. Available from: https://www.ncbi.nlm.nih.gov/books/NBK62258/

Bailey, H. N., Moran, G., Pederson, D. R., & Bento, S. (2007). Understanding the transmission of attachment using variable- and relationship-centered approaches. Development and psychopathology, 19(2), 313–343. https://doi.org/10.1017/S0954579407070162

Baillargeon, R., & DeVos, J. (1991). Object permanence in young infants: Further evidence. Child Development, 62(6), 1227–1246. https://doi.org/10.2307/1130803

Baillargeon, R., & Graber, M. (1987). Where's the rabbit? 5.5-month-old infants' representation of the height of a hidden object. Cognitive Development, 2(4), 375–392. https://doi.org/10.1016/S0885-2014(87)80014-X

Bandura, A. (1977). Self-efficacy: toward a unifying theory of behavioral change. Psychological review, 84(2), 191–215. https://doi.org/10.1037//0033-295x.84.2.191

Bandura, A., & Walters, R.H. (1963). Social learning and personality development. Holt Rinehart and Winston: New York.

Bandura, A., Ross, D., & Ross, S. A. (1961). Transmission of aggression through imitation of aggressive models. The Journal of Abnormal and Social Psychology, 63(3), 575–582. https://doi.org/10.1037/h0045925

Baron-Cohen, S., Leslie, A. M., & Frith, U. (1985). Does the autistic child have a "theory of mind"?. Cognition, 21(1), 37–46. https://doi.org/10.1016/0010-0277(85)90022-8

Barry, H. III, Bacon, M. K., & Child, I. L. (1957). A cross-cultural survey of some sex differences in socialization. The Journal of Abnormal and Social Psychology, 55(3), 327–332. https://doi.org/10.1037/h0041178

Bateson, G., Jackson, D. D., Haley, J., & Weakland, J. (1956). Toward a theory of schizophrenia. Behavioral Science, 1, 251–264. https://doi.org/10.1002/bs.3830010402

Bauman, K. E., & Ennett, S. T. (1996). On the importance of peer influence for adolescent drug use: commonly neglected considerations. Addiction (Abingdon, England), 91(2), 185–198.

Baylis, C., et al. (1996) Hypothalamic lesions induce obesity and sex-dependent glomerular damage and increases in blood pressure in rats, Hypertension, 27(4), (pp. 926–932). Available at: https://doi.org/10.1161/01.hyp.27.4.926.

Beck, A. T., Shaw, B. F., Rush, A. J., Emery, G. (1979). Cognitive Therapy of Depression. United Kingdom: Guilford Publications.

Beck, A. T., Ward, C. H., Mendelson, M., Mock, J. E., & Erbaugh, J. K. (1962). Reliability of psychiatric diagnosis. 2. A study of consistency of clinical judgments and ratings. The American journal of psychiatry, 119, 351–357. https://doi.org/10.1176/ajp.119.4.351

Beltman, M. W., Voshaar, R. C., & Speckens, A. E. (2010). Cognitive-behavioural therapy for depression in people with a somatic disease: meta-analysis of randomised controlled trials. The British journal of psychiatry : the journal of mental science, 197(1), 11–19. https://doi.org/10.1192/bjp.bp.109.064675

Bem, S. L. (1974). The measurement of psychological androgyny. Journal of Consulting and Clinical Psychology, 42(2), 155–162. https://doi.org/10.1037/h0036215

Bem, S. L. (1981). Gender schema theory: A cognitive account of sex typing. Psychological Review, 88(4), 354–364. https://doi.org/10.1037/0033-295X.88.4.354

Benton, D., & Young, H. A. (2016). A meta-analysis of the relationship between brain dopamine receptors and obesity: a matter of changes in behavior rather than food addiction?. International journal of obesity (2005), 40 Suppl 1(Suppl 1), S12–S21. https://doi.org/10.1038/ijo.2016.9

Bergh, C., Sabin, M., Shield, J., Hellers, G., Zandian, M., Palmberg, K., Olofsson, B., Lindeberg, K., Björnström, M., & Södersten, P. (2009). A Framework for the Treatment of obesity: Early Support. In Obesity: Causes, Mechanisms and Prevention (pp.1-27). Sinauer.

Berman, M. E., McCloskey, M. S., Fanning, J. R., Schumacher, J. A., & Coccaro, E. F. (2009). Serotonin augmentation reduces response to attack in aggressive individuals. Psychological science, 20(6), 714–720. https://doi.org/10.1111/j.1467-9280.2009.02355.x

Berry, J. W. (1969). On cross-cultural comparability.International Journal of Psychology,4,119–128. Available at: https://psycnet.apa.org/record/1970-12414-001

Bickman, L. (1974). The social power of a uniform. Journal of Applied Social Psychology, 4(1), 47–61. https://doi.org/10.1111/j.1559-1816.1974.tb02599.x

BIBLIOGRAPHY AND REFERENCES

Birch, L. L., McPhee, L., Shoba, B. C., Pirok, E., & Steinberg, L. (1987). What kind of exposure reduces children's food neophobia? Looking vs. tasting. Appetite, 9(3), 171–178. https://doi.org/10.1016/s0195-6663(87)80011-9

Blackburn, R. (1993). The psychology of criminal conduct: Theory, research and practice. John Wiley & Sons.

Blass, T. (1991). Understanding behavior in the Milgram obedience experiment: The role of personality, situations, and their interactions. Journal of Personality and Social Psychology, 60(3), 398–413. https://doi.org/10.1037/0022-3514.60.3.398

Boca, S., Garro, M., Giammusso, I., & Abbate, C. S. (2018). The effect of perspective taking on the mediation process. Psychology research and behavior management, 11, 411–416. https://doi.org/10.2147/PRBM.S168956

Bogartz, R. S., Shinskey, J. L., & Schilling, T. H. (2000). Object permanence in five-and-a half-month-old infants? Infancy, 1(4), 403–428. https://doi.org/10.1207/S15327078IN0104_3

Boos, H. B., Cahn, W., van Haren, N. E., Derks, E. M., Brouwer, R. M., Schnack, H. G., Hulshoff Pol, H. E., & Kahn, R. S. (2012). Focal and global brain measurements in siblings of patients with schizophrenia. Schizophrenia bulletin, 38(4), 814–825. https://doi.org/10.1093/schbul/sbq147

Bosma, H., Marmot, M. G., Hemingway, H., Nicholson, A. C., Brunner, E., & Stansfeld, S. A. (1997). Low job control and risk of coronary heart disease in Whitehall II (prospective cohort) study. BMJ (Clinical research ed.), 314(7080), 558–565. https://doi.org/10.1136/bmj.314.7080.558

Bouchard T. J. (2013). The Wilson Effect: the increase in heritability of IQ with age. Twin research and human genetics: the official journal of the International Society for Twin Studies, 16(5), 923–930. https://doi.org/10.1017/thg.2013.54

Boury, M., Treadwell, T., & Kumar, V. K. (2001). Integrating psychodrama and cognitive therapy--an exploratory study. International Journal of Action Methods: Psychodrama, Skill Training, and Role Playing, 54(1), 13–37.

Bovet, J., & Raymond, M. (2015). Preferred women's waist-to-hip ratio variation over the last 2,500 years. PLoS one, 10(4), e0123284. https://doi.org/10.1371/journal.pone.0123284

Bowlby, J. (1944). Forty-four juvenile thieves: their characters and home-life. The International Journal of Psychoanalysis, 25, 19–53.

Brody, A. L., Olmstead, R. E., London, E. D., Farahi, J., Meyer, J. H., Grossman, P., Lee, G. S., Huang, J., Hahn, E. L., & Mandelkern, M. A. (2004). Smoking-induced ventral striatum dopamine release. The American journal of psychiatry, 161(7), 1211–1218. https://doi.org/10.1176/appi.ajp.161.7.1211

Bruch, H. (1979). The golden cage: The enigma of anorexia nervosa. Vintage Books.

Brunner, H. G., Nelen, M., Breakefield, X. O., Ropers, H. H., & van Oost, B. A. (1993). Abnormal behavior associated with a point mutation in the structural gene for monoamine oxidase A. Science, 262(5133), 578–580. https://doi.org/10.1126/science.8211186

Bulik, C. M., Sullivan, P. F., Tozzi, F., Furberg, H., Lichtenstein, P., & Pedersen, N. L. (2006). Prevalence, heritability, and prospective risk factors for anorexia nervosa. Archives of general psychiatry, 63(3), 305–312. https://doi.org/10.1001/archpsyc.63.3.305

Burger, J. M. (2009). Replicating Milgram: Would people still obey today? American Psychologist, 64(1), 1–11. https://doi.org/10.1037/a0010932

Burt, C. (1955). The evidence for the concept of intelligence. British Journal of Educational Psychology, 25, 158–177. https://doi.org/10.1111/j.2044-8279.1955.tb03305.x

Buss, A. H. (1966). Instrumentality of aggression, feedback, and frustration as determinants of physical aggression. Journal of Personality and Social Psychology, 3(2), 153–162. https://doi.org/10.1037/h0022826

Buss, D. M. (1989). Sex differences in human mate preferences: Evolutionary hypotheses tested in 37 cultures. Behavioral and Brain Sciences, 12(1), 1–49. https://doi.org/10.1017/S0140525X00023992

Bussey, K., & Bandura, A. (1999). Social cognitive theory of gender development and differentiation. Psychological Review, 106(4), 676–713. https://doi.org/10.1037/0033-295X.106.4.676

Caldera, Y. M., Huston, A. C., & O'Brien, M. (1989). Social interactions and play patterns of parents and toddlers with feminine, masculine, and neutral toys. Child development, 60(1), 70–76. https://doi.org/10.1111/j.1467-8624.1989.tb02696.x

Camp, S.D. & Gaes, G. (2005). Criminogenic Effects of the Prison Environment on Inmate Behavior: Some Experimental Evidence. Crime & Delinquency - CRIME DELINQUEN. 51. 425-442. 10.1177/0011128704271471.

Canter, D. (1994). Criminal Shadows: Inside the Mind of the Serial Killer. HarperCollins.

Canter, D., & Larkin, P. (1993). The environmental range of serial rapists. Journal of Environmental Psychology, 13(1), 63–69. https://doi.org/10.1016/S0272-4944(05)80215-4

Cardno, A. G., Marshall, E. J., Coid, B., Macdonald, A. M., Ribchester, T. R., Davies, N. J., Venturi, P., Jones, L. A., Lewis, S. W., Sham, P. C., Gottesman, I. I., Farmer, A. E., McGuffin, P., Reveley, A. M., & Murray, R. M. (1999). Heritability estimates for psychotic disorders: the Maudsley twin psychosis series. Archives of general psychiatry, 56(2), 162–168. https://doi.org/10.1001/archpsyc.56.2.162

Carter, B. L., & Tiffany, S. T. (1999). Meta-analysis of cue-reactivity in addiction research. Addiction (Abingdon, England), 94(3), 327–340.

Cashon, C. H., & Cohen, L. B. (2000). Eight-month-old infants' perceptions of possible and impossible events. Infancy, 1(4), 429–446. https://doi.org/10.1207/S15327078IN0104_4

Cheniaux, E., Landeira-Fernandez, J., & Versiani, M. (2009). The diagnoses of schizophrenia, schizoaffective disorder, bipolar disorder and unipolar depression: interrater reliability and congruence between DSM-IV and ICD-10. Psychopathology, 42(5), 293–298. https://doi.org/10.1159/000228838

Christiansen, K.O., & Mednick, S. A. (1977). Biosocial bases of criminal behavior. Gardner Press.

Christianson, S.-Å., & Hübinette, B. (1993). Hands upp A study of witnesses' emotional reactions and memories associated with bank robberies. Applied Cognitive Psychology, 7(5), 365–379. https://doi.org/10.1002/acp.2350070502

Clark, R. D., & Hatfield, E. (1989). Gender differences in receptivity to sexual offers. Journal of Psychology & Human Sexuality, 2(1), 39–55. https://doi.org/10.1300/J056v02n01_04

Cloninger, C. R. (1987). A systematic method for clinical description and classification of personality variants: A proposal. Archives of General Psychiatry, 44(6), 573–588. https://doi.org/10.1001/archpsyc.1987.01800180093014

Coccaro, E. F., Bergeman, C. S., Kavoussi, R. J., & Seroczynski, A.D. (1997). Heritability of aggression and irritability: A twin study of the Buss-Durkee aggression scales in adult male subjects. Biological Psychiatry, 41(3), 273–284. https://doi.org/10.1016/S0006-3223(96)00257-0

Cochrane, R. (1977). Mental illness in immigrants to England and Wales: An analysis of mental hospital admissions, 1971. Social Psychiatry, 12(1), 25–35. https://doi.org/10.1007/BF00578979

Condon, W. S., & Sander, L. W. (1974). Neonate movement is synchronized with adult speech: Interactional participation and language acquisition. Science, 183(4120), 99–101. https://doi.org/10.1126/science.183.4120.99

Copson, G. (1995). Coals to Newcastle? Police Use of Offender Profiling. Accessed 09/04/23 from: https://www.politieacademie.nl/kennisenonderzoek/kennis/mediatheek/PDF/3974.pdf

Cornelissen, P. L., Johns, A., & Tovée, M. J. (2013). Body size over-estimation in women with anorexia nervosa is not qualitatively different from female controls. Body image, 10(1), 103–111. https://doi.org/10.1016/j.bodyim.2012.09.003

BIBLIOGRAPHY AND REFERENCES

Cotton, S. M., Lambert, M., Schimmelmann, B. G., Foley, D. L., Morley, K. I., McGorry, P. D., & Conus, P. (2009). Gender differences in premorbid, entry, treatment, and outcome characteristics in a treated epidemiological sample of 661 patients with first episode psychosis. Schizophrenia research, 114(1-3), 17–24. https://doi.org/10.1016/j.schres.2009.07.002

Cowlishaw, S., Merkouris, S., Dowling, N., Anderson, C., Jackson, A., & Thomas, S. (2012). Psychological therapies for pathological and problem gambling. The Cochrane database of systematic reviews, 11, CD008937. https://doi.org/10.1002/14651858.CD008937.pub2

Creese, I., Burt, D. R., & Snyder, S. H. (1976). Dopamine receptor binding predicts clinical and pharmacological potencies of antischizophrenic drugs. Science (New York, N.Y.), 192(4238), 481–483. https://doi.org/10.1126/science.3854

Cunningham, M. R., Roberts, A. R., Barbee, A. P., Druen, P. B., & Wu, C.-H. (1995). "Their ideas of beauty are, on the whole, the same as ours": Consistency and variability in the cross-cultural perception of female physical attractiveness. Journal of Personality and Social Psychology, 68(2), 261–279. https://doi.org/10.1037/0022-3514.68.2.261

Dabbs, J. M., Carr, T. S., Frady, R. L., & Riad, J. K. (1995). Testosterone, crime, and misbehavior among 692 male prison inmates. Personality and Individual Differences, 18(5), 627–633. https://doi.org/10.1016/0191-8869(94)00177-T

Dalle Grave, R., Calugi, S., El Ghoch, M., Conti, M., & Fairburn, C. G. (2014). Inpatient cognitive behavior therapy for adolescents with anorexia nervosa: immediate and longer-term effects. Frontiers in psychiatry, 5, 14. https://doi.org/10.3389/fpsyt.2014.00014

Danelli, L., Cossu, G., Berlingeri, M., Bottini, G., Sberna, M., & Paulesu, E. (2013). Is a lone right hemisphere enough? Neurolinguistic architecture in a case with a very early left hemispherectomy. Neurocase, 19(3), 209–231. https://doi.org/10.1080/13554794.2011.654226

Davis, J. L., & Rusbult, C. E. (2001). Attitude alignment in close relationships. Journal of Personality and Social Psychology, 81(1), 65–84. https://doi.org/10.1037/0022-3514.81.1.65

Davis, L. K., et al. (2013). Partitioning the heritability of Tourette syndrome and obsessive compulsive disorder reveals differences in genetic architecture. PLoS genetics, 9(10), e1003864. https://doi.org/10.1371/journal.pgen.1003864

Deffenbacher, K. A. (1983). The influence of arousal on reliability of testimony. In S. M. A. Lloyd-Bostock & B. R. Clifford (Eds.), Evaluating witness evidence (pp. 235–251). Chichester, England: Wiley.

Delisi, M., Berg, M.T., & Hochstetler, A. (2005). Gang members, career criminals and prison violence: Further specification of the importation model of inmate behavior. Criminal Justice Studies. 17. 369-383. 10.1080/1478601042000314883.

DeLongis, A., Coyne, J. C., Dakof, G., Folkman, S., & Lazarus, R. S. (1982). Relationship of daily hassles, uplifts, and major life events to health status. Health Psychology, 1(2), 119–136. https://doi.org/10.1037/0278-6133.1.2.119

Deutsch, M., & Gerard, H. B. (1955). A study of normative and informational social influences upon individual judgment. The Journal of Abnormal and Social Psychology, 51(3), 629–636. https://doi.org/10.1037/h0046408

Diamond, M. (2013). Transsexuality among twins: Identity concordance, transition, rearing, and orientation. International Journal of Transgenderism, 14(1), 24–38. https://doi.org/10.1080/15532739.2013.750222

Dinstein, I., Thomas, C., Humphreys, K., Minshew, N., Behrmann, M., & Heeger, D. J. (2010). Normal movement selectivity in autism. Neuron, 66(3), 461–469. https://doi.org/10.1016/j.neuron.2010.03.034

Dittmar, H., Halliwell, E., & Ive, S. (2006). Does Barbie make girls want to be thin? The effect of experimental exposure to images of dolls on the body image of 5- to 8-year-old girls. Developmental Psychology, 42(2), 283–292. https://doi.org/10.1037/0012-1649.42.2.283

Dodd, D. K. (1985). Robbers in the classroom: A deindividuation exercise. Teaching of Psychology, 12(2), 89–91. https://doi.org/10.1207/s15328023top1202_9

Douglas, J. E., Ressler, R. K., Burgess, A. W., & Hartman, C. R. (1986). Criminal profiling from crime scene analysis. Behavioral Sciences & the Law, 4(4), 401–421. https://doi.org/10.1002/bsl.2370040405

Elkins R. L. (1991). An appraisal of chemical aversion (emetic therapy) approaches to alcoholism treatment. Behaviour research and therapy, 29(5), 387–413. https://doi.org/10.1016/0005-7967(91)90123-k

Ellis, A. (1962). Reason and emotion in psychotherapy. Lyle Stuart.

Elms, A. C., & Milgram, S. (1966). Personality characteristics associated with obedience and defiance toward authoritative command. Journal of Experimental Research in Personality, 1(4), 282–289.

Embling S. (2002). The effectiveness of cognitive behavioural therapy in depression. Nursing standard (Royal College of Nursing (Great Britain) : 1987), 17(14-15), 33–41. https://doi.org/10.7748/ns2002.12.17.14.33.c3318

Epstein, J. N., Saunders, B. E., Kilpatrick, D. G., & Resnick, H. S. (1998). PTSD as a mediator between childhood rape and alcohol use in adult women. Child abuse & neglect, 22(3), 223–234. https://doi.org/10.1016/s0145-2134(97)00133-6

Erickson-Schroth, L. (2013). Update on the Biology of Transgender Identity. Journal of Gay & Lesbian Mental Health, 17, 150 - 174.

Errington, F.K., & Gewertz, D.B. (1987). Cultural Alternatives and a Feminist Anthropology: An Analysis of Culturally Constructed Gender Interests in Papua New Guinea.

Eysenck, H. J. (1947). Dimensions of personality. Kegan Paul.

Fall, T., & Ingelsson, E. (2014). Genome-wide association studies of obesity and metabolic syndrome. Molecular and cellular endocrinology, 382(1), 740–757. https://doi.org/10.1016/j.mce.2012.08.018

Farde, L., Wiesel, F. A., Stone-Elander, S., Halldin, C., Nordström, A. L., Hall, H., & Sedvall, G. (1990). D2 dopamine receptors in neuroleptic-naive schizophrenic patients. A positron emission tomography study with [11C]raclopride. Archives of general psychiatry, 47(3), 213–219. https://doi.org/10.1001/archpsyc.1990.01810150013003

Fazel, S., Grann, M., Kling, B., & Hawton, K. (2011). Prison suicide in 12 countries: an ecological study of 861 suicides during 2003-2007. Social psychiatry and psychiatric epidemiology, 46(3), 191–195. https://doi.org/10.1007/s00127-010-0184-4

Festinger, L., Pepitone, A., & Newcomb, T. (1952). Some consequences of de-individuation in a group. The Journal of Abnormal and Social Psychology, 47(2, Suppl), 382–389. https://doi.org/10.1037/h0057906

Fox N. (1977). Attachment of kibbutz infants to mother and metapelet. Child development, 48(4), 1228–1239.

Frayling, T. M., Timpson, N. J., Weedon, M. N., Zeggini, E., Freathy, R. M., Lindgren, C. M., Perry, J. R., Elliott, K. S., Lango, H., Rayner, N. W., Shields, B., Harries, L. W., Barrett, J. C., Ellard, S., Groves, C. J., Knight, B., Patch, A. M., Ness, A. R., Ebrahim, S., Lawlor, D. A., … McCarthy, M. I. (2007). A common variant in the FTO gene is associated with body mass index and predisposes to childhood and adult obesity. Science (New York, N.Y.), 316(5826), 889–894. https://doi.org/10.1126/science.1141634

Freud, S. (1909). Analysis of a phobia in a five-year-old boy.

Friedman, M., & Rosenman, R. H. (1959). Association of specific overt behavior pattern with blood and cardiovascular findings; blood cholesterol level, blood clotting time, incidence of arcus senilis, and clinical coronary artery disease. Journal of the American Medical Association, 169(12), 1286–1296. https://doi.org/10.1001/jama.1959.03000290012005

BIBLIOGRAPHY AND REFERENCES

Funk S. C. (1992). Hardiness: a review of theory and research. Health psychology : official journal of the Division of Health Psychology, American Psychological Association, 11(5), 335–345. https://doi.org/10.1037//0278-6133.11.5.335

Furnham, A. (1984). Personality, social skills, anomie and delinquency: A self-report study of a group of normal non-delinquent adolescents. Child Psychology & Psychiatry & Allied Disciplines, 25(3), 409–420. https://doi.org/10.1111/j.1469-7610.1984.tb00160.x

Geen, R. G. (1968). Effects of frustration, attack, and prior training in aggressiveness upon aggressive behavior. Journal of Personality and Social Psychology, 9(4), 316–321. https://doi.org/10.1037/h0026054

Geiger, B. (1996). Fathers as primary caregivers. Greenwood Press/Greenwood Publishing Group.

Geiselman, R. E., Fisher, R. P., MacKinnon, D. P., & Holland, H. L. (1985). Eyewitness memory enhancement in the police interview: Cognitive retrieval mnemonics versus hypnosis. Journal of Applied Psychology, 70(2), 401–412. https://doi.org/10.1037/0021-9010.70.2.401

Gergen, K.J., Gergen, M.M., & Barton, W.H. (1973). Deviance in the dark. Psychology Today. 7. 129-130.

Gospic, K., Mohlin, E., Fransson, P., Petrovic, P., Johannesson, M., & Ingvar, M. (2011). Limbic justice--amygdala involvement in immediate rejection in the Ultimatum Game. PLoS biology, 9(5), e1001054. https://doi.org/10.1371/journal.pbio.1001054

Gottesman, I. I. (1991). Schizophrenia genesis: The origins of madness. W H Freeman/Times Books/ Henry Holt & Co.

Greenhalgh, J., Dickson, R., & Dundar, Y. (2010). Biofeedback for hypertension: a systematic review. Journal of hypertension, 28(4), 644–652. https://doi.org/10.1097/HJH.0b013e3283370e20

Greer, S., & Watson, M. (1985). Towards a psychobiological model of cancer: psychological considerations. Social science & medicine (1982), 20(8), 773–777. https://doi.org/10.1016/0277-9536(85)90330-2

Griffiths, M.D. (1994). The role of cognitive bias and skill in fruit machine gambling. British Journal of Psychology, 85, 351-369.

Gurucharri, C., & Selman, R. L. (1982). The development of interpersonal understanding during childhood, preadolescence, and adolescence: A longitudinal follow-up study. Child Development, 53(4), 924–927. https://doi.org/10.2307/1129129

Hagger, M. S., Lonsdale, A., & Chatzisarantis, N. L. (2011). Effectiveness of a brief intervention using mental simulations in reducing alcohol consumption in corporate employees. Psychology, health & medicine, 16(4), 375–392. https://doi.org/10.1080/13548506.2011.554568

Hajek, P., & Stead, L. F. (2004). Aversive smoking for smoking cessation. The Cochrane database of systematic reviews, 2001(3), CD000546. https://doi.org/10.1002/14651858.CD000546.pub2

Haker, H., Kawohl, W., Herwig, U., & Rössler, W. (2013). Mirror neuron activity during contagious yawning--an fMRI study. Brain imaging and behavior, 7(1), 28–34. https://doi.org/10.1007/s11682-012-9189-9

Haney, C., Banks, C., & Zimbardo, P. (1973). Interpersonal dynamics in a simulated prison. International Journal of Criminology & Penology, 1(1), 69–97.

Happé, F., Ehlers, S., Fletcher, P., Frith, U., Johansson, M., Gillberg, C., Dolan, R., Frackowiak, R., & Frith, C. (1996). 'Theory of mind' in the brain. Evidence from a PET scan study of Asperger syndrome. Neuroreport, 8(1), 197–201. https://doi.org/10.1097/00001756-199612200-00040

Haracz J. L. (1982). The dopamine hypothesis: an overview of studies with schizophrenic patients. Schizophrenia bulletin, 8(3), 438–469. https://doi.org/10.1093/schbul/8.3.438

Hare, L., Bernard, P., Sánchez, F. J., Baird, P. N., Vilain, E., Kennedy, T., & Harley, V. R. (2009). Androgen receptor repeat length polymorphism associated with male-to-female transsexualism. Biological psychiatry, 65(1), 93–96. https://doi.org/10.1016/j.biopsych.2008.08.033

Harlow, H. F., & Zimmermann, R. R. (1959). Affectional Responses in the Infant Monkey. Science, 130, 421-432. https://doi.org/10.1126/science.130.3373.421

Hassett, J. M., Siebert, E. R., & Wallen, K. (2008). Sex differences in rhesus monkey toy preferences parallel those of children. Hormones and behavior, 54(3), 359–364. https://doi.org/10.1016/j.yhbeh.2008.03.008

Hazan, C., & Shaver, P. (1987). Romantic love conceptualized as an attachment process. Journal of personality and social psychology, 52(3), 511–524. https://doi.org/10.1037//0022-3514.52.3.511

Healy, D. (2004). The Creation of Psychopharmacology. Harvard University Press.

Herman, C. P., & Mack, D. (1975). Restrained and unrestrained eating. Journal of Personality, 43(4), 647–660. https://doi.org/10.1111/j.1467-6494.1975.tb00727.x

Herman, C. P., & Polivy, J. (1984). A boundary model for the regulation of eating. Research publications - Association for Research in Nervous and Mental Disease, 62, 141–156.

Heymsfield, S. B., Greenberg, A. S., Fujioka, K., Dixon, R. M., Kushner, R., Hunt, T., Lubina, J. A., Patane, J., Self, B., Hunt, P., & McCamish, M. (1999). Recombinant leptin for weight loss in obese and lean adults: a randomized, controlled, dose-escalation trial. JAMA, 282(16), 1568–1575. https://doi.org/10.1001/jama.282.16.1568

Hickok G. (2009). Eight problems for the mirror neuron theory of action understanding in monkeys and humans. Journal of cognitive neuroscience, 21(7), 1229–1243. https://doi.org/10.1162/jocn.2009.21189

Hilker, R., Helenius, D., Fagerlund, B., Skytthe, A., Christensen, K., Werge, T. M., Nordentoft, M., & Glenthøj, B. (2018). Heritability of Schizophrenia and Schizophrenia Spectrum Based on the Nationwide Danish Twin Register. Biological psychiatry, 83(6), 492–498. https://doi.org/10.1016/j.biopsych.2017.08.017

Holland, A. J., Sicotte, N., & Treasure, J. (1988). Anorexia nervosa: evidence for a genetic basis. Journal of psychosomatic research, 32(6), 561–571. https://doi.org/10.1016/0022-3999(88)90004-9

Holmes, T. H., & Rahe, R. H. (1967). The Social Readjustment Rating Scale. Journal of psychosomatic research, 11(2), 213–218. https://doi.org/10.1016/0022-3999(67)90010-4

Holtom-Viesel, A., & Allan, S. (2014). A systematic review of the literature on family functioning across all eating disorder diagnoses in comparison to control families. Clinical psychology review, 34(1), 29–43. https://doi.org/10.1016/j.cpr.2013.10.005

Howard, M. O., Kivlahan, D., & Walker, R. D. (1997). Cloninger's tridimensional theory of personality and psychopathology: applications to substance use disorders. Journal of studies on alcohol, 58(1), 48–66. https://doi.org/10.15288/jsa.1997.58.48

Hu, X. Z., Lipsky, R. H., Zhu, G., Akhtar, L. A., Taubman, J., Greenberg, B. D., Xu, K., Arnold, P. D., Richter, M. A., Kennedy, J. L., Murphy, D. L., & Goldman, D. (2006). Serotonin transporter promoter gain-of-function genotypes are linked to obsessive-compulsive disorder. American journal of human genetics, 78(5), 815–826. https://doi.org/10.1086/503850

Hughes, J. R., Shiffman, S., Callas, P., & Zhang, J. (2003). A meta-analysis of the efficacy of over-the-counter nicotine replacement. Tobacco control, 12(1), 21–27. https://doi.org/10.1136/tc.12.1.21

Hughes, M. (1975). Egocentrism in preschool children.

Hulshoff Pol, H., Cohen-Kettenis, P., Haren, N.E.M., Peper, J.S., Brans, R.G.H., Cahn, W., Schnack, H.G., Gooren, L., & Kahn, R.S. (2006). Changing your sex changes your brain: Influences of testosterone and estrogen on adult human brain structure. European Journal of Endocrinology, Supplement. 155. 10.1530/eje.1.02248.

Huseman, R. C., Hatfield, J. D., & Miles, E. W. (1987). A new perspective on equity theory: The equity sensitivity construct. The Academy of Management Review, 12(2), 222–234. https://doi.org/10.2307/258531

BIBLIOGRAPHY AND REFERENCES

Ireland, J.L. (2004). Anger management therapy with young male offenders: An evaluation of treatment outcome. Aggressive Behaviour, 30(2), 174–185.

Irwin, J., & Cressey, D.R. (1962). Thieves, Convicts and the Inmate Culture. Social Problems, Volume 10, Issue 2, (pp. 142–155), https://doi.org/10.2307/799047

Isabella, R. A., Belsky, J., & von Eye, A. (1989). Origins of infant-mother attachment: An examination of interactional synchrony during the infant's first year. Developmental Psychology, 25(1), 12–21. https://doi.org/10.1037/0012-1649.25.1.12

Jacobs, J. (1887). Experiments on Prehension. American Journal of Psychology, 1, 193.

Jahoda, M. (1958). Current concepts of positive mental health. Basic Books. https://doi.org/10.1037/11258-000

Jakobsen, K. D., Frederiksen, J. N., Hansen, T., Jansson, L. B., Parnas, J., & Werge, T. (2005). Reliability of clinical ICD-10 schizophrenia diagnoses. Nordic journal of psychiatry, 59(3), 209–212. https://doi.org/10.1080/08039480510027698

Jauhar, S., McKenna, P. J., Radua, J., Fung, E., Salvador, R., & Laws, K. R. (2014). Cognitive-behavioural therapy for the symptoms of schizophrenia: systematic review and meta-analysis with examination of potential bias. The British journal of psychiatry : the journal of mental science, 204(1), 20–29. https://doi.org/10.1192/bjp.bp.112.116285

Jiang, L.C., Bazarova, N.N. and Hancock, J.T. (2010), The Disclosure–Intimacy Link in Computer-Mediated Communication: An Attributional Extension of the Hyperpersonal Model. Human Communication Research, 37: 58-77. https://doi.org/10.1111/j.1468-2958.2010.01393.x

Jiang, S., & Fisher-Giorlando, M. (2002). Inmate misconduct: A test of the deprivation, importation, and situational models. The Prison Journal, 82(3), 335–358. https://doi.org/10.1177/003288550208200303

Johnstone, E. C., Crow, T. J., Frith, C. D., Husband, J., & Kreel, L. (1976). Cerebral ventricular size and cognitive impairment in chronic schizophrenia. Lancet (London, England), 2(7992), 924–926. https://doi.org/10.1016/s0140-6736(76)90890-4

Jones, M. C. (1924). A Laboratory Study of Fear: The Case Of Peter, The Pedagogical Seminary and Journal of Genetic Psychology, 31:4, 308-315, DOI: 10.1080/08856559.1924.9944851

Jónsson, H., & Hougaard, E. (2009). Group cognitive behavioural therapy for obsessive-compulsive disorder: a systematic review and meta-analysis. Acta psychiatrica Scandinavica, 119(2), 98–106. https://doi.org/10.1111/j.1600-0447.2008.01270.x

Kanner, A. D., Coyne, J. C., Schaefer, C., & Lazarus, R. S. (1981). Comparison of two modes of stress measurement: daily hassles and uplifts versus major life events. Journal of behavioral medicine, 4(1), 1–39. https://doi.org/10.1007/BF00844845

Karasek, R. A. (1979). Job Demands, Job Decision Latitude, and Mental Strain: Implications for Job Redesign. Administrative Science Quarterly, 24(2), 285–308. https://doi.org/10.2307/2392498

Kaye, W. H., Fudge, J. L., & Paulus, M. (2009). New insights into symptoms and neurocircuit function of anorexia nervosa. Nature reviews. Neuroscience, 10(8), 573–584. https://doi.org/10.1038/nrn2682

Kelman, H.C. (1958). Compliance, identification, and internalization three processes of attitude change. Journal of Conflict Resolution, 2, 51 - 60.

Kerckhoff, A. C., & Davis, K. E. (1962). Value consensus and need complementarity in mate selection. American Sociological Review, 27(3), 295–303. https://doi.org/10.2307/2089791

Kiecolt-Glaser, J. K., Garner, W., Speicher, C., Penn, G. M., Holliday, J., & Glaser, R. (1984). Psychosocial modifiers of immunocompetence in medical students. Psychosomatic medicine, 46(1), 7–14. https://doi.org/10.1097/00006842-198401000-00003

Kivimäki, M., Virtanen, M., Elovainio, M., Kouvonen, A., Väänänen, A., & Vahtera, J. (2006). Work stress in the etiology of coronary heart disease--a meta-analysis. Scandinavian journal of work, environment & health, 32(6), 431–442. https://doi.org/10.5271/sjweh.1049

Kobasa, S. C. (1979). Stressful life events, personality, and health: An inquiry into hardiness. Journal of Personality and Social Psychology, 37(1), 1–11. https://doi.org/10.1037/0022-3514.37.1.1

Kohlberg, L. (1966). Cognitive Stages and Preschool Education. Human Development, 9(1/2), 5–17. http://www.jstor.org/stable/26761699

Kohlberg, L. (1984). The Psychology of Moral Development: the Nature and Validity of Moral Stages. Harper & Row

Köhnken, G., Milne, R., Memon, A., & Bull, R. (1999). The Cognitive Interview: A Meta-Analysis. Psychology Crime & Law - PSYCHOL CRIME LAW. 5. 3-27. 10.1080/10683169908414991.

Kontis, D., & Theochari, E. (2012). Dopamine in anorexia nervosa: a systematic review. Behavioural pharmacology, 23(5-6), 496–515. https://doi.org/10.1097/FBP.0b013e328357e115

Kortegaard, L. S., Hoerder, K., Joergensen, J., Gillberg, C., & Kyvik, K. O. (2001). A preliminary population-based twin study of self-reported eating disorder. Psychological medicine, 31(2), 361–365. https://doi.org/10.1017/s0033291701003087

Krahé, B., Möller, I., Huesmann, L. R., Kirwil, L., Felber, J., & Berger, A. (2011). Desensitization to media violence: links with habitual media violence exposure, aggressive cognitions, and aggressive behavior. Journal of personality and social psychology, 100(4), 630–646. https://doi.org/10.1037/a0021711

Kruijver, F. P., Zhou, J. N., Pool, C. W., Hofman, M. A., Gooren, L. J., & Swaab, D. F. (2000). Male-to-female transsexuals have female neuron numbers in a limbic nucleus. The Journal of clinical endocrinology and metabolism, 85(5), 2034–2041. https://doi.org/10.1210/jcem.85.5.6564

Kuhn, T. (1970) The Structure of Scientific Revolutions. University of Chicago Press, Chicago.

Kurniawan, H., Maslov, A.V., & Pechenizkiy, M. (2013). Stress detection from speech and Galvanic Skin Response signals. Proceedings of the 26th IEEE International Symposium on Computer-Based Medical Systems, 209-214.

Lashley, K. S. (1950). In search of the engram. In Society for Experimental Biology, Physiological mechanisms in animal behavior. (Society's Symposium IV.) (pp. 454–482). Academic Press.

Latimer, J., Dowden, C., & Muise, D. (2005). The Effectiveness of Restorative Justice Practices: A Meta-Analysis. The Prison Journal, 85(2), 127–144. https://doi.org/10.1177/0032885505276969

Le, B., & Agnew, C. (2003). Commitment and Its Theorized Determinants: A Meta-analysis of the Investment Model. Personal Relationships. 10. 37 - 57. 10.1111/1475-6811.00035.

Lemaire, J. B., Wallace, J. E., Lewin, A. M., de Grood, J., & Schaefer, J. P. (2011). The effect of a biofeedback-based stress management tool on physician stress: a randomized controlled clinical trial. Open medicine : a peer-reviewed, independent, open-access journal, 5(4), e154–e163.

Leucht, S., Cipriani, A., Spineli, L., Mavridis, D., Orey, D., Richter, F., Samara, M., Barbui, C., Engel, R. R., Geddes, J. R., Kissling, W., Stapf, M. P., Lässig, B., Salanti, G., & Davis, J. M. (2013). Comparative efficacy and tolerability of 15 antipsychotic drugs in schizophrenia: a multiple-treatments meta-analysis. Lancet (London, England), 382(9896), 951–962. https://doi.org/10.1016/S0140-6736(13)60733-3

Levin, E. D., Hampton, D., & Rose, J. E. (2010). IV nicotine self-administration in rats using the consummatory operant licking response. Physiology & behavior, 101(5), 755–758. https://doi.org/10.1016/j.physbeh.2010.08.015

Li, H., Chan, R. C., McAlonan, G. M., & Gong, Q. Y. (2010). Facial emotion processing in schizophrenia: a meta-analysis of functional neuroimaging data. Schizophrenia bulletin, 36(5), 1029–1039. https://doi.org/10.1093/schbul/sbn190

BIBLIOGRAPHY AND REFERENCES

Lieberman, J. A., Stroup, T. S., McEvoy, J. P., Swartz, M. S., Rosenheck, R. A., Perkins, D. O., Keefe, R. S., Davis, S. M., Davis, C. E., Lebowitz, B. D., Severe, J., Hsiao, J. K., & Clinical Antipsychotic Trials of Intervention Effectiveness (CATIE) Investigators (2005). Effectiveness of antipsychotic drugs in patients with chronic schizophrenia. The New England journal of medicine, 353(12), 1209–1223. https://doi.org/10.1056/NEJMoa051688

Lindström, L. H., Gefvert, O., Hagberg, G., Lundberg, T., Bergström, M., Hartvig, P., & Långström, B. (1999). Increased dopamine synthesis rate in medial prefrontal cortex and striatum in schizophrenia indicated by L-(beta-11C) DOPA and PET. Biological psychiatry, 46(5), 681–688. https://doi.org/10.1016/s0006-3223(99)00109-2

Loftus, E. F., & Palmer, J. C. (1974). Reconstruction of automobile destruction: An example of the interaction between language and memory. Journal of Verbal Learning & Verbal Behavior, 13(5), 585–589. https://doi.org/10.1016/S0022-5371(74)80011-3

Logie, R. H. (1995). Visuo-spatial working memory. Lawrence Erlbaum Associates, Inc.

Lorenz, K. (1935). Der Kumpan in der Umwelt des Vogels. Der Artgenosse als auslösendes Moment sozialer Verhaltungsweisen [The companion in the bird's world. The fellow-member of the species as releasing factor of social behavior]. Journal für Ornithologie. Beiblatt. (Leipzig), 83, 137–213. https://doi.org/10.1007/BF01905355

Lorenz, K. (1966). On Aggression. (M. Latzke, Trans.) Methuen.

Marsman, A., van den Heuvel, M. P., Klomp, D. W., Kahn, R. S., Luijten, P. R., & Hulshoff Pol, H. E. (2013). Glutamate in schizophrenia: a focused review and meta-analysis of ^{1}H-MRS studies. Schizophrenia bulletin, 39(1), 120–129. https://doi.org/10.1093/schbul/sbr069

Martin, C. L., & Halverson, C. F. (1981). A Schematic Processing Model of Sex Typing and Stereotyping in Children. Child Development, 52(4), 1119–1134. https://doi.org/10.2307/1129498

Martin, C. L., & Halverson, C. F. (1983). The effects of sex-typing schemas on young children's memory. Child Development, 54(3), 563–574. https://doi.org/10.2307/1130043

Martin, C. L., & Little, J. K. (1990). The relation of gender understanding to children's sex-typed preferences and gender stereotypes. Child development, 61(5), 1427–1439.

Maslow, A. H. (1943). A theory of human motivation. Psychological Review, 50(4), 370–396. https://doi.org/10.1037/h0054346

Mason, J. W. (1971). A re-evaluation of the concept of "non-specificity" in stress theory. Journal of Psychiatric Research, 8(3-4), 323–333. https://doi.org/10.1016/0022-3956(71)90028-8

Mason, P., Harrison, G., Croudace, T., Glazebrook, C., & Medley, I. (1997). The predictive validity of a diagnosis of schizophrenia. A report from the International Study of Schizophrenia (ISoS) coordinated by the World Health Organization and the Department of Psychiatry, University of Nottingham. The British journal of psychiatry : the journal of mental science, 170, 321–327. https://doi.org/10.1192/bjp.170.4.321

Matthews, K. A., & Haynes, S. G. (1986). Type A behavior pattern and coronary disease risk. Update and critical evaluation. American journal of epidemiology, 123(6), 923–960. https://doi.org/10.1093/oxfordjournals.aje.a114347

McCutcheon, L. E., Lange, R., & Houran, J. (2002). Conceptualization and measurement of celebrity worship. British journal of psychology (London, England : 1953), 93(Pt 1), 67–87. https://doi.org/10.1348/000712602162454

McCutcheon, L.E., Scott, V.B., Aruguete, M.S., & Parker, J. (2006). Exploring the link between attachment and the inclination to obsess about or stalk celebrities. North American Journal of Psychology. 8. 289-300.

Mcghee, P.E., & Frueh, T. (1980). Television viewing and the learning of sex-role stereotypes. Sex Roles, 6, 179-188.

McKenna, K., Green, A., & Gleason, M. (2002). Relationship Formation on the Internet: What's the Big Attraction?. Journal of Social Issues - J SOC ISSUES. 58. 9-31. 10.1111/1540-4560.00246.

McKenna, K.Y., & Bargh, J.A. (1999). Causes and Consequences of Social Interaction on the Internet: A Conceptual Framework. Media Psychology, 1, 249-269.

McMonagle, T., & Sultana, A. (2000). Token economy for schizophrenia. The Cochrane database of systematic reviews, (3), CD001473. https://doi.org/10.1002/14651858.CD001473

Mead, M. (1935). Sex and Temperament in Three Primitive Societies. William Morrow.

Mednick, S. A., & Christiansen, K. O. (1977). Biosocial bases of criminal behavior. Gardner Press.

Mednick, S.A., Gabrielli, W.F., Jr, & Hutchings, B. (1984). Genetic influences in criminal convictions: evidence from an adoption cohort. Science (New York, N.Y.), 224(4651), 891–894. https://doi.org/10.1126/science.6719119

Meehl, P. E. (1962). Schizotaxia, schizotypy, schizophrenia. American Psychologist, 17(12), 827–838. https://doi.org/10.1037/h0041029

Meichenbaum, D. (1985). Stress Inoculation Training. Pergamon Press.

Meier, L. L., Semmer, N. K., Elfering, A., & Jacobshagen, N. (2008). The double meaning of control: Three-way interactions between internal resources, job control, and stressors at work. Journal of Occupational Health Psychology, 13(3), 244–258. https://doi.org/10.1037/1076-8998.13.3.244

Mennella, J. A., Pepino, M. Y., & Reed, D. R. (2005). Genetic and environmental determinants of bitter perception and sweet preferences. Pediatrics, 115(2), e216–e222. https://doi.org/10.1542/peds.2004-1582

Milan, M. A., & McKee, J. M. (1976). The cellblock token economy: token reinforcement procedures in a maximum security correctional institution for adult male felons. Journal of applied behavior analysis, 9(3), 253–275. https://doi.org/10.1901/jaba.1976.9-253

Milgram, S. (1963). Behavioral Study of obedience. The Journal of Abnormal and Social Psychology, 67(4), 371–378. https://doi.org/10.1037/h0040525

Milgram, S. (1974). Obedience to Authority: An Experimental View. Harper and Row.

Milne, R., & Bull, R. (2002). Back to basics: A componential analysis of the original cognitive interview mnemonics with three age groups. Applied Cognitive Psychology, 16(7), 743–753. https://doi.org/10.1002/acp.825

Ministry of Justice. (2013). Proven Reoffending Quarterly Statistics: Last Updated 26 January 2023. Accessed 09/04/23 from: https://www.gov.uk/government/collections/proven-reoffending-statistics

Minuchin, S., Rosman, B. L., & Baker, L. (1978). Psychosomatic families: Anorexia nervosa in context. Harvard U Press. https://doi.org/10.4159/harvard.9780674418233

Miyake A, Friedman NP, Emerson MJ, Witzki AH, Howerter A, Wager TD. The unity and diversity of executive functions and their contributions to complex "Frontal Lobe" tasks: a latent variable analysis. Cogn Psychol. 2000 Aug;41(1):49-100. doi: 10.1006/cogp.1999.0734. PMID: 10945922.

Moscovici, S., Lage, E., & Naffrechoux, M. (1969). Influence of a consistent minority on the responses of a majority in a color perception task. Sociometry, 32(4), 365–380. https://doi.org/10.2307/2786541

Munroe, R. H., Shimmin, H. S., & Munroe, R. L. (1984). Gender understanding and sex role preference in four cultures. Developmental Psychology, 20(4), 673–682. https://doi.org/10.1037/0012-1649.20.4.673

Nemeth, C. J. (1986). Differential contributions of majority and minority influence. Psychological Review, 93(1), 23–32. https://doi.org/10.1037/0033-295X.93.1.23

O'Connor, K., Todorov, C., Robillard, S., Borgeat, F., & Brault, M. (1999). Cognitive-behaviour therapy and medication in the treatment of obsessive-compulsive disorder: A controlled study. The Canadian Journal of Psychiatry / La Revue canadienne de psychiatrie, 44(1), 64–71. https://doi.org/10.1177/070674379904400108

BIBLIOGRAPHY AND REFERENCES

O'Kearney, R. T., Anstey, K. J., & von Sanden, C. (2006). Behavioural and cognitive behavioural therapy for obsessive compulsive disorder in children and adolescents. The Cochrane database of systematic reviews, 2006(4), CD004856. https://doi.org/10.1002/14651858.CD004856.pub2

Offman, A., & Kleinplatz, P. (2004). Does PMDD belong in the DSM? Challenging the medicalization of women's bodies. Canadian Journal of Human Sexuality. 13. 17-27.

Orth-Gomér K, Rosengren A, Wilhelmsen L. Lack of social support and incidence of coronary heart disease in middle-aged Swedish men. Psychosom Med. 1993 Jan-Feb;55(1):37-43. doi: 10.1097/00006842-199301000-00007. PMID: 8446739.

Orth-Gomér, K., Rosengren, A., & Wilhelmsen, L. (1993). Lack of social support and incidence of coronary heart disease in middle-aged Swedish men. Psychosomatic medicine, 55(1), 37–43. https://doi.org/10.1097/00006842-199301000-00007

Palmer, E. J., & Hollin, C. R. (1998). A comparison of patterns of moral development in young offenders and non-offenders. Legal and Criminological Psychology, 3(Part 2), 225–235. https://doi.org/10.1111/j.2044-8333.1998.tb00363.x

Parke, J., & Griffiths, M. (2004). Gambling addiction and the evolution of the "near miss" [Editorial]. Addiction Research & Theory, 12(5), 407–411. https://doi.org/10.1080/16066350410001728118

Pavlov P. I. (1927). Conditioned reflexes: An investigation of the physiological activity of the cerebral cortex. Annals of neurosciences, 17(3), 136–141. https://doi.org/10.5214/ans.0972-7531.1017309

Penney, C. G. (1975). Modality effects in short-term verbal memory. Psychological Bulletin, 82(1), 68–84. https://doi.org/10.1037/h0076166

Petry, N. M., Ammerman, Y., Bohl, J., Doersch, A., Gay, H., Kadden, R., Molina, C., & Steinberg, K. (2006). Cognitive-behavioral therapy for pathological gamblers. Journal of consulting and clinical psychology, 74(3), 555–567. https://doi.org/10.1037/0022-006X.74.3.555

Piaget, J. (1952). The origins of intelligence in children. (M. Cook, Trans.). W W Norton & Co. https://doi.org/10.1037/11494-000

Piaget, J., & Inhelder, B. (1956). The Child's Conception of Space. (F.J. Langdon, & J.L. Lunzer, Trans.). W W Norton & Co.

Pigott, T. A., & Seay, S. M. (1999). A review of the efficacy of selective serotonin reuptake inhibitors in obsessive-compulsive disorder. The Journal of clinical psychiatry, 60(2), 101–106. https://doi.org/10.4088/jcp.v60n0206

Pilling, S., Bebbington, P., Kuipers, E., Garety, P., Geddes, J., Orbach, G., & Morgan, C. (2002). Psychological treatments in schizophrenia: I. Meta-analysis of family intervention and cognitive behaviour therapy. Psychological medicine, 32(5), 763–782. https://doi.org/10.1017/s0033291702005895

Pinizzotto, A. J., & Finkel, N. J. (1990). Criminal personality profiling: An outcome and process study. Law and Human Behavior, 14(3), 215–233. https://doi.org/10.1007/BF01352750

Pinker, S. (1997). How the mind works. W W Norton & Co.

Pollock, N. L., & Hashmall, J. M. (1991). The excuses of child molesters. Behavioral Sciences & the Law, 9(1), 53–59. https://doi.org/10.1002/bsl.2370090107

Popper, K. (1959). The logic of scientific discovery. Basic Books.

Prochaska, J. O., & DiClemente, C. C. (1983). Stages and processes of self-change of smoking: toward an integrative model of change. Journal of consulting and clinical psychology, 51(3), 390–395. https://doi.org/10.1037/0022-006x.51.3.390

Puts, D. A., McDaniel, M. A., Jordan, C. L., & Breedlove, S. M. (2008). Spatial ability and prenatal androgens: meta-analyses of congenital adrenal hyperplasia and digit ratio (2D:4D) studies. Archives of sexual behavior, 37(1), 100–111. https://doi.org/10.1007/s10508-007-9271-3

Ragland, D. R., & Brand, R. J. (1988). Type A behavior and mortality from coronary heart disease. The New England journal of medicine, 318(2), 65–69. https://doi.org/10.1056/NEJM198801143180201

Rahe, R. H., Mahan, J. L., & Arthur, R. J. (1970). Prediction of near-future health change from subjects' preceding life changes. Journal of Psychosomatic Research, 14(4), 401–406. https://doi.org/10.1022-3999(70)90008-5

Raine A. (1996). Autonomic nervous system factors underlying disinhibited, antisocial, and violent behavior. Biosocial perspectives and treatment implications. Annals of the New York Academy of Sciences, 794, 46–59. https://doi.org/10.1111/j.1749-6632.1996.tb32508.x

Raine, A., Buchsbaum, M., & LaCasse, L. (1997). Brain abnormalities in murderers indicated by positron emission tomography. Biological psychiatry, 42(6), 495–508. https://doi.org/10.1016/S0006-3223(96)00362-9

Ramachandran, V. S., & Oberman, L. M. (2006). Broken mirrors: a theory of autism. Scientific American, 295(5), 62–69. https://doi.org/10.1038/scientificamerican1106-62

Rehfeldt, R. A., Dillen, J. E., Ziomek, M. M., & Kowalchuk, R. K. (2007). Assessing Relational Learning Deficits in Perspective-Taking in Children with High-Functioning Autism Spectrum Disorder. The Psychological Record, 57(1), 23–47.

Rekers, G. A., & Lovaas, O. I. (1974). Behavioral treatment of deviant sex-role behaviors in a male child. Journal of applied behavior analysis, 7(2), 173–190. https://doi.org/10.1901/jaba.1974.7-173

Richardson, A.H., & Winch, R.F. (1959). Mate-Selection: A Study of Complementary Needs.

Rivera, S. M., Wakeley, A., & Langer, J. (1999). The drawbridge phenomenon: Representational reasoning or perceptual preference? Developmental Psychology, 35(2), 427–435. https://doi.org/10.1037/0012-1649.35.2.427

Rizzolatti, G., Fadiga, L., Gallese, V., & Fogassi, L. (1996). Premotor cortex and the recognition of motor actions. Brain research. Cognitive brain research, 3(2), 131–141. https://doi.org/10.1016/0926-6410(95)00038-0

Robin, A. L., Siegel, P. T., Moye, A. W., Gilroy, M., Dennis, A. B., & Sikand, A. (1999). A controlled comparison of family versus individual therapy for adolescents with anorexia nervosa. Journal of the American Academy of Child and Adolescent Psychiatry, 38(12), 1482–1489. https://doi.org/10.1097/00004583-199912000-00008

Robin, A. L., Siegel, P. T., Moye, A. W., Gilroy, M., Dennis, A. B., & Sikand, A. (1999). A controlled comparison of family versus individual therapy for adolescents with anorexia nervosa. Journal of the American Academy of Child and Adolescent Psychiatry, 38(12), 1482–1489. https://doi.org/10.1097/00004583-199912000-00008

Rodin M. (1992). The social construction of premenstrual syndrome. Social science & medicine (1982), 35(1), 49–56. https://doi.org/10.1016/0277-9536(92)90118-a

Rogers, Carl. (1951). Client-Centered Therapy: Its Current Practice, Implications and Theory. London: Constable. ISBN 1-84119-840-4.

Rollie, S. S., & Duck, S. (2006). Divorce and Dissolution of Romantic Relationships: Stage Models and Their Limitations. In M. A. Fine & J. H. Harvey (Eds.), Handbook of divorce and relationship dissolution (pp. 223–240). Lawrence Erlbaum Associates Publishers.

Rosenhan D. L. (1973). On being sane in insane places. Science (New York, N.Y.), 179(4070), 250–258. https://doi.org/10.1126/science.179.4070.250

Rosenhan, D. L., & Seligman, M. E. P. (1989). Abnormal psychology (2nd ed.). W W Norton & Co.

Rosenman, R. H., Brand, R. J., Sholtz, R. I., & Friedman, M. (1976). Multivariate prediction of coronary heart disease during 8.5 year follow-up in the Western Collaborative Group Study. The American journal of cardiology, 37(6), 903–910. https://doi.org/10.1016/0002-9149(76)90117-x

Rosenstein, D., & Oster, H. (1988). Differential facial responses to four basic tastes in newborns. Child development, 59(6), 1555–1568.

Roth, W., Tinklenberg, J.R., Whitaker, C.A., Darley, C.F., Kopell, B.S., & Hollister, L.E. (1973). The effect of marihuana on tracking task perfomance. Psychopharmacologia. 33. 259-265. 10.1007/BF00423060.

Rotter, J. B. (1966). Generalized expectancies for internal versus external control of reinforcement. Psychological Monographs: General and Applied, 80(1), 1–28. https://doi.org/10.1037/h0092976

BIBLIOGRAPHY AND REFERENCES

Rusbult, C. E. (1980). Commitment and satisfaction in romantic associations: A test of the investment model. Journal of Experimental Social Psychology, 16(2), 172–186. https://doi.org/10.1016/0022-1031(80)90007-4

Rusbult, C. E. (1983). A longitudinal test of the investment model: The development (and deterioration) of satisfaction and commitment in heterosexual involvements. Journal of Personality and Social Psychology, 45(1), 101–117. https://doi.org/10.1037/0022-3514.45.1.101

Rutter M. (1998). Developmental catch-up, and deficit, following adoption after severe global early privation. English and Romanian Adoptees (ERA) Study Team. Journal of child psychology and psychiatry, and allied disciplines, 39(4), 465–476.

Saunders, T., Driskell, J. E., Johnston, J. H., & Salas, E. (1996). The effect of stress inoculation training on anxiety and performance. Journal of Occupational Health Psychology, 1(2), 170–186. https://doi.org/10.1037/1076-8998.1.2.170

Savage, J. S., Hoffman, L., & Birch, L. L. (2009). Dieting, restraint, and disinhibition predict women's weight change over 6 y. The American journal of clinical nutrition, 90(1), 33–40. https://doi.org/10.3945/ajcn.2008.26558

Saxena, S., & Rauch, S.L. (2000). Functional neuroimaging and the neuroanatomy of obsessive-compulsive disorder. The Psychiatric clinics of North America, 23 3, 563-86.

Scarr, S. (1988). Race and gender as psychological variables: Social and ethical issues. American Psychologist, 43(1), 56–59. https://doi.org/10.1037/0003-066X.43.1.56

Schaeffer, H. R., & Emerson, P. E. (1964). The development of social attachments in infancy. Monographs of the Society for Research in Child Development, 29(3, Whole No. 94), 1–77. https://doi.org/10.2307/1165727

Schedlowski, M., Jacobs, R., Stratmann, G., Richter, S., Hädicke, A., Tewes, U., Wagner, T. O., & Schmidt, R. E. (1993). Changes of natural killer cells during acute psychological stress. Journal of clinical immunology, 13(2), 119–126. https://doi.org/10.1007/BF00919268

Schizophrenia Working Group of the Psychiatric Genomics Consortium (2014). Biological insights from 108 schizophrenia-associated genetic loci. Nature, 511(7510), 421–427. https://doi.org/10.1038/nature13595

Schleidt W. M. (1974). How "fixed" is the fixed action pattern?. Zeitschrift fur Tierpsychologie, 36, 184–211. https://doi.org/10.1111/j.1439-0310.1974.tb02131.x

Schönenberg, M., & Jusyte, A. (2014). Investigation of the hostile attribution bias toward ambiguous facial cues in antisocial violent offenders. European archives of psychiatry and clinical neuroscience, 264(1), 61–69. https://doi.org/10.1007/s00406-013-0440-1

Schultheiss, O. C., Köllner, M. G., Busch, H., & Hofer, J. (2021). Evidence for a robust, estradiol-associated sex difference in narrative-writing fluency. Neuropsychology, 35(3), 323–333. https://doi.org/10.1037/neu0000706

Scott-Van Zeeland, A. A., Bloss, C. S., Tewhey, R., Bansal, V., Torkamani, A., Libiger, O., Duvvuri, V., Wineinger, N., Galvez, L., Darst, B. F., Smith, E. N., Carson, A., Pham, P., Phillips, T., Villarasa, N., Tisch, R., Zhang, G., Levy, S., Murray, S., Chen, W., … Schork, N. J. (2014). Evidence for the role of EPHX2 gene variants in anorexia nervosa. Molecular psychiatry, 19(6), 724–732. https://doi.org/10.1038/mp.2013.91

Seeman, P., Lee, T., Chau-Wong, M., & Wong, K. (1976). Antipsychotic drug doses and neuroleptic/dopamine receptors. Nature, 261(5562), 717–719. https://doi.org/10.1038/261717a0

Seligman M. E. (2016). Phobias and Preparedness - Republished Article. Behavior therapy, 47(5), 577–584. https://doi.org/10.1016/j.beth.2016.08.006

Selman, R.L. (1980). The growth of interpersonal understanding : developmental and clinical analyses. Academic Press.

Selye, H. (1936). A syndrome produced by diverse nocuous agents. Nature, 138, 32. https://doi.org/10.1038/138032a0

Shackelford, T. K., & Larsen, R. J. (1997). Facial asymmetry as an indicator of psychological, emotional, and physiological distress. Journal of Personality and Social Psychology, 72(2), 456–466. https://doi.org/10.1037/0022-3514.72.2.456

Sieber, J. E., & Stanley, B. (1988). Ethical and professional dimensions of socially sensitive research. The American psychologist, 43(1), 49–55. https://doi.org/10.1037//0003-066x.43.1.49

Siegmann, E. M., Müller, T., Dziadeck, I., Mühle, C., Lenz, B., & Kornhuber, J. (2020). Digit ratio (2D:4D) and transgender identity: new original data and a meta-analysis. Scientific reports, 10(1), 19326. https://doi.org/10.1038/s41598-020-72486-6

Skinner, B. F. (1938). The behavior of organisms: an experimental analysis. Appleton-Century.

Skinner, B. F. (1948). 'Superstition' in the pigeon. Journal of Experimental Psychology, 38(2), 168–172. https://doi.org/10.1037/h0055873

Skinner, B. F. (1953). Science and human behavior. Macmillan.

Slaby, R. G., & Frey, K. S. (1975). Development of gender constancy and selective attention to same-sex models. Child Development, 46(4), 849–856. https://doi.org/10.2307/1128389

Smith, E. E., & Jonides, J. (1997). Working memory: a view from neuroimaging. Cognitive psychology, 33(1), 5–42. https://doi.org/10.1006/cogp.1997.0658

Snyder S. H. (1976). The dopamine hypothesis of schizophrenia: focus on the dopamine receptor. The American journal of psychiatry, 133(2), 197–202. https://doi.org/10.1176/ajp.133.2.197

Söderberg, P., Tungström, S., & Armelius, B. A. (2005). Reliability of global assessment of functioning ratings made by clinical psychiatric staff. Psychiatric services (Washington, D.C.), 56(4), 434–438. https://doi.org/10.1176/appi.ps.56.4.434

Soomro GM, Altman DG, Rajagopal S, Oakley Browne M. Selective serotonin re-uptake inhibitors (SSRIs) versus placebo for obsessive compulsive disorder (OCD). Cochrane Database of Systematic Reviews 2008, Issue 1. Art. No.: CD001765. DOI: 10.1002/14651858.CD001765.pub3

Soon, C. S., Brass, M., Heinze, H. J., & Haynes, J. D. (2008). Unconscious determinants of free decisions in the human brain. Nature neuroscience, 11(5), 543–545. https://doi.org/10.1038/nn.2112

Sperry R. W. (1968). Hemisphere deconnection and unity in conscious awareness. The American psychologist, 23(10), 723–733. https://doi.org/10.1037/h0026839

Sprecher, S., & Hendrick, S. S. (2004). Self-Disclosure in Intimate Relationships: Associations With Individual and Relationship Characteristics Over Time. Journal of Social and Clinical Psychology, 23(6), 857–877. https://doi.org/10.1521/jscp.23.6.857.54803

Stachour, V.M., (1998). The Role of Social Support in Mediating Stress and Illness. Honors Projects. 57. https://digitalcommons.iwu.edu/psych_honproj/57

Steiner J. E. (1979). Human facial expressions in response to taste and smell stimulation. Advances in child development and behavior, 13, 257–295. https://doi.org/10.1016/s0065-2407(08)60349-3

Stern, K., & McClintock, M. K. (1998). Regulation of ovulation by human pheromones. Nature, 392(6672), 177–179. https://doi.org/10.1038/32408

Stunkard, A. J., Harris, J. R., Pedersen, N. L., & McClearn, G. E. (1990). The body-mass index of twins who have been reared apart. The New England journal of medicine, 322(21), 1483–1487. https://doi.org/10.1056/NEJM199005243222102

Suddath, R. L., Christison, G. W., Torrey, E. F., Casanova, M. F., & Weinberger, D. R. (1990). Anatomical abnormalities in the brains of monozygotic twins discordant for schizophrenia. The New England journal of medicine, 322(12), 789–794. https://doi.org/10.1056/NEJM199003223221201

Sutherland, E. H. (1947). Principles of criminology (4th ed.). J. B. Lippincott.

Sykes, G.M. (1958). The Society of Captives: A Study of a Maximum Security Prison. Princeton University Press.

BIBLIOGRAPHY AND REFERENCES

Tager-Flusberg, H. (2007). Evaluating the theory-of-mind hypothesis of autism. Current Directions in Psychological Science, 16(6), 311–315. https://doi.org/10.1111/j.1467-8721.2007.00527.x

Tamres, L. K., Janicki, D., & Helgeson, V. S. (2002). Sex Differences in Coping Behavior: A Meta-Analytic Review and an Examination of Relative Coping. Personality and Social Psychology Review, 6(1), 2–30. https://doi.org/10.1207/S15327957PSPR0601_1

Tang, N., Bensman, L., & Hatfield, E. (2013). Culture and Sexual Self-Disclosure in Intimate Relationships. Interpersona: An International Journal on Personal Relationships. 7. 227-245. 10.5964/ijpr.v7i2.141.

Tavolacci, M. P., Ladner, J., Grigioni, S., Richard, L., Villet, H., & Dechelotte, P. (2013). Prevalence and association of perceived stress, substance use and behavioral addictions: a cross-sectional study among university students in France, 2009-2011. BMC public health, 13, 724. https://doi.org/10.1186/1471-2458-13-724

Taylor, S. E., Klein, L. C., Lewis, B. P., Gruenewald, T. L., Gurung, R. A., & Updegraff, J. A. (2000). Biobehavioral responses to stress in females: tend-and-befriend, not fight-or-flight. Psychological review, 107(3), 411–429. https://doi.org/10.1037/0033-295x.107.3.411

Temoshok L. (1987). Personality, coping style, emotion and cancer: towards an integrative model. Cancer surveys, 6(3), 545–567.

The Schizophrenia Commission. (2012). The Abandoned Illness. Accessed 07/04/23 from: https://www.rethink.org/media/2637/the-abandoned-illness-final.pdf

Thompson S. K. (1975). Gender labels and early sex role development. Child development, 46(2), 339–347.

Thornton, D., & Reid, R. L. (1982). Moral reasoning and type of criminal offence. British Journal of Social Psychology, 21(3), 231–238. https://doi.org/10.1111/j.2044-8309.1982.tb00544.x

Tienari, P., Wynne, L. C., Sorri, A., Lahti, I., Läksy, K., Moring, J., Naarala, M., Nieminen, P., & Wahlberg, K. E. (2004). Genotype-environment interaction in schizophrenia-spectrum disorder. Long-term follow-up study of Finnish adoptees. The British journal of psychiatry : the journal of mental science, 184, 216–222. https://doi.org/10.1192/bjp.184.3.216

Tinebergen, N. (1952). The curious behavior of the stickleback. Scientific American, 187(6), 22–26. https://doi.org/10.1038/scientificamerican1252-22

Tricker, R., Casaburi, R., Storer, T. W., Clevenger, B., Berman, N., Shirazi, A., & Bhasin, S. (1996). The effects of supraphysiological doses of testosterone on angry behavior in healthy eugonadal men--a clinical research center study. The Journal of clinical endocrinology and metabolism, 81(10), 3754–3758. https://doi.org/10.1210/jcem.81.10.8855834

Tulving, E., & Thomson, D. M. (1973). Encoding specificity and retrieval processes in episodic memory. Psychological Review, 80(5), 352–373. https://doi.org/10.1037/h0020071

Utne, M.K., Hatfield, E., Traupmann, J., & Greenberger, D.B. (1984). Equity, Marital Satisfaction, and Stability. Journal of Social and Personal Relationships, 1, 323 - 332.

Van Goozen, S. H., Cohen-Kettenis, P. T., Gooren, L. J., Frijda, N. H., & Van de Poll, N. E. (1995). Gender differences in behaviour: activating effects of cross-sex hormones. Psychoneuroendocrinology, 20(4), 343–363. https://doi.org/10.1016/0306-4530(94)00076-x

Van Grootheest, D. S., Cath, D. C., Beekman, A. T., & Boomsma, D. I. (2005). Twin studies on obsessive-compulsive disorder: a review. Twin research and human genetics : the official journal of the International Society for Twin Studies, 8(5), 450–458. https://doi.org/10.1375/183242705774310060

Van IJzendoorn, M. H., & Kroonenberg, P. M. (1988). Cross-cultural patterns of attachment: A meta-analysis of the strange situation. Child Development, 59(1), 147–156. https://doi.org/10.2307/1130396

Van Keer, H., & Verhaeghe, J.P. (2005). Effects of Explicit Reading Strategies Instruction and Peer Tutoring on Second and Fifth Graders' Reading Comprehension and Self-Efficacy Perceptions. The Journal of Experimental Education, 73, 291 - 329.

Varese, F., Smeets, F., Drukker, M., Lieverse, R., Lataster, T., Viechtbauer, W., Read, J., van Os, J., & Bentall, R. P. (2012). Childhood adversities increase the risk of psychosis: a meta-analysis of patient-control, prospective- and cross-sectional cohort studies. Schizophrenia bulletin, 38(4), 661–671. https://doi.org/10.1093/schbul/sbs050

Velicer, W. F., Redding, C. A., Sun, X., & Prochaska, J. O. (2007). Demographic variables, smoking variables, and outcome across five studies. Health psychology : official journal of the Division of Health Psychology, American Psychological Association, 26(3), 278–287. https://doi.org/10.1037/0278-6133.26.3.278

Virkkunen, M., Kallio, E., Rawlings, R., Tokola, R., Poland, R. E., Guidotti, A., Nemeroff, C., Bissette, G., Kalogeras, K., Karonen, S.-L., & Linnoila, M. (1994). Personality profiles and state aggressiveness in Finnish alcoholic, violent offenders, fire setters, and healthy volunteers. Archives of General Psychiatry, 51(1), 28–33. https://doi.org/10.1001/archpsyc.1994.03950010028004

Volkow, N. D., Wang, G. J., Telang, F., Fowler, J. S., Thanos, P. K., Logan, J., Alexoff, D., Ding, Y. S., Wong, C., Ma, Y., & Pradhan, K. (2008). Low dopamine striatal D2 receptors are associated with prefrontal metabolism in obese subjects: possible contributing factors. NeuroImage, 42(4), 1537–1543. https://doi.org/10.1016/j.neuroimage.2008.06.002

Wall P. D. (1977). The presence of ineffective synapses and the circumstances which unmask them. Philosophical transactions of the Royal Society of London. Series B, Biological sciences, 278(961), 361–372. https://doi.org/10.1098/rstb.1977.0040

Walster, E., Aronson, V., Abrahams, D., & Rottman, L. (1966). Importance of physical attractiveness in dating behavior. Journal of Personality and Social Psychology, 4(5), 508–516. https://doi.org/10.1037/h0021188

Walther, J. (1996). Computer-mediated communication: Impersonal, interpersonal, and hypersonal interaction. Communication Research. 39. 274-279.

Wang, G. J., Volkow, N. D., Logan, J., Pappas, N. R., Wong, C. T., Zhu, W., Netusil, N., & Fowler, J. S. (2001). Brain dopamine and obesity. Lancet (London, England), 357(9253), 354–357. https://doi.org/10.1016/s0140-6736(00)03643-6

Wang, K., Zhang, H., Bloss, C. S., Duvvuri, V., Kaye, W., Schork, N. J., Berrettini, W., Hakonarson, H., & Price Foundation Collaborative Group (2011). A genome-wide association study on common SNPs and rare CNVs in anorexia nervosa. Molecular psychiatry, 16(9), 949–959. https://doi.org/10.1038/mp.2010.107

Watson, J. B., & Rayner, R. (2000). Conditioned emotional reactions. 1920. The American psychologist, 55(3), 313–317. https://doi.org/10.1037//0003-066x.55.3.313

Webb, T. L., & Sheeran, P. (2006). Does changing behavioral intentions engender behavior change? A meta-analysis of the experimental evidence. Psychological bulletin, 132(2), 249–268. https://doi.org/10.1037/0033-2909.132.2.249

Wender, P. H., Kety, S. S., Rosenthal, D., Schulsinger, F., Ortmann, J., & Lunde, I. (1986). Psychiatric disorders in the biological and adoptive families of adopted individuals with affective disorders. Archives of general psychiatry, 43(10), 923–929. https://doi.org/10.1001/archpsyc.1986.01800100013003

Williamson, D. A., Cubic, B. A., & Gleaves, D. H. (1993). Equivalence of body image disturbances in anorexia and bulimia nervosa. Journal of Abnormal Psychology, 102(1), 177–180. https://doi.org/10.1037/0021-843X.102.1.177

Wilson, M. I., & Daly, M. (1996). Male sexual proprietariness and violence against wives. Current Directions in Psychological Science, 5(1), 2–7. https://doi.org/10.1111/1467-8721.ep10772668

Wing, R. R., & Jeffery, R. W. (1999). Benefits of recruiting participants with friends and increasing social support for weight loss and maintenance. Journal of consulting and clinical psychology, 67(1), 132–138. https://doi.org/10.1037//0022-006x.67.1.132

Wolpe, J. (1969). The practice of behavior therapy. Pergamon Press.

Wood, D., Bruner, J. S., & Ross, G. (1976). The role of tutoring in problem solving. Child Psychology & Psychiatry & Allied Disciplines, 17(2), 89–100. https://doi.org/10.1111/j.1469-7610.1976.tb00381.x

BIBLIOGRAPHY AND REFERENCES

Youngblade, L. M., & Belsky, J. (1992). Parent-child antecedents of 5-year-olds' close friendships: A longitudinal analysis. Developmental Psychology, 28(4), 700–713. https://doi.org/10.1037/0012-1649.28.4.700

Yusuf, S., Hawken, S., Ôunpuu, S., Dans, T., Avezum, A., Lanas, F., Budaj, A., Pais, P., Varigos, J., & Lisheng, L. (2004). Effect of potentially modifiable risk factors associated with myocardial infarction in 52 countries (the INTERHEART study): Case-control study. The Lancet, 364(9438), 937–952. https://doi.org/10.1016/S0140-6736(04)17018-9

Zhou, J. N., Hofman, M. A., Gooren, L. J., & Swaab, D. F. (1995). A sex difference in the human brain and its relation to transsexuality. Nature, 378(6552), 68–70. https://doi.org/10.1038/378068a0

Zimbardo, P. G. (1969). The human choice: Individuation, reason, and order versus deindividuation, impulse, and chaos. Nebraska Symposium on Motivation, 17, 237–307.

Zimmermann, G., Favrod, J., Trieu, V. H., & Pomini, V. (2005). The effect of cognitive behavioral treatment on the positive symptoms of schizophrenia spectrum disorders: a meta-analysis. Schizophrenia research, 77(1), 1–9. https://doi.org/10.1016/j.schres.2005.02.018

GLOSSARY

Addiction: A physical and/or psychological dependence on something that produces reward stimuli, such as drugs or gaming. Individuals with addictions develop a *tolerance* to their addictions (needing more to produce the same effect) and suffer *withdrawal syndrome* (unpleasant symptoms, such as anxiety) when they are taken away.

Agentic state: A state where an individual mentally considers themselves as an agent (tool) of an authority figure and thus not personally responsible for their actions. It is the opposite of the *autonomous state*.

Attachment: An emotional connection between an individual and another person (an attachment figure). For example, a baby will typically develop an attachment to its caregiver.

Androcentrism: A bias that sees the male perspective as default. For example, using all-male participants in a study and assuming the findings apply to all humans.

Anisogamy: A form of sexual reproduction where gametes of different size – the male sperm and the female egg – fuse. Differences between these male and female sex cells give rise to different reproductive pressures and different reproductive behaviours.

Anorexia nervosa: An eating disorder characterised by an obsession with losing weight, body image distortion, restriction of food consumption, and low bodyweight.

Anxiety: An unpleasant emotional state of unease, worry, and/or fear. It is often accompanied by physical symptoms such as increased heart rate and behaviours such as fidgeting.

Autism: A developmental disorder characterised, in part, by difficulties with social cognition. For example, people with autism may have difficulties interacting and communicating with other people.

Autonomous state: A state where an individual is freely and consciously in control of their actions and thus takes responsibility for them. It is the opposite of the *agentic state*.

Aversion therapy: A form of classical conditioning that seeks to create negative associations with a substance or behaviour in order to make that substance or behaviour less desirable. For example, emetic drugs cause sickness and so can be combined with alcohol in order to create an association with drinking alcohol and feeling sick. This reduces the desire to drink alcohol.

Avolition: A lack of desire or motivation to do anything. It is a common symptom of schizophrenia.

Axon: The long part of a neuron through which an electrical signal is carried away from the cell body towards the axon terminal and terminal boutons.

Behaviourism: See *behavioural approach*.

Behavioural approach: A learning approach to psychology that analyses the mind based on external observations of stimulus and behaviour as opposed to, for example, the inner workings of the mind (cognitive approach) or as a consequence of physical and chemical processes (biological approach).

Bias: A systematic deviation from an accurate perception of reality in favour of some less accurate interpretation. For example, a person with an optimism bias may believe they have a better than 50/50 chance of winning a coin flip, even though the true odds are 50/50.

GLOSSARY

Biological approach: An approach to psychology that analyses the mind physiologically, looking at things like genetics and the chemical processes that cause mental states and behaviours. The biological approach can be contrasted against other approaches to psychology, such as those that focus on the inner workings of the mind (cognitive approach) or external observations of stimulus and behaviour (behavioural approach).

Biological rhythms: The regular cycles of bodily processes. These cycles may be *circadian* (~24 hours in length), *infradian* (>24 hours in length) or *ultradian* (<24 hours in length).

Biopsychology: See *biological approach*.

(Storage) Capacity: How much information can be stored in a given component of memory.

(Neuron) Cell body: The part of a neuron that contains the cell nucleus and genetic information.

Central executive: The component of the working memory model of short term memory that filters and co-ordinates the various components of working memory. This filtering process involves sending information to its 3 slave systems: the phonological loop, the visuo-spatial sketchpad, and the episodic buffer.

Coding: The *format* that information in memory is stored as.

Cognitive approach: An approach to psychology that analyses the mind from the perspective of the subject's thoughts and thought processes by inferring them from behaviour. The cognitive approach can be contrasted against other approaches to psychology, such as those that analyse the mind in terms of physical and chemical processes (biological approach) or external observations of stimulus and behaviour only (behavioural approach).

Cognitive behavioural therapy (CBT): A treatment approach for psychological disorders that seeks to identify and challenge the irrational and maladaptive thought patterns that cause them. Patients are encouraged to replace these thought patterns, which in turn changes their behaviour.

Cognitive dissonance: An uncomfortable feeling caused by holding two or more beliefs that contradict each other.

Compliance: The weakest type of conformity where a person publicly changes their behaviour and beliefs to fit that of a group and avoid disapproval. Privately, though, the person does not accept these behaviours and beliefs. For example, pretending to like a film you hate so as not to stand out from the group.

Concordance rate: The extent to which twins in a twin study share a trait. A high concordance rate – particularly among identical twins – suggests that the trait is genetically determined.

Concurrent validity: The extent to which a study's results are consistent with similar studies. A study has high concurrent validity if its results are the same as a similar study.

(Classical) Conditioning: When someone is conditioned to associate a neutral stimulus with a natural (unconditioned) response. For example, psychologist Ivan Pavlov demonstrated how dogs could be conditioned to salivate (a natural response to food) in response to a bell ringing (a neutral stimulus) by ringing the bell at the same time as presenting the dog with food. The repeated occurrence of the bell ringing with the presentation of food eventually produced a conditioned response in the dogs, who would salivate at the sound of the bell even when there was no food.

GLOSSARY

(Operant) Conditioning: When a behaviour is reinforced because of consequences, making it more likely that the behaviour is repeated. Reinforcement can be positive (e.g. getting praised for doing your homework), negative (e.g. doing your homework to avoid getting told off for not doing it), or as a result of punishment (e.g. getting told off by your teacher for not doing your homework, so you do it next time).

Confederate: A fake subject (actor/stooge) in an experiment who is pretending to be part of the experiment.

Conformity: A form of social influence where a person changes their beliefs or behaviours to fit with those of a larger group.

Contralateral: Information from the left side of the body is processed by the right hemisphere of the brain and information from the right side of the body is processed by the left hemisphere of the brain. For example, images presented to the left visual field will be processed in the right hemisphere.

Control group: A group of participants who are not exposed to the independent variable being tested. This group provides a benchmark against which you can compare whether the independent variable had an effect or not. For example, in order to test whether caffeine has an effect on test scores, you need to have a control group that doesn't take caffeine to compare against the group that does take caffeine.

Covert sensitisation: A form of classical conditioning similar to aversion therapy but using imagination rather than real-life unpleasant stimuli in order to make a substance or behaviour less desirable. For example, a therapist may get a cigarette addict to imagine smoking cigarettes covered in faeces and feeling sick, which reduces their desire to smoke cigarettes.

Cue reactivity: A form of classical conditioning where neutral stimuli associated with an addictive substance cause urges to use that addictive substance. For example, an alcoholic may condition himself to feel a strong urge to drink alcohol when going inside the environment of a pub. In isolation, the pub is a neutral stimulus but because it becomes associated with the pleasant sensations of alcohol, it causes a conditioned response (urge to drink alcohol).

Cultural bias: A bias where the researcher assumes their own culture is the default. For example, conducting a study on British teenagers and assuming the findings apply to all teenagers in the world.

De-individuation: When a person loses their sense of personal identity and responsibility due to anonymity. For example, a person wearing a mask, or in a dark area where they can't be seen, or in a large crowd may become de-individuated.

Dendrite: The part of a neuron that receives a signal (in the form of a neurotransmitter) from another neuron.

Dependence: A symptom of addiction where a person feels like they need a substance. Physical dependence is when someone experiences withdrawal syndrome without the substance. Psychological dependence is when a person has a strong desire to use the substance.

GLOSSARY

Dependent variable: Something that is *measured* by researchers in an experiment. For example, participant reaction times.

Depression: A mental disorder characterised by feelings of low mood, loss of motivation, and inability to feel pleasure.

(Hard) Determinism: The belief that human behaviour is entirely caused by physical processes beyond our control. This means free will is impossible.

(Soft) Determinism: The belief that human behaviour is to a large extent caused by processes beyond our control (e.g. biology, upbringing, etc.) but that we can overrule these processes and exert free will when necessary.

Diathesis-stress model: An explanation of schizophrenia that explains the disorder as the result of interaction between biological factors (biological diathesis) and environmental factors (stress).

DSM: The *Diagnostic and Statistical Manual of Mental Disorders*, a manual produced by the American Psychiatric Association to diagnose psychological disorders.

(Storage) Duration: *How long* information can be stored for in a given component of memory.

Ecological validity: The extent to which findings from a study apply in real-life situations outside the study. A study where the same results are seen in similar real world situations has high ecological validity.

Endogenous pacemaker: Things *within* the body that regulate biological rhythms (your 'body clock').

Enmeshment: Where the family members have little individual identity but instead blur into one single unit. According to the family systems theory of anorexia, people with the disorder often come from such enmeshed families.

Episodic buffer: The component of the working memory model of short term memory that combines and temporarily stores information coded in all forms. For example, visual and semantic information may be combined in the episodic buffer to create a coherent working memory of a story.

Episodic (long-term) memory: A type of long-term memory for autobiographical events in a person's own life. For example, remembering your first holiday.

Ethics: Whether something is morally right or wrong, good or bad. Psychological studies must consider ethical issues in the study design (e.g. any harm that might be inflicted on the participants) as well as ethical implications of the results for society in general (e.g. whether the study's results could be used to justify discrimination).

Ethnocentrism: A bias where researchers assume behaviour from one culture is the default and normal, and so (falsely) conclude that behaviours considered normal in other cultures are abnormal.

Exogenous zeitgebers: Cues in the *external environment* that inform endogenous pacemakers to regulate biological rhythms. For example, light is an exogenous zeitgeber because it is used to regulate the sleep/wake cycle.

Extraneous variable: An unwanted variable in an experiment that might skew the results.

GLOSSARY

Face validity: The extent to which a test looks like it is an accurate measure of what it is supposed to measure. A test has high face validity if it is highly plausible (at face value) that the test is an accurate measure of what it is supposed to measure.

Falsifiability: A theory or hypothesis is falsifiable if there is some possible observation that could disprove it. For example, the hypothesis "water boils at 100°c" is falsifiable because it is conceivable that you could heat water to 9999°c and it doesn't boil over. Even though this would never physically happen, it is a possible observation that would count against the hypothesis. An unfalsifiable hypothesis, in contrast, is consistent with every possible observation and so cannot be disproved – this is considered unscientific.

Forensic psychology: The application of psychology to criminal behaviour.

Free will: The belief that humans are able to freely choose their thoughts and actions. It is the opposite view of determinism.

Gender: Whether a person's psychology, personality, and behaviour is masculine and/or feminine. It is related to, but not the same as, a person's biological sex (i.e. whether they are male or female).

(Alpha) Gender bias: A bias that *exaggerates* differences between genders.

(Beta) Gender bias: A bias that *ignores* differences between genders.

Gender dysphoria: When a person's psychological gender does not match their biological sex. For example, a person born biologically female (XX chromosomes) may have a male gender.

Gender identity disorder: See *gender dysphoria*.

Gene: A biological unit of information inherited from either the mother or the father that encodes for a physical or psychological trait. For example, if someone inherits the SLC1A1 gene from their parents, it increases their risk of obsessive-compulsive disorder.

Gland: An organ of the body that produces and releases hormones. For example, the thyroid gland produces and releases the thyroxine hormone.

Heredity: The passing of traits (e.g. psychological or physical) from parents to children via genes.

Holism: An approach to psychology that seeks to understand behaviour using all levels of explanation. For example, a holistic approach to depression would look at the biological, cognitive, and social causes rather than just zooming in on one. It is the opposite approach to reductionism.

Homeostasis: A state of stable and normal functioning within the body. For example, drinking alcohol disrupts homeostasis and so the body processes the alcohol in order to return the body to homeostasis.

Hormone: A chemical produced in a gland of the body that communicates information and has an effect in the body. For example, the growth hormone stimulates cell division and growth.

Humanistic psychology: An approach to psychology that emphasises the subjective experience and free will of the individual, encouraging them to achieve self-actualisation.

Hypothesis: A scientific theory or explanation for something. The hypothesis is tested by comparing its predictions with the results of an experiment.

GLOSSARY

ICD: The *International Statistical Classification of Diseases and Related Health Problems*, a manual produced by the World Health Organisation to diagnose psychological and other health disorders.

Identification: A type of conformity where a person both publicly and privately changes their behaviour and beliefs to fit that of a group they want to be part of. Identification is a stronger form of conformity than compliance due to the additional private acceptance, but a weaker form of conformity than internalisation because the individual does not maintain the beliefs and behaviours after leaving the group. For example, adopting the same music tastes and fashion as your friendship group.

Idiographic: An approach to psychology that seeks to understand each individual as a unique case rather than through general laws that apply to all humans. It is the opposite of the nomothetic approach.

Informational social influence (ISI): When an individual is motivated to look to the behaviours and beliefs of a group in order to be correct. For example, if you are at a formal restaurant and don't know which cutlery to use, you might look to what someone else is doing for information as to the correct course of action.

Independent variable: Something that is *changed* by researchers to see if it has an effect on the dependent variable. For example, researchers might change the independent variable of the time of day in some experiments to see if this has an effect on the dependent variable of reaction times.

Insecure-avoidant attachment: A type of infant attachment characterised by low stranger anxiety, low separation anxiety, and minimal reaction upon reunion with the mother.

Insecure-resistant attachment: A type of infant attachment characterised by wariness of strangers, high separation anxiety, and rejection upon reunion with the mother.

Interactional synchrony: In the context of attachment, interactional synchrony is the way interactions between caregivers and infants are synchronised (i.e. co-ordinated). For example, a baby and mother may 'take turns' in a synchronised manner that is similar to the way adults take turns to talk in a conversation.

Internalisation: The strongest type of conformity where a person both publicly and privately changes their behaviour and beliefs to those of a group. Unlike identification, individuals who internalise beliefs and behaviours maintain them even after leaving the social group. For example, a person who undergoes a genuine religious conversion will still pray and believe in God even if they move away from the social group of their church.

Introspection: Looking 'inward' and examining one's thoughts, emotions, and sensations. For example, a person might be shown a picture and then asked to examine how it makes them feel. Psychologist Wilhelm Wundt pioneered introspection as an experimental technique. In Wundt's experiments, subjects were trained to report their inner experiences in a highly systematic and controlled way.

Learning approach: An approach to psychology that explains behaviour as the result of learning experiences from environment. Examples of learning approaches are behaviourism and social learning theory.

GLOSSARY

Locus of control: A way of characterising how much control a person believes they have over their life. If someone has an internal locus of control, they believe their own choices shape their life. If someone has an external locus of control, they believe their life is primarily shaped by forces outside their control such as luck and fate.

Long-term memory: A long-lasting or permanent store of information. It is the third system of the multi-store model of memory. Some psychologists differentiate between 3 types of long-term memory: episodic, semantic, and procedural.

Longitudinal study: A type of study that involves following someone or something over an extended time period.

Majority influence: See *conformity*.

Mediating processes: A term from social learning theory that covers the cognitive processes after observing another person's behaviour that determine whether the observer imitates that behaviour. They are attention, retention, reproduction, and motivation.

Meta-analysis: A study of studies. Researchers take several smaller studies within a certain research area and use statistics to identify trends across those studies to create a larger study.

Minority influence: A form of social influence where a person rejects the beliefs and behaviours of the majority and instead adopts those of a smaller group.

Mirror neuron: A neuron that fires both when an action is performed and when that action is observed being performed by someone else.

Multi-store model (MSM): A cognitive theory that explains memory as information flowing through 3 storage systems: sensory register, short-term memory, and long-term memory. Each system uses different coding for the information, and has different storage capacity and duration.

Neophobia: A dislike or phobia of anything new. Innate neophobia may explain food preferences, as new foods could potentially be poisonous.

Nervous system: The main system that controls the mind and body. It consists of the central nervous system (the brain and spinal cord), which is connected to the external world and the rest of the body via the peripheral nervous system.

Neuron: The components through which information is transmitted through the nervous system. For example, a sensory neuron may transmit information from the fingertips (via an electrical impulse) to the central nervous system.

Neuroplasticity: The ability of the brain to change its physical structure in order to perform different functions.

Neurotransmitter: A chemical used by neurons to communicate with each other. A neurotransmitter is released by a neuron, where it crosses a synapse and binds to a receptor in the next neuron.

Nomothetic: An approach to psychology that seeks to identify general laws of human behaviour by looking at the similarities between them. It is the opposite of the idiographic approach.

GLOSSARY

Normative social influence (NSI): When an individual is motivated to look to the behaviours and beliefs of a group in order to be accepted by the group and not stand out. For example, pretending to agree with the group's opinions on politics.

Obedience: A form of social influence where a person complies with the instructions of an authority figure.

Objective: Something that takes place in the external world. It is the opposite of subjective, which is something that takes place in the inner world of the mind.

Obsessive-compulsive disorder (OCD): An anxiety disorder characterised by continuous and repeated thoughts (obsessions) and uncontrollable behaviours and rituals resulting from these thoughts (compulsions). For example, an obsessive fixation on germs may lead to compulsive hand-washing behaviour.

Parasocial relationship: One-sided relationships where a person gets attached to someone they don't know in real life. For example, someone might engage in a parasocial relationship with a celebrity or social media star.

Phobia: An anxiety disorder characterised by extreme and irrational fear towards something. For example, arachnophobia is an extreme fear of spiders.

Phonological loop: The component of the working memory model of short term memory that deals with auditory information (i.e. sound) – in particular, words.

Privation: An extreme form of deprivation which, in the context of attachment, means an infant never forms an attachment bond with a caregiver.

Procedural (long-term) memory: A type of long-term memory for skills, actions, and how to do things. For example, remembering how to ride a bike.

Psychodynamic approach: An approach to psychology that analyses behaviour as a consequence of conflicts between different parts of the mind. For example, Freud believed unconscious desires (e.g. towards violence or sex) often conflict with one's conscious beliefs and attitudes (e.g. a moral belief that punching people is wrong).

Psychopathology: The study of psychological conditions whereby an individual's behaviour and mental states are considered abnormal. Abnormality can be defined in several ways: Deviation from social norms, failure to function adequately, statistical infrequency, and deviation from ideal mental health.

Reactance: When an individual is motivated to assert their free will by rebelling against rules or authority figures that the individual believes are attempting to restrict their free will.

Recidivism: Committing further crime(s) after being sentenced for a previous crime.

Reciprocity: In the context of attachment, reciprocity is the way interactions are reciprocal (i.e. two-way). For example, when a baby smiles, the mother will smile back.

Reductionism: An approach to psychology that seeks to understand behaviour by breaking it down into smaller parts. For example, biological approaches may analyse depression purely on the basis of neurochemistry without considering higher levels of explanation such as thought patterns or social factors. It is the opposite view to holism.

GLOSSARY

Reliability: A study's results are reliable if the same results can be replicated under the same circumstances (i.e. the results are consistent).

Schema: Patterns of thought developed from experience that the individual uses to categorise information and experiences more easily. Stereotypes (e.g. dark alley at night = dangerous) are an example of schema.

Schizophrenia: A psychological disorder characterised by loss of contact with reality. Positive symptoms of schizophrenia include hallucinations and delusions, negative symptoms include avolition and speech poverty.

Secure attachment: A type of infant attachment characterised by low stranger anxiety when the mother is present, high separation anxiety, and happiness upon reunion with the mother.

Semantic (long-term) memory: A type of long-term memory for meaning, understanding, and general knowledge. For example, remembering "Paris is the capital of France".

Sensory register: The first storage system in the multi-store model of memory. It temporarily stores the immediate 'raw' data that comes in from the senses.

Separation anxiety: When an infant demonstrates symptoms of anxiety when separated from an attachment figure.

Social change: The process through which the social norms of society (which are generally determined by majority influence) change to give way to new social norms. For example, the suffragette movement inspired the social change of acceptance of women's voting rights.

Social learning approach: A learning approach to psychology that explains behaviour in terms of observing and imitating others' behaviour (in addition to learning via standard behaviourist principles).

Social learning theory: See *social learning approach*.

Social roles: The different roles we play in order to conform to the social norms of the situation. For example, in the role of customer in a shop, you are expected to join the queue and pay for your items. In the role of employee at a company, you are expected to show up on time and go to meetings.

Soma: See *cell body*.

Short-term memory: A temporary store of information (i.e. less than 30 seconds). Short-term memory is the second system of the multi-store model of memory. The working memory model adds further detail to this system by differentiating between 4 separate information-processing components.

Stress: The physiological response and unpleasant feeling a person gets when they feel that they are unable to cope with the demands of a situation. For example, if you feel that you don't know enough to pass your psychology exam (whether this is true or not), this will cause feelings of stress.

Stressor: Something that causes stress.

Subjective: Something that takes place in the inner world of the mind. It is the opposite of objective, which is something that takes place in the external world.

GLOSSARY

Symptoms: A characteristic of a disorder or disease. Positive symptoms are behaviours/experiences in addition to normal functioning whereas negative symptoms are a lack of behaviours/experiences associated with normal functioning.

Synapse: A gap between two neurons.

Synaptic transmission: The process of sending information from one neuron to another over a synapse.

Temporal validity: The extent to which a study's results stay true over time. A study has high temporal validity if its results are still accurate and valid decades later.

Terminal bouton: The part of a neuron at the end of the axon that contains the neurotransmitters which are released in order to pass information on to the next neuron.

Theory of mind: The ability to imagine and model the mental states of other people's minds. For example, if you see someone crying, your theory of mind tells you that this person is feeling upset.

Twin study: A study that compares the concordance rate of a trait among sets of twins. If the concordance rate for a trait is higher among monozygotic (identical) twins than dizygotic (non-identical) twins, that suggests the trait is genetically inherited rather than environmentally determined.

Validity: A study's results are valid if the accurately measure what they are supposed to (i.e. the results are true and correct). There are several forms of validity, including ecological validity, concurrent validity, face validity, and temporal validity.

Variable: A factor in an experiment. Different kinds of variables include independent variables, dependent variables, and extraneous variables.

Vicarious reinforcement: A term from social learning theory whereby a person is more likely to imitate the behaviour of someone else if they see that person being rewarded for it. Or vice versa: where a person is less likely to imitate someone else's behaviour if they observe them being punished for it.

Visuo-spatial sketchpad: The component of the working memory model of short term memory that deals with visual information and its location in space (i.e. pictures). Also called the mind's inner eye.

Withdrawal syndrome: A symptom of addiction where a person develops unpleasant symptoms – e.g. shaking, headaches, anxiety – upon stopping use of an addictive substance.

Working memory model (WMM): A model of short-term memory consisting of 4 components, which hold and process different types of information. The components of the WMM are: the central executive, the phonological loop, the visuo-spatial sketchpad, and the episodic buffer.

Printed in Great Britain
by Amazon